Lauer Series in Rhetoric and Composition

Series Editors, Catherine Hobbs and Patricia Sullivan

Lauer Series in Rhetoric and Composition

Series Editors, Catherine Hobbs and Patricia Sullivan

The Lauer Series in Rhetoric and Composition honors the contributions Janice Lauer Hutton has made to the emergence of Rhetoric and Composition as a disciplinary study. It publishes scholarship that carries on Professor Lauer's varied work in the history of written rhetoric, disciplinarity in composition studies, contemporary pedagogical theory, and written literacy theory and research.

Other Books in the Series

Historical Studies of Writing Program Administration: Individuals, Communities, and the Formation of a Discipline, edited by Barbara L'Eplattenier and Lisa Mastrangelo (2004)

Rhetorics, Poetics, and Cultures: Refiguring College English Studies (Expanded Edition) by James A. Berlin (2003)

Composing a Community

A History of Writing Across the Curriculum

Editors

Susan H. McLeod

Margot Iris Soven

Parlor Press
West Lafayette, Indiana
www.parlorpress.com

Parlor Press LLC, West Lafayette, Indiana 47906

© 2006 by Parlor Press
All rights reserved.
Printed in the United States of America

SAN: 254-8879

Library of Congress Cataloging-in-Publication Data

Composing a community : a history of writing across the curriculum /
    edited by Susan H. McLeod and Margot Iris Soven.
        p. cm. -- (Lauer series in rhetoric and composition)
    Includes bibliographical references and index.
    ISBN 1-932559-17-5 (pbk. : alk. paper) -- ISBN 1-932559-25-6 (alk.
paper) -- ISBN 1-932559-81-7 (adobe ebook) 1. English language--
Rhetoric--Study and teaching. 2. Report writing--Study and teaching
(Higher) 3. Interdisciplinary approach in education. 4. Writing centers-
-Administration. I. McLeod, Susan H. II. Soven, Margot. III. Title. IV.
Series.

    PE1404.C61757 2006
    808'.0420711--dc22

                                        2006006627

Cover design by David Blakesley.
Cover illustration: "Reading by Candle Light" © 2006, by Adrian Moisei.
    Used by permission.
Printed on acid-free paper.

Parlor Press, LLC is an independent publisher of scholarly and trade titles
in print and multimedia formats. This book is available in paper, cloth
and Adobe eBook formats from Parlor Press on the World Wide Web
at http://www.parlorpress.com or through online and brick-and mortar
bookstores. For submission information or to find out about Parlor Press
publications, write to Parlor Press, 816 Robinson St., West Lafayette,
Indiana, 47906, or e-mail editor@parlorpress.com.

Contents

Composing a Community

Introduction

WAC's Beginnings: Developing a Community of Change Agents

David R. Russell

This collection is an informal history of the early years of the writing across the curriculum (WAC) movement, as told by some of the people who made that history. If you are reading this, you probably already know that the WAC movement is an effort to improve education by encouraging students to write in many fields (or content areas). What you may not know is that the WAC movement is an extraordinary example of grassroots change in education. In 1984, when the WAC movement was 14 years old, I first started researching the history of attempts to improve students' writing across the curriculum, dating back to the beginnings of mass education in the waning years of the nineteenth century (Russell, *Writing*). What struck me most often and most forcefully in the early 1990s was that the WAC movement had lasted longer—and involved far more students and teachers—than any previous attempt to improve writing across the curriculum—and there had been many, I found. Now, twenty years later, WAC may well be the largest and longest-lived educational reform movement in the history of American higher education that did not develop a formal organizational structure—with the possible exception of the general education movement. How did that happen?

This book is by and about the people who made that history, people who began, often, as newcomers to education and went on—largely through their involvement in WAC—to become provosts, directors of core curricula, department chairs, deans, heads of teaching and learning centers, as well as WAC program coordinators. And so WAC spread and gained such staying power, to the extent that it has brought about systemic changes rather than just individual classroom change. Though WAC has been important in secondary schools (and is increasingly so), the most visible institutional change came in higher education, the focus of this book. WAC appeals to the way professors work and think (they have more time to ponder questions and do research), and it appeals to something many of them sense they are lacking (more knowledge about teaching and learning). Further, faculty can and do become administrators, who then have the power to change practice in a way that secondary teachers do not (unfortunately, in my view). Thus, WAC has been a training ground for change agents: WAC coordinators who then go on to support other innovative programs that are in line with WAC principles, forging alliances and spreading the insights that into teaching and learning that come though focusing on learning to write and writing to learn.

The book has three main purposes and three audiences—overlapping, I suspect. First, it's for people interested in the process of educational change, especially when that change takes the form of a movement. From this perspective, the book is a kind of loose case study of one of the longest-lasting and most widespread movements in the history of American education. The WAC movement began with—and maintained—a very informal structure, relying on a network of personal relationships in a community of practitioners in many disciplines, rather than a formal organization (Walvoord). The trade-offs involved offer educational reformers—in WAC and other movements—much food for thought.

Second, it's for people interested in the WAC movement as part of the larger enterprise of literacy teaching and research. The teaching of writing became a professional field at the same time as the WAC movement began. And the emerging field of composition (as it is still usually called) owes much to the WAC movement. This collection makes that debt clear—and also reveals the complex relation between general writing courses, such as first-year composition, and efforts to develop students writing and learning in other courses.

Third, it's for people interested in the history—and future—of WAC. The movement has over the thirty-odd years of its existence involved hundreds (perhaps thousands) of K12 and higher education institutions, tens of thousands of teachers, and millions of students.

The stories collected here enrich the meaning of that diverse and ongoing work, providing (as history often does) new ideas and insights for the future as it opens up the past. I was asked to contribute this introduction because I wrote a book-length history of attempts to improve writing across the curriculum, *Writing in the Academic Disciplines: A Curricular History,* which devotes a chapter to the WAC movement. And readers wanting a more formal overview might begin there. But much is left out in this and other published accounts—very much. And this collection fills in important gaps in the published historical studies.

I'll take up these three purposes one by one, providing some background for the stories that follow and suggesting some of the many themes those stories offer.

WAC: CASE STUDY IN GRASSROOTS EDUCATIONAL CHANGE MOVEMENTS

Movements are begun as responses to social needs, but they are begun by human beings, shaped by the decisions of those people, their loves and fears and desires and interests (Giddens). People, not "forces," make a movement happen. These are very much personal stories, stories of intellectual interests developing out of not only institutions and books, but also personal networks, human communities. These sustained and spread the movement despite its lack of formal organization.

As I suggested earlier, the WAC movement did not have an elaborated theory but rather a few powerful ideas, which might be summarized as "Writing to learn; learning to write." Nor did it have a single curricular agenda, but rather a wide range of possible models, to be adapted or rejected according to local institutional needs and personalities. Nor did it have any formal or well-articulated research agenda, but rather a bricolage of theories and methods, without refereed journals or graduate courses or conferences specific to it. It did not, in other words, have the usual means of disseminating ideas and practices in academia.

What it did have was a community. In the stories that follow, we see that community develop in several key ways, mainly relying on personal, face-to-face contact. Over and over we hear of ideas developed in a faculty workshop passed on to another institution when the workshop leader served as a consultant for a day or two. Or spread through a semester or summer visiting professorship, (Maimon to

Penn [see Peterson and Kuriloff this volume]; Weiner to South Dakota [see Bean, this volume]). Or disseminated at a seminar or small conference organized at an institution, as at Beaver College (see Maimon, this volume) or Chicago (see Soven, this volume). Or a rump meeting or special interest group meeting quietly held as a small part of a national conference, as with the National WAC network at CCCC the NCTE conference (see Thaiss, this volume). With enough time and records, one could create a map of dissemination by tracing the visits of a few consultants, influencing program directors where they visited, who then became consultants themselves, and so on, to form the network of personal relationships that created the movement. This is evident in the stories that follow, as the contributors tell of a visit that became another node in the network.

Barbara Walvoord, in her essay "The Future of WAC," subtly analyzes this phenomenon well in terms of social movement theory. WAC's early emphasis on "micro, rather than macro, concerns," such as individual faculty adoption, local curricular change, membership, and resources, led to a "quiet and local flowering" (61). It did not seek national publicity, form an agenda—or spawn a counter-movement.

What the movement did do is form useful, if often tentative, alliances with other movements, opportunistically and often serendipitously. Early on, it allied itself in informal and local ways with the National Writing Project (NWP), a program begun in the Bay Area for secondary school teachers that quickly spread nation-wide. WAC borrowed its workshop methods and egalitarian ethic. One may also note, in the stories that follow, alliances formed and reformed with such movements as critical thinking, assessment, general education reform, learning communities (Freshman Interest Groups), writing centers and other student support units, teaching centers, literacy movements, and many others.

This flexibility allowed WAC to get funding from very disparate sources, local, regional, and national. And the quest for funding forms an important theme in these stories as well. Early WAC programs did particularly well in getting federal and foundation monies, not only because they had good ideas for meeting real needs in an environment of expanding access and, later, greater calls for accountability, but also because they could ally themselves with any number of other reforms. Writing is everywhere and everywhere necessary. And the funding followed good ideas on how to use writing to accomplish something beyond "fixing" students' writing.

The flexible, informal organizational structure also allowed WAC to negotiate the treacherous political battles that education, like all organizations, is heir to. As a grassroots movement, protean in form, WAC could "fly under the radar" and escape the fire of more visible and agenda-driven movements, as Walvoord points out (62).

However, the lack of formal organization also involves trade-offs. Thaiss, in his chapter on the National Network of WAC Programs (this volume) provides a very personal and soul-searching inquiry into many of the questions Walvoord and others have raised. He writes, "A mere network lacks the ability of a more formal organization to do many things: create an agenda to focus efforts, issue position statements, establish and publicize standards, conduct statistical surveys of members, and, maybe most basic, ensure continuity through an orderly process of succeeding leadership" I agree with Thaiss that the lack of organization is most evident in the relative slowness of WAC to be adopted in secondary schools, where it might be extremely useful to the profound and contentious reforms (particularly in assessment) affecting secondary education from the 1990s on. And I would add that WAC's relationship to the professional organization most closely associated with it, the Conference on College Composition and Communication, has become weaker, in many ways, as the direction of CCCC has moved toward a focus on critical pedagogy within courses and away from building articulations between general writing courses and courses in the disciplines and professions—which can and do include critical pedagogy as well.

Whatever directions WAC may take will still depend for their conception and initial execution on the agency and dedication of individuals in the network of personal relationships that formed WAC. And it's worth noting here that many of the people who created WAC (including many of the contributors to this volume) are now heads of Teaching and Learning centers, department chairs, deans, provosts, and chancellors, as well as leaders in professional organizations that shape secondary and higher education policies and directions. They are in a position to make a difference in ways that were unthinkable twenty or thirty years ago because of the movement they created and sustained.

But the leadership (however dedicated) and organization (however loose) are certainly not the most important factor in WAC's longevity, as these essays make abundantly clear. The crucial move was to make faculty from many disciplines into what the literature on educational reform calls "change agents," those who actually make educational reform happen. As McLeod and Miraglia pointed out, extensive research on change agents in school reform found that "pedagogical and curricular change was a problem of the smallest unit, of local capacity and teacher motivation. The most effective change agents were not in fact outside consultants and external developers brought in for the various projects, but rather the teachers themselves" (*WAC* 21). It was faculty who took insights from workshops into their classrooms and departments that, as Thaiss has pointed out, "remains the basic strategy of WAC faculty development" and a central reason for its longevity (358). It is indeed a grassroots movement, and one that has evolved as faculty have developed in their careers to increasingly influential roles within institutions, carrying with them those colleagues and friends who formed a long-lasting community—and made an increasingly influential movement.

WAC's Role in the Professionalization of Composition as a Field

WAC's growth coincided with—and in many ways helped create and shape—the professionalization of composition as a field. In this collection, we sense the excitement of young professionals in English and other fields discovering that the study and teaching of writing could be serious intellectual work, something worth devoting a one's professional life to. Most were trained in literature (a surprising number in Renaissance literature, oddly enough). But through their contacts with one another at WAC seminars and at professional meetings, they came to find new purpose in their work and create a community that became a movement. Particularly important was the annual meeting of the Conference on College Composition and Communication (CCCC), which had begun after WWII as a place for composition teachers to meet but grew in the 1970s into a full-fledged professional organization.

The social context of the 1960s and 1970s provided motivation for the professionalization of composition and the creation of WAC. Many of the authors in this collection, like others in the emerging

field of composition, saw their work as having important social signifi-
cance. Most were students during the campus upheavals of the 1960s,
and they came to see teaching writing as a humane and socially responsible way to help previously excluded groups succeed in higher
education, as open admissions policies brought an influx of students
who had difficulty learning and writing in this new environment.
Many colleges, universities, and funding agencies began programs to
help these new students. WAC coordinators found administrative and
grant support to enlist the aid of faculty in all disciplines to improve
students' writing and learning—and success rate. As teachers and researchers of composition interacted with faculty in other disciplines,
through workshops and consulting, they glimpsed the great variety
and richness of the uses of writing and began to rethink fundamental
assumptions that have undergirded general compositions courses for
a century.

The formal teaching of writing had been based on skill drills (on
the behaviorist model) and the teaching of general strategies focused
on forms ("modes"), not processes. This has come to be called the "current-traditional paradigm" of writing instruction. And the research on
writing instruction was also primarily behaviorist and focused on in-
culcating general skills, which were assumed to be readily transferred
by students to their writing in other disciplines.

In the 1970s came the first research on writing process, based in
cognitive psychology and centered at Carnegie-Mellon University.
Cognitive models of how students develop as writers and/or learners
(e.g., William Perry, Jean Piaget) were an important topic of discussion in the WAC community, as they might offer help across the disciplines. Graduate programs in composition began, along with expanded research. And classroom practice in general composition courses
began to change as a result of this research.

However, as writing teachers began interacting with faculty in
other disciplines, through WAC programs, they saw the profound
limitations of the current-traditional model and of cognitive models.
Cross-disciplinary rhetorical comparisons, spurred by the WAC movement, made the limitations of these generalized approaches even more
apparent. Writing came to be seen as a social process, dependent on
the communities, organizations, and purposes for which students—
and professionals—write. Thus the personal and social as well as be-
havioral and cognitive psychological dimensions of writing came to be

an object of focus (Nystrand et al.). Drawing on Britton's theory and the experience of NWP and WAC workshops, classrooms began using more informal and personal writing as a way of involving students. Kenneth Bruffee's collaborative model of writing development, developed in a cross-curricular writing center, was influential ("Collaborative"; *Collaborative*). There came to be much more small group work, collaborative writing, and peer editing. As researchers and theorists looked more widely and deeply at disciplinary activity systems extending beyond the classroom, some began to focus on the ways discourse carries on disciplinary and professional activities, and they ways students learn in a discipline.

A few researchers began to use ethnographic methods to explore the variety of ways writing shapes learning in specific disciplines. They found that students are like "strangers in strange lands" when they are asked to write in a variety of new disciplines, to borrow the title of one of the most influential early ethnographic/linguistic studies of WAC (McCarthy). And research began on what writing in the disciplines is really like, how, for example, the seemingly humble and ubiquitous "research paper" takes many forms and has many functions across the curriculum, reflecting the methods, values, and epistemology of the discipline. Many general composition courses began to teach students that writing was different in different disciplines and tied to the kinds of learning going on in those disciplines. Textbooks by two authors in this volume, Bazerman (*The Informed Writer*) and Maimon (*Writing in the Arts and Sciences*) (both 1981) were particularly influential in this regard.

Similarly, the experience of WAC influenced the assessment of writing. Several of the stories in this collection begin with a composition director needing to do assessment and finding the old behaviorist and formalist ideas of assessment inadequate. How do students use writing to succeed in college? they asked. And to answer that question, they began to look beyond the traditional composition classroom and talk to colleagues across the curriculum.

So WAC benefited mightily from the professionalization of composition in the 1970s and early 1980s. But WAC also contributed mightily, in broadening the focus to the role of writing in whole curriculum, in the development of the whole student, and to the whole range of writing that the general composition courses were—quite unrealistically—expected, traditionally, to prepare students for. Indeed, the WAC movement raised the level of awareness of the university community (and in a more modest way, the K-12 community) to writing, thus raising its professional status by making it more widely and directly useful.

WAC's History and Future

Today the WAC movement—called variously writing in the disciplines (WID) or communication across the curriculum (CAC), depending on the emphasis—takes a vast number of forms at different institutions, K-graduate school. Perhaps one third of U.S. institutions have some WAC program (McLeod and Soven). These programs are often (but not always) connected with or a part of the general writing courses (first-year and/or upper level), specialized writing courses, composition courses linked to courses or departments in another field, or a writing center/tutoring center. Many WAC programs also exist without any specific curricular connection; instead they are part of faculty development efforts, often under the umbrella of a teaching support center. But they are almost always charged with integrating writing development into the teaching and learning in the various specialized academic programs, through building partnerships. The vast number of forms WAC takes is well illustrated in this volume (for more specific discussions of WAC models, see McLeod, et al.).

The first programs, however, began with faculty in various disciplines sitting down to talk about a felt need—poor writing (or thinking) among students. The "ur-form" of WAC, as I noted above, is a faculty workshop, led by a faculty member from English, ordinarily, but decidedly in the role of leader or facilitator—not trainer or teacher. The model was egalitarian. The faculty workshop was a place to share ideas and practices, not a place to learn from an expert, ordinarily. There faculty not only discussed the particular needs and resources for their students' writing but also how writing works differently in each of their disciplines, how it brings students to deeper involvement with the unique ways of knowing in each—the epistemology—and how they write themselves, professionally and, sometimes, personally. (Fulwiler and Young, this volume) This was a revelation, often, to both English and other faculty, as was the experience of sitting down together and talking seriously about their teaching—a rare experience, unfortunately, for most faculty.

How is such an informal, grassroots practice disseminated to become a movement? The model of dissemination was, as things evolved, that of the "itinerant preacher"—the workshop facilitator (Walvoord 61). Institutions tended to bring in workshop leaders or "WAC consultants" for the faculty. Thus a loose network formed.

The model for many workshops was the NWP. In the NWP model, teachers in a region gather, usually in the summer, to share teaching ideas on improving students writing—and to write themselves. They write and talk and grow together in an egalitarian and collegial community. Though NWP summer retreats attracted mainly English and language arts teachers, teachers from other content areas were welcomed. Often local, regional, or state NWP sites were attached to universities, and the NWP site came to inspire college faculty looking for a way to improve teaching and learning through writing across the curriculum. As the WAC movement spread in higher education more rapidly than in secondary education, the connection between WAC and the NWP became less common or deep, though there are important exceptions (see Thaiss, this volume).

WAC, then, originated as a grassroots effort to improve teaching and learning through writing, without any specific curricular or theoretical agenda. And it has remained that. But WAC quickly found intellectual roots. Actually the WAC movement in the U.S. was directly inspired by a British researcher named James Britton and his colleagues at the University of London Institute of Education, who coined the term WAC. Several of his colleagues figure in the stories told here, such as Nancy Martin and Robert Parker. Britton and his colleagues viewed writing (and talk) as a gradually developing accomplishment, thoroughly bound up with the particular intellectual goals and traditions of each discipline or profession, not as a single set of readily-generalizable skills learned once and for all. Learning to write goes hand in hand with writing to learn, in James Britton's famous phrase. WAC aims not only to develop students' writing but, more importantly, *to develop learning through writing.* The basic idea is that students best learn to communicate when they're communicating about course material and preparing for professional roles where effective writing (and speaking and visual design) will be vital to their success—and preparing for roles as critically-aware citizens. They learn to write as they write to learn.

In the U.S., this theory of secondary-school writing development was adapted to higher education, which made sense because in U.S. colleges and universities, unlike those in Britain, students take courses in a range of fields rather than specializing immediately. With this basic theory and a basic form of grassroots organization—the faculty workshop and itinerant consultants—the WAC movement was set to contribute to the professionalization of composition and to the reform of American secondary and, especially, higher education.

It is these crucial formative years that the essays in this volume focus on. And an equally rich volume might be written on the years of development in the late 1980s and 1990s when WAC became woven into the fabric of American higher education brought us to the present sprawling diversity of approaches and national—indeed international—awareness. WAC is now becoming an important reform movement in European higher education, with the formation of a professional association, the European Association of Teachers of Academic Writing, conferences, national and international, and investments in research and pedagogy (Rienecker et al.). The WAC community is helping to produce 'change agents' worldwide. What then of the future?

The future of WAC has been the subject of much discussion and some controversy—as it must and should be in any growing movement. But what is certain is that this grassroots movement will continue to depend on the kind of personal and collegial commitment that these essays illustrate: a community of change agents.

I have tried here to suggest some themes and issues that struck me as I read these stories. Readers will doubtless find their own, and, I hope, new possibilities for their own work, whether in WAC or in other educational reforms. But in closing, I'd like to remember the breadth and depth of the challenge that the WAC movement took up, to put in perspective its remarkable accomplishments. The WAC movement has taken what is still widely regarded as a single, generalizable skill, learned once and for all at and early age—writing—and reconceived it as a ubiquitous and powerful tool for developing students and their teachers at all levels in all disciplines in all kinds of institutions. Even more ambitiously, WAC has attempted to simultaneously raise the awareness of students, teaching staff, and policy makers to writing's powerful and varied role in learning and teaching and work, while at the same time integrating efforts to improve writing into the specialized studies and activities writing serves—instead of segregating it and holding it in the domain of some discipline, or, worse, keeping it on the margins, where it has historically been in academia.

The movement has succeeded to the extent that now educators in other nations are looking to the WAC movement for inspiration and ideas for transforming their systems of education. WAC has expanded because it meets a deep need of people in modern societies, to connect with each other. It connects us to one another in powerful ways. And by learning to write in new ways, students are expanding their learning and thinking—and their involvement with different worlds that make up our world. The WAC movement has found and is continually finding ways to help students enter and eventually transform powerful organizations of people, lives linked by the written word, in ways so pervasive and daily that we forget sometimes how powerful writing is to our futures—and the futures of our students. So if students learn by expanding their involvements, so too must the WAC movement learn by expanding, as it has for a third of a century now. The future of WAC, like its past, is about forging alliances, expanding with new connections. And I'm terribly optimistic about its future.

As Barbara Walvoord pointed out, WAC—like so many other movements—may be transformed through its alliances and involvements into something that looks very different than the movement today. It might not even be called WAC. But the deep principles on which the WAC movement was founded, and to which it has persistently held, should continue to undergird whatever new transformations we create. These principles were articulated beautifully at the 1997 National WAC conference by Elaine Maimon ("Time"). Here they are:

- Writing is a complex process integrally related to thinking.
- WAC means active learning across the curriculum.
- Curriculum change depends on scholarly exchange among faculty members.
- Writing helps students make connections.
- WAC helps faculty members make connections, with students and with each other.
- WAC leads to other reforms in pedagogy, curriculum, and administration.

In the stories that follow, we see these principles in the making, in the words of several of the makers.

Works Cited

Bazerman, Charles. *The Informed Writer*. Boston: Houghton, 1981.

Bruffee, Kenneth. *Collaborative Learning: Higher Education, Interdependence and the Authority of Knowledge*. Baltimore: Johns Hopkins UP, 1993.

—. "Collaborative Learning and the Conversation of Mankind." *College English* 46.7 (1984): 635-52.

Giddens, Anthony. *Central Problems in Social Theory: Action, Structure and Contradiction in Social Analysis*. London: MacMillan, 1979.

Maimon, Elaine P. "Time Future Contained in Time Past." National Writing Across the Curriculum Conference. Charleston, SC, 1997.

Maimon, Elaine P., Gerald L. Belcher, Gail W. Hearn, Barbara F. Nodine, and Finbarr W. O'Connor. *Writing in the Arts and Sciences*. Boston: Little Brown, 1981.

McCarthy, Lucille P. "A Stranger in Strange Lands: A College Student Writing Across the Curriculum." *Research in the Teaching of English* 21 (1987): 233–65.

McLeod, Susan H., et al., eds. *WAC for the New Millennium: Strategies for Continuing Writing across the Curriculum Programs*. Urbana, IL: National Council of Teachers of English, 2001.

McLeod, Susan H., and Margot Soven, eds. *Writing across the Curriculum: A Guide to Developing Programs*. Newberry Park, CA: Sage, 1992. Academic.Writing Landmark Publications in Writing Series. Available: http://aw.colostate.edu/books/mcleod_soven. October 20 2001.

Nystrand, Martin, Stuart Greene, and Jeffrey Wiemelt. "Where Did Composition Studies Come From? An Intellectual History." *Written Communication* 10.3 (1993): 267–333.

Rienecker, Lotte, Peter Stray Jorgensen, Gerd Brauer, and Lennert Bjork, eds. *Teaching Academic Writing in European Higher Education*. Amsterdam: Kluwer, 2003.

Russell, David R. *Writing in the Academic Disciplines, 1870–1990: A Curricular History*. Carbondale: Southern Illinois UP, 1991.

Thaiss, Chris. "Writing across the Curriculum." *Theorizing Composition*. Ed. Mary Lynch Kennedy. Westport, CT: Greenwood Press, 1998. 356–64.

Walvoord, Barbara E. "The Future of WAC." *College English* 58.1 (1996): 58–79.

1 It Takes a Campus to Teach a Writer: WAC and the Reform of Undergraduate Education

Elaine P. Maimon

The first time I heard the actual phrase, "writing across the curriculum," was in a discussion, probably in 1974 or 1975 of the book by Nancy Martin et al., entitled, Writing and Learning Across the Curriculum, *11–16. The phrase truly resonated with me a few years later when I spent a day visiting the National Endowment for the Humanities (NEH) seminar at Rutgers called "Writing in the Humanities." Robert Parker, one of Nancy Martin's co-authors, was among the people whom I met on that visit. Toby Fulwiler, a participant in that seminar, was undoubtedly in attendance on that summer day when my colleague Barbara Nodine and I made the one-hour-drive from Beaver College (now Arcadia University) in suburban Philadelphia) to Rutgers, but I do not recall that he and I connected on that day. That would come later.*

Let me begin this essay with a specific date in that same summer of 1977: July 14. That particular Bastille Day was revolutionary in an educational sense for Beaver College, the small, liberal arts college, where I then served as Assistant Professor of English (completing my second year as a full-time faculty member) and as Director of Composition. It was on that day that we received official word from the National Endowment for the Humanities (NEH) that the College had received an Institutional Development Grant in the amount of $207,726 (a fortune in those days and the largest federal grant ever received to that date in the history of Beaver College) for "A Program to Strengthen the Humanities at Beaver College through an Emphasis on Instruction in Writing and Reading by all Faculty, September 1977 to August 1980."

I have snapshots of the impromptu celebration that took place at my house that afternoon. My seven-year-old daughter, who now conducts writing workshops herself, looks on dazed, as professors and administrators, fully sober and fully clothed, jump into the backyard swimming pool in an expression of joy and affirmation of community.

What led up to that joyous *Quatorze Juillet* of 1977? Let's turn back the clock to September, 1973. (One of the wonders of the written word is the power that it gives us over time!) After two-and-a-half years at Haverford College, as a substitute for professors on leave (and consequently teaching just about every post-Renaissance literature course in the Haverford catalogue), I became a part-time composition instructor at Beaver College. Married, with two children, ages three-and-a-half and six months, at a time when the job market for English professors had gone into its first major slump, I was ready to accept any college teaching job in the Philadelphia metropolitan area. In fact, the prospect of teaching freshman composition—in multiple sections but with one preparation—seemed at first to offer the prospect of more time to play with my babies.

So why was I working harder than ever? Most of the students at Beaver were hungry to learn more about writing. Unlike Haverford College students, a pretty elite bunch, Beaver College students wanted to find a way in. Cracking the secret codes of the university—manifest in writing—seemed like a good place to start. And I really wanted to help them. But how? My PhD in English, conferred with distinction by the University of Pennsylvania, had not taught me much about teaching writing. But I had learned how to be a scholar, to find out what I needed to know. My first instinct was to take a course. So I looked for one in the Penn catalogue and decided upon linguistics. Not a bad choice. What else was available in Philadelphia-area universities in the early 1970s?

But the most important thing I did was to read journals, attend conferences, and talk with colleagues. Fortunately, the 1976 Conference on College Composition and Communication Conference (4Cs) was held in Philadelphia. Knowing absolutely no one at the conference, I remember going from session to session, happy to be in structured settings, so that I could use them as the basis for conversation during the lonely coffee breaks. Beyond stimuli for academic chats, I found much-needed information at 4Cs and resolved to attend subsequent meetings. And, in fact, ever since the mid-1970s I have faithfully attended 4Cs, except on those occasions in these later years when administrative duties have posed irresolvable conflicts.

As the 1974–75 academic year came to an end, Beaver College had (*mirabile dictu*) appointed me to a full-time position on the tenure-track as an Assistant Professor of English and Director of Composition. It was the custom in those days, a custom that, I am told, still prevails in some academic institutions, to appoint the youngest and most vulnerable person on the faculty to the position of Composition Director. It was convenient to do so because one of the major responsibilities of the position was to accept abuse from colleagues, who used faculty meetings as the occasion to heap blame on the English department for what they saw as the generally woeful state of student writing.

During the Fall 1975 semester, writing instruction was a matter of particular contention. Student admissions had not yet begun to accelerate at the college, and faculty members were in a competitive mood over course enrollments. Why, they wondered, did the English department require a full year of freshman composition? What was actually achieved in the second semester? Several faculty members insisted that the Director of Composition should undertake to measure increased student achievement in order to justify the two-semester composition requirement.

So, I embarked on a personal research project to discover the state of knowledge on measuring growth in writing abilities. I studied standardized tests and discovered that they were tests of usage, not of writing. After a literature search of books and articles, I realized that no one had anything better than a primitive grasp of this area of knowledge. Actually, this futile search piqued my interest in a number of research questions about measuring growth in writing—questions that my PhD in English literature left me unprepared to explore—without a knowledgeable partner. So, in desperation, I approached a tenured cognitive psychologist, who also happened to be the Chair of the College Curriculum Committee, the very committee and, in fact, the very person who had been demanding evidence of further student development in writing through the second semester.

"Barbara," I said, "I think it's a great idea to measure growth in student writing achievement, but to me a measure means iambic pentameter. If you really want to explore this matter, we will have to do it together."

And that's what we did, forming a research partnership that lasted through several articles and three books. Barbara Nodine learned, among other things, that growth in writing ability was not a neat linear process, although we did our best to find something that was linear in our first published article, "Measuring Syntactic Growth: Errors and Expectations in Sentence-Combining Practice with College Freshmen." As time went on, she was in much better position than I to explain complexities to other empiricists on the Beaver College faculty. For my own part, I learned a great deal about the joys and limitations of the scientific method. But the most important lesson I learned was that research—especially research partnerships across the disciplines—was the best foundation for growth and change in academic institutions.

In fact, I was already engaged in another partnership with another colleague, Gail Hearn, who had sought my help in writing an instruction manual for biology students to improve their observation of zoo animals. In another kind of partnership, I had teamed up with a popular anthropology professor, Bette Landman, who later became Dean and is now President of Arcadia University (neé Beaver College). In 1975, we were two assistant professors forming what is now called a learning community. Nothing fancy here. Bette always had high freshman enrollments, so it was a sure bet that I would have a number of her students in my composition section. I assigned the same collection of anthropology essays that she assigned to her class, and we invited the students we had in common to do drafting across the curriculum, submitting a draft for comments to either one of us and then the finished paper for a grade to the other.

This kind of collaboration on research and teaching was going on by December of 1975, as the fall semester catapulted toward final exams. Then on December 9, 1975, *Newsweek* published a cover story on "Why Johnny Can't Write." The new dean (whose tenure lasted only one year) summoned me to his office and threw the magazine at me. "What are you going to do about this?" he demanded. At the end of that month, at the MLA (Modern Language Association) meeting in San Francisco, I found the answer.

During my days at Haverford College, I had started attending the
MLA, when it was scheduled in New York City. In late 1974, the Call
for Papers appeared for the December 1975 MLA meeting, which
would be held in San Francisco. Inspired by my linguistics course, I
wrote a paper and, without expecting it to be accepted, submitted it
for consideration at a session on linguistics and the teaching of writing, organized by Paul Eschholz and Albert Rosa of the University
of Vermont. When I found out that my paper had been selected for
presentation at the San Francisco meeting, Beaver College offered me
$50.00 for the cross-country trip, actually a generous amount, consid-
ering that I was still on a part-time appointment. I was determined to
attend, even though it meant pretty much paying my own way. Conferences are important sites for developing new ideas. The 1975 MLA
meeting, besides giving Beaver College its money's worth for a $50.00
investment, was a turning point in my professional life.

1975 was the year that many young English professors, traditionally trained in literature, discovered that the teaching of writing was
a scholarly field. This realization may have been building for a time,
e.g., my own investigations into the growth of writing abilities. But
lightning struck in a San Francisco ballroom when we heard Mina
Shaughnessy present a talk entitled, "Diving In." It was highly unusual
for the MLA to devote a ballroom to a forum on the teaching of writing. Never before or since, at least in my MLA experience, was there
a greater buzz in a ballroom. Shaughnessy, the director of the writing
program at City College (CUNY), challenged the standing-room-only
crowd to react against conservative academics who saw the teaching of
writing as a matter of "guarding the gates" or "converting the natives."
Shaughnessy urged us to dive into a new scholarly field—a field that
we could help create.

Like many others whom I did not yet know, I left that session in
a transformed state of mind. It was lunchtime, and I had made plans
to join a friend for a cable car ride and lunch on Fisherman's Wharf.
My unfortunate friend, who had not attended the session—and, indeed, everyone else in proximity to me on that cable car—heard me
extol Mina Shaughnessy's inspiring challenge to devote our scholarly
energies toward creating a new field of composition studies. One of
my fellow cable-car travelers was Harriet Sheridan, then the Acting
President and Dean of Carleton College in Northfield, Minnesota. I
have written about this first meeting with Harriet Sheridan elsewhere

("Teaching Across the Curriculum"). Suffice it to say that community building takes place in the pages of journals and in formal conference sessions but also on cable cars and in restaurants. Harriet joined my friend and me for lunch at Fisherman's Wharf and then invited me to spend some time with her the next day so that she could tell me about the Carleton Plan.

As a result of that San Francisco MLA meeting, I returned to Beaver College with a plan for writing across the curriculum—the Carleton Plan. Here is a partial description of the Carleton Plan in Harriet Sheridan's own words, from *Course Information for Freshmen*, "Writing at Carleton," 1975–76:

> Each summer a group of faculty from diverse departments joins with student rhetoric assistants in a Rhetoric Institute to talk over common principles and standards for writing courses, and to analyze each other's prose minutely and frankly. Although the emphasis we give to the different aspects of writing may differ from course to course, proof of a vigorous diversity that is one of the strengths of the College, we are all agreed about a core of objectives and methods. We value coherent organization and the exact expression of ideas. We look for the human voice that speaks to the human ear. We agree to explain the function of a writing assignment before you are thrust upon it, and to record our reactions to your essays in legible comment. We agree to schedule writing assignments that allow time before and after for your questions and revisions. We agree to emphasize revision as a way to help you become your own best editor. Although a Rhetoric Seminar offers more writing and more conference time, each of the other kinds of writing courses will pursue its way towards our common ends.

With the help of a grant from the Northwest Area Foundation, Harriet Sheridan had been conducting Rhetoric Institutes for Carleton faculty members, since the summer of 1973. These faculty members would then teach courses called "extra-territorials," meaning that they were in disciplines beyond the territory of English. Assisting the faculty members in these classes were rhetoric fellows—undergraduate tutors who had participated in the summer Rhetoric Institute. Dean Sheridan had thus created the first Writing Fellows program in the United States. When she became Dean of the College at Brown University in the early 1980s, she took that concept with her. In fact, the major contribution of the 1970s Carleton College program was national, rather than local. Brown University Writing Fellows have been emulated in many places. The Carleton Rhetoric Institute was the model for faculty writing workshops at Beaver College, which then influenced writing workshops across the country. And the Carleton approach of involving the campus in writing instruction influenced the full-immersion model at Beaver College.

By very good luck, Harriet Sheridan had plans to visit Philadelphia for a deans' conference on February 7, 1976. (The Philadelphia celebration of the nation's Bicentennial Year, blessedly, brought many conferences to the City of Brotherly Love, including the 1976 CCCC, as mentioned above.) Luck is always a factor in human endeavor, but human relationships are more important than luck. Harriet agreed to use part of her time in Philadelphia in a visit to the Dean and top administration of Beaver College. This visit gave credibility to the ideas that I as an untenured assistant professor had brought back from the MLA.

Beaver College was ready for luck—and for Harriet Sheridan's good counsel. On February 27, 1976, twenty days after Dean Sheridan's visit, the Beaver College Committee on Educational Policy gave preliminary approval to the Carleton Plan. Here are some excerpts from the minutes to that meeting:

> The Carleton Plan would be adopted gradually with modifications appropriate to Beaver's needs. . . . Each summer, or in January, a group of faculty from various disciplines, together with prospective student tutors, would enroll in a nine-day training seminar, taught by the English department. They would learn to teach writing skills and assess writing competency. . . . Carleton College has seen an increased emphasis on writing throughout the institution since the inception of this program. The need for students to improve their writing skills has become widely recognized.

(Beaver College, *Committee on Education Policy,* Tenth Meeting, 1975–76, February 27, 1976)

On April 6, 1976, the Beaver College faculty approved a plan for writing across the curriculum. The two-semester composition requirement was affirmed, although the course name was changed from Literature and Expression to Thought and Expression. Because the composition year was now understood as the foundation for writing across the campus, the faculty approved a policy of no exemptions. What a difference a few months and Harriet Sheridan had made.

The faculty had also approved, in principle, the institution of faculty writing workshops, with the first one to be held during the January break in 1977. The problem was that Beaver College in those days was a poorly endowed college, with very little to spare for faculty development (cf. the $50.00 travel grant for the San Francisco trip). Although the faculty had approved the idea of the English department's teaching the rest of the faculty to teach writing, I knew that we needed to bring in outside consultants, if we wanted to expand the teaching of writing beyond the teaching of literature. In fact, I wanted to bring to Beaver one of the few English professors in the nation who actually could help faculty members incorporate writing into their courses. I wanted to invite Harriet Sheridan. I thought that I could persuade Harriet to forgo a stipend, but I did want to pay her travel expenses and to provide a few amenities for the workshop. But when I asked the dean for $1500, he suggested that I raise the money myself. And so began my career as a fund-raiser.

Working with the Executive Vice President, I wrote a proposal to a small, Philadelphia-based foundation, Dolfinger-McMahon, for $2,500 in seed money to conduct a nine-day faculty workshop in January 1977. The Executive Vice President thought that it would be a good idea, simultaneously, to begin drafting a much larger proposal for a campus-wide writing program. He was not at all sure who might be interested in funding such a proposal, but he knew that we were embarked upon an important idea.

I immediately suggested the National Endowment for the Humanities for the larger proposal. But the Executive Vice President, who spent a portion of his time haunting the halls of Washington agencies, told me that NEH viewed writing as a skill and therefore under the purview of the Office of Education. When I reviewed previous grants from the Office Education, it was clear that their interest was quite literally in discrete skills, e.g. usage and punctuation. I knew from journals and conferences that NEH had funded the Berkeley Bay Area Writing Project and believed that the time might be right to reaffirm rhetoric as one of the key humanities disciplines. It took my own trip to NEH in November 1976, to convince the Executive Vice President that we should, indeed, submit a proposal to NEH.

Right before Thanksgiving I returned to Beaver with a sample NEH proposal the size of my doctoral dissertation. The deadline was January 2. Even though I had the five-page Dolfinger-McMahon proposal and a few additional ideas drafted, it looked impossible to submit a full-fledged proposal by the deadline. In those days before word processors, secretaries had to type and retype grant proposals, and Beaver College secretaries would be on the job only through December 23. We had four weeks to prepare the proposal.

It did not seem doable. I was teaching three courses and supervising student teachers. But the Executive Vice President was by this time convinced that we were dealing with an idea whose time had come and that if we did not get our proposal to NEH in January, five better known institutions would submit their proposals six months later. He told me to use his secretary for anything I needed and—this was true heresy—to get my grades in late, if I had to.

Well, we got the proposal—and my grades—in on time. The short time-frame inspired the most incredible team-work on the part of faculty and administration. Art professors produced flow charts that were suitable for framing; history professors helped with the history of the institution; and everybody read and commented on multiple drafts.

Meanwhile, we were also soliciting participation in the Dolfinger-McMahon workshop, scheduled for January. Since we had no stipends to offer for the nine-day workshop, we used the general momentum to promise that only those who participated in January would be eligible for summer stipends under the proposed NEH grant. It worked. Twenty-five faculty members signed up, including a large representation of senior faculty members and department chairs.

In December 1976, the MLA met in New York City, obviating the need for another $50.00 travel grant for this Philadelphia professor. But in many ways, the 1976 MLA meeting was as momentous as the San Francisco meeting in 1975. Professor Kenneth Bruffee of Brooklyn College, the chair of the newly formed Teaching of Writing Division, scheduled an informal meeting on the last day of the convention for those division members who were writing program administrators. At that standing-room-only meeting, the National Association of Writing Program Administrators (WPA) was born.

Since I had spoken up at this organizational meeting from the small-college perspective, I found myself on the planning committee for this new organization. That was pretty amazing, since the award of the NEH grant was still six months away and my only publication at that time was about F. Scott Fitzgerald. But I left the meeting room with Harvey Wiener and Donald McQuade, both already names in the field of writing, to make concrete plans for creating WPA, an organization that would provide support for those in another newly-emerging subfield of composition, writing program administration. The founding of WPA demonstrates the collegiality, openness, and non-hierarchical spirit that created the entrepreneurial energy in the field of rhetoric and composition in general and in writing across the curriculum in particular. From a pragmatic standpoint, my work in WPA put me in contact with an expanding network of scholars, who contributed to the writing workshops at Beaver College. Many emerging WAC leaders also became leaders in the Council of Writing Program Administrators (Linda Peterson, for example, served as its president, and many of those who have contributed to this volume have served or are serving on the WPA executive board and on the editorial board of the journal).

Back in Philadelphia after that second momentous MLA meeting, my colleagues and I prepared for the first writing workshop, supported by the Dolfinger-McMahon Foundation in January 1977. Harriet Sheridan, during her five days with us, set the tone for writing across the curriculum at Beaver College by assigning Aristotle's *Rhetoric* as our only text. Those who had previously thought that a writing workshop would be about commas and semi-colons, or, at best, about gerunds and gerundives, found out that writing was an ancient art, a challenging craft, and, in many ways, thinking made visible. For the final four days of the workshop, Harriet Sheridan's colleague, Wayne Carver, was the workshop leader. As editor of the Carleton Miscellany, Professor Carver spent most of his time in one-on-one conferences with faculty members about their own plans for publication. By doing so, he established the connection between the teaching of writing and faculty members' own writing and publication. I believe that this continuum linking student writing and professional writing makes manifest the complexity of the writing process. The empathy between students and faculty members as writers has done more than almost anything else, I believe, to sustain writing across the curriculum (as it has for the National Writing Project).

And then on July 14, 1977, we found out that the faculty commitment to the Dolfinger-McMahon workshop in January would be the first step in a sustained program. The NEH grant provided for two-week January workshops, followed each June by a five-week seminar. No stipend was offered for January, since it fell under faculty members' "Winterim" obligation, but January participation was prerequisite for membership in the June seminar, which did carry a stipend.

One key to success was the sustained commitment required of faculty members. Another was the emphasis on scholarly inquiry, rather than on a "how-to" approach. We benefited from the fact that no one in 1977 actually knew "how-to" in writing across the curriculum. But we structured the workshops and seminars to give maximum emphasis to the inquiry mode. We invited a variety of people who were doing interesting work on writing from various perspectives. Thanks to MLA, CCCC, WPA, and other occasions for networking, we were able to compile an amazing list: Edward P. J. Corbett, James Kinneavy, Linda Flower, Lynn Bloom, Winifred Horner, Harvey Wiener, Donald McQuade, Kenneth Bruffee, Richard Young, Nancy Sommers, John R. Hayes; the list goes on and on. We asked scholars to visit us for four days each and to engage faculty workshop participants as interactively as possible in their approaches to the teaching of writing. On the fifth day of each week, we met on our own to discuss the implications for us at Beaver College. In other words, we drew on a variety of interesting and contrasting perspectives to develop our own definitions and procedures for writing across the curriculum.

Some workshop leaders led us through discussions of student writing examples; others asked us to write and to discuss our own writing. Most asked us to read theoretical material; many suggested articles summarizing best practices. For three years, each January and June offered quite an intellectual feast. Each June workshop leader gave a public lecture on the Wednesday evening of his or her stay, and in that way we shared perspectives on the teaching of writing with the metropolitan Philadelphia community.

We also had parties. We understood that change has a crucial social dimension and that those who break bread together might very well go on to create innovative programs and even break conventions together.

My colleagues and I were also aware of the importance of regional connections. We helped form the Delaware Valley Writing Council to link people interested in writing instruction from all over metropolitan Philadelphia, extending to northern Delaware and southern New Jersey. In October of 1978, the Delaware Valley Writing Council held a conference on the Beaver College campus. We planned the conference for about 75 people; 300 showed up. They came in busloads from New York City and beyond. Chuck Bazerman was among them, as he reports in his chapter. We ran out of chairs. The ventilation system was sorely inadequate. But at that moment it dawned on us that Beaver College was becoming a name for writing across the curriculum.

I found myself developing a missionary zeal to make writing across the curriculum a national movement. I remember the 1978 4C's meeting in Denver, when Toby Fulwiler, Art Young, and I literally pursued Frank D'Angelo, the program chair for the 1979 4C's, on and off elevators, to convince him to make writing across the curriculum the theme for the meeting in Minneapolis—and he did. That 1979 4C's was a true tipping point for WAC, as several writers in this volume have reported.

Today as I think about that heady time in the late 1970s, I am amazed at the artless innovation we engaged in. So much that is current in educational theory and practice today had its seeds in the early days of writing across the curriculum. Learner-centered education and learning communities were parts of our projects. In addition to faculty workshops and seminars, the Beaver College NEH project included a provision for "cluster courses," in which three or more professors worked together to find linkages among what otherwise might have been discrete subject matter. Cluster courses were originally conceived as a means for ongoing faculty development. A composition instructor was always part of the cluster, ostensibly to provide ongoing writing assistance to the other professors in the cluster. And, indeed, we did further develop the practice of drafting across the curriculum, inviting students to develop a topic appropriate to two or more courses and then submit a draft to one instructor for comments and then a finished paper to a second instructor for a final grade applicable to both courses. As a serendipitous benefit, we planned interdisciplinary, thematic intersections among the three courses. A cluster that involved a course in nineteenth-century literature, a course in nineteenth-century history, and a course in Human Evolution found a focal point in the works of Charles Darwin, viewed as history, literature, and biology. The connections were remarkable.

The NEH project offered a course release each academic year to an English professor who had participated in the January and June workshops. The idea was to provide incentive for English department members, whose participation in the workshops was crucial, to attend (and learn) without their insisting on leading the discussions. In exchange for the course release, the English professor had the added responsibility of coordinating several course clusters and directing a Writing Center, transformed from a "clinic" to a place where trained undergraduate writing consultants were available for peer review.

This stratagem had several positive results. Nearly all full-time English professors participated in the workshops. Their participation led to real dialogue between first-year composition instructors and faculty in other departments. As a consequence, Beaver College developed a model for writing across the curriculum that had its foundation in freshman composition. The goals for that first-year course shifted radically from unreasonable expectations about students learning to write once and forever more to students gaining experience that other faculty members could build on: with writing as a complex set of processes, often involving multiple drafts; with peer review and collaborative learning; and with the use of a handbook as a reference tool. As the 1970s became the 1980s, the composition course became so highly regarded by the faculty as a whole that the English department was asked to develop an upper-division composition course for transfer students.

The immersion model was appropriate to Beaver because the culture of the college as a whole was transformed by writing across the curriculum. Beaver was too small for writing intensive courses because they might have led to a narrowing of students' writing experience rather than a persistent reinforcement throughout the curriculum. I recall one clever student's comment in early September of 1979 or 1980, after she had reviewed syllabi for her new fall courses to find that course after course listed the handbook that had been purchased in freshman composition as a required text, assigned papers in draft stages, and mandated peer review: "Good heavens, they've gone to another writing workshop. It's like the "'Stepford Wives.'"

During this period, five of us—Barbara Nodine in psychology, Gail Hearn in biology, Barry O'Connor in philosophy, Jerry Belcher in history, and I—were collaborating on the writing of two textbooks, so that other colleges and universities could institute writing across the curriculum and make the freshman composition course the foundation of the program. The process of writing these books—*Writing in the Arts and Sciences* and *Readings in the Arts and Sciences*—gave added legitimacy to the writing across the curriculum program at the college. Each co-author brought additional credibility to the curricular project by devoting years of scholarly endeavor to the textbooks.

By 1980, "across the curriculum" had such panache with the Beaver College faculty and, increasingly, with the educational community across the country, that Beaver College successfully applied to FIPSE (the Fund for the Improvement of Post-Secondary Education) for a project in problem-solving across the curriculum. That project eventually linked Beaver College faculty members with John Bean and others (see Bean, this volume). In addition, Beaver College received two additional grants from NEH, to disseminate writing across the curriculum to universities, colleges, and high schools across the country and, intensively to K-12 school districts in metropolitan Philadelphia. In 1983, in Philadelphia, as part of one of these later grant projects, Beaver College organized the first national conference in writing across the curriculum, entitled, "Writing in the Humanities."

Principles and practices of writing across the curriculum were also communicated through invited consultancies. During one consultancy, extending from 1981–83, I had the opportunity to assist my Alma Mater, the University of Pennsylvania, in creating their Writing Across the University program. It is gratifying to see ideas that I developed and reports that I wrote cited in Linda Peterson's chapter on the Ivy League Consortium.

The 1980s was the decade for organized dissemination of the principles of writing across the curriculum, manifested most dramatically in the twelve conferences sponsored by the University of Chicago on writing and critical thinking. The first of these conferences was originally intended to focus on cognitive development and adult learning. But at a meeting in New York City in 1981, for FIPSE project directors, I met Marilyn Stocker, who was assisting Carol Schneider in planning the first Chicago conference. In several long talks and walks through the streets of Manhattan, Marilyn and I discovered that her community of cognitive development and my community of writing across the curriculum had enormous amounts in common, even though we were reading different bibliographies and attending different conferences. In twenty-first-century terminology, both communities were "learner-centered." Marilyn communicated this information to Carol, and Carol and I talked. We thought it would be highly beneficial—and great fun—to bring these communities together. Thus, the Chicago conferences, which others in this volume have written about in greater detail. By the way, Carol Schneider is now the President of the Association of American Colleges and Universities (AAC&U) and in that role continues to organize national conferences on the cutting edge of teaching and learning.

So where are we today? We can say with confidence that writing across the curriculum is a reform movement that has outlived the century in which it was first articulated. In fact, WAC has outlived the name of the college, where it had early prominence. Beaver College has changed its name to Arcadia University. I asked JoAnn Weiner, the Chair of the Arcadia University English department (also a colleague during the late 1970s), to comment on writing across the curriculum at Arcadia today:

> As I see it, there are four manifestations of WAC (broadly defined) here:
>
> 1. the composition courses are still the gateway to writing in the university in that they aim to help the student develop her own writing process and a conscious understanding of it;
>
> 2. many faculty outside the English department incorporate writing into their courses—graduate as well as undergraduate—in one way or another;
>
> 3. the Writing Center has a faculty director, newly hired, who trains and supervises student consultants;
>
> 4. our two required interdisciplinary core curriculum courses—Interpretations of Justice (ID111) and Pluralism in the United States (ID222) are advancing writing and critical thinking at the University.

Across the country in classrooms, grade school through grad school, ideas that were radical in the 1970s are taken for granted now: writing as process, writing as critical thinking, peer review, etc. I remember when naysayers predicted that WAC would have a short life like every other educational fad. But a movement that uncovers fundamental, simple truths is the opposite of faddish. It takes a campus to teach a writer. How could we ever have thought otherwise?

WORKS CITED

Maimon, Elaine P. "'Teaching' Across the Curriculum." *Handbook of the Undergraduate Curriculum.* Ed. Jerry G. Gaff, James L. Ratcliffe, and Associates. San Francisco: Jossey-Bass, 1997. 377–91.

Maimon, Elaine P., et al. *Readings in the Arts and Sciences.* Boston: Little Brown, 1984.

Maimon, Elaine P., et al. *Writing in the Arts and Sciences.* Boston: Little Brown, 1981.

Maimon, Elaine P., and Barbara Nodine. "Measuring Syntactic Growth: Errors and Expectations in Sentence-Combining Practice with College Freshmen." *Research in the Teaching of English* 12 (1978): 233–44.

Shaughnessy, Mina. "Diving In: An Introduction to Basic Writing." MLA Convention. San Francisco, 1975. Published in *College Composition and Communication,* 27 (1976): 234–39.

2 A University-Schools Partnership: WAC and the National Writing Project at George Mason University

Christopher Thaiss

> *I don't recall the first time I heard the term "writing across the curriculum," but it was probably in our Northern Virginia Writing Project planning for a guest presentation by Janet Emig in our first summer institute. Emig was the first director of the New Jersey Writing Project, also just beginning, and her presentation emphasized her research in "writing as a mode of learning" and its applications across disciplines.*

When WAC began at George Mason in 1978, the university was but six years old. The college from which it grew, George Mason College of the University of Virginia, was only twenty. But GMU was in the fastest-growing part of the state, the burgeoning suburbs of Washington, D.C., and by the mid-1970s was adding a thousand students a year, most of them commuters, most holding jobs, a rich mix from around the globe. Growth and diversity were the catalysts for WAC at GMU, as they were for most of what happened in those days at this new university.

As this essay will detail, WAC at GMU grew up in close connection with the Northern Virginia site of the National Writing Project (NWP), which began in 1974 as the Bay Area Writing Project in California and expanded nationally after receiving a challenge grant from the National Endowment for the Humanities. The GMU WAC-NVWP relationship was indeed, as I'll show, vital to the shape and progress of our local development of writing across the curriculum, but it was hardly the only example of NWP influence on university WAC. At least two other early WAC ventures storied in the volume: the Baltimore Area Consortium for Writing Across the Curriculum (BACWAC), described by Barbara Walvoord, and the WAC program at Michigan Tech, described by Toby Fulwiler, were built by many of the same people who created the NWP sites in those areas and were moved by the same theoretical and pedagogical principles that inspired the NWP.

The Setting for WAC at GMU and My Place in It

I'd been hired as a Renaissance specialist by the English department in 1976 after having taught there and at Northern Virginia Community College for a year as an adjunct, during which I had taught mostly composition. As typical in those days, I'd had no training as a comp teacher; I'd had little teaching background at all, having been a TA for two semesters in literature while doing my PhD at Northwestern, which I completed in 1975. Though I had to learn to teach writing on the job, I found that I loved working with student writers, especially the very diverse populations at both GMU and NVCC. When I was hired full-time by Mason, I looked forward to teaching both writing and literature. Then, in 1977, at the start of my second year, our Faculty Senate picked up on the national furor over "Why Johnny Can't Write" (as the *Newsweek* cover had proclaimed in December 1975) to question why so many GMU juniors and seniors seemed to have severe trouble putting together coherent essays with correctly constructed sentences. Senate leaders surveyed faculty in all fields as to their general perceptions of student writing, and faculty took the opportunity to vent their frustrations with "foreign" students' "poor grammar," their suspicions of the many students (about 30 percent) who were transferring in ever-increasing numbers from the community colleges, and their concerns about an English department that just didn't seem to be "doing its job" in its freshman comp courses. All the "evidence" in the survey was anecdotal and emotional; no actual student work had been collected or studied as part of the research. Nevertheless, a crisis atmosphere pretty quickly developed.

When the Senate turned to the English department (where else would one turn in those days?) for answers, the English chair at the time, Michael Sundell, replied in a letter to the Senate that the Department was doing its level best in its two freshman courses (capped at 29 students in those days) to cure the various writing ills that our students brought with them from high school, but that it was an unmanageable task; still, he maintained, who else was qualified to attempt it? Besides, the Department could do nothing about all those who had transferred from NVCC having already completed the composition requirement there. The Senate replied as Senates do, with establishment of a Literacy Task Force, and with tentative suggestions, including a junior-level test that all students would have to pass and "remedial" courses for deficient incoming students, both freshmen and transfers. The task force would study these options and others. But there was no question in anyone's mind that something needed to be done, and at that point in the debate that "something" didn't include faculty development. Never was it questioned during the debate just what students were being asked to write in those courses where they were allegedly performing so poorly, nor had anyone asked what faculty in those courses were doing with and to the writing and for the writers. But this was, of course, pre-WAC.

Mike Sundell turned to Donald Gallehr, an eighteenth-century scholar and linguist who at age 36 had already been a member of the faculty for eleven years and who had begun with a few other faculty to build a writing program. The program included a few advanced undergraduate sections in creative and technical writing and a master's level course in the teaching of writing, taught by Don. The program also included a "writing lab": use of a cubicle amid a warren of faculty cubicles for twenty hours a week to counsel concerned student writers.

BIRTH OF THE NORTHERN VIRGINIA WRITING PROJECT

At the time of the 1977 crisis, Don had been engaged in his most ambitious project yet, creation of a Northern Virginia site as part of the new National Writing Project, a groundbreaking collaboration between public school and university faculties that had started in the Bay Area in 1974. The Bay Area Writing Project had just secured a challenge grant from the National Endowment for the Humanities, had become the National Writing Project (NWP), and was seeking site applications from around the U.S. Don and education professor Larry Bowen had met with NWP leaders James Gray and Miles Myers in Berkeley in summer 1977 to talk about a possible Northern Virginia

Writing Project, and they and Fairfax County Public Schools language arts supervisor Betty Blaisdell applied that fall. The first summer institute for teachers, K-University, would be held in July-August 1978.

Gallehr was the best choice, probably the only choice, to lead the Department's response to the Senate, as his work with the expanding writing program and his development of the NVWP had made him uniquely conversant in this almost exclusively literature-oriented Department (typical for the time) with the ideas and texts of the nascent field of composition and rhetoric. The theoretical basis of the NWP, which Don brought to his work with the Senate, was embodied in two essential principles: "teachers teaching teachers" and "teachers of writing must write" (Gray). These principles would not only support the new NVWP but would also become part of the basis for Don's and the English department's response to the Senate. "Teachers teaching teachers" meant that the primary agents of the Project would always be classroom teachers, not the administrators or outside experts central to most faculty development schemes. The "faculty," as it were, of any Project site would be excellent classroom teachers who would be invited to take part in a summer institute, and who would develop presentations on aspects of the teaching of writing that they would then be qualified to give in workshops and in-service courses. The rationale was that actual teachers would have greater credibility in a faculty development situation than would a non-teacher, regardless of expertise, and would be better able to understand and adapt to the audience's needs.

"Teachers of writing must write" recognized the great credibility gap that existed in schools at all levels between what writing teachers preached and their own, usually limited, writing experience. So every NWP summer institute and every NWP in-service course would include a large proportion of time devoted to the participant teachers' own writing. Here they would learn how difficult it was to write, thus learning not only empathy for students but typical problems writers face. They would learn how to offer solutions to writers by having to confront problems in their own composing. They would also work with fellow writers in the Project and learn how to give and receive commentary. What the BAWP leaders discovered, and what other site directors discovered in their first workshops based on this principle, was the deep and largely unfulfilled desire by teachers for just this time and attention to their own writing. As it turned out, a similar desire was latent in the GMU faculty, and would be adapted productively in the GMU program that emerged.

Gallehr was named the English department representative to the Literacy Task Force. Meanwhile, as the new Northern Virginia Writing Project prepared for its first invitational summer institute for classroom teachers, Gallehr asked me to join him on the Department team in planning the event. I still consider this one of the most important moments in my development as a teacher and scholar. Though I'd been hired into the assistant professorship to teach Shakespeare and other Renaissance literature (in 1977 I was teaching classics, the Bible in literature, and 17th century poets, too, besides the early modern lit survey), I'd already been bitten by the composition bug. I'd first come to GMU in 1975, while finishing my Renaissance dissertation at the Folger Library in DC, to serve as a ten-hour a week volunteer in the new writing lab that Don had founded. I'd had little teaching experience as a grad student at Northwestern, and I saw this as a way to make myself more attractive on the job market. That bit of tutoring experience gave me my first taste of the euphoria one can feel in helping others learn to write. Soon thereafter I was hired as an adjunct to teach freshman composition, both at GMU and at Northern Virginia Community College. I marveled at the diversity of the students, the individuality of their imaginations and lives, the depth of their desire to be accepted as competent, even excellent, writers. Don introduced me to NCTE publications and to the books of such writers as Donald Murray, James Britton, James Moffett, and Ken Macrorie, and I used these influences to mold my teaching of writing. I was thrilled when Don asked me join him in planning the NVWP summer institute and in reviewing what he would propose to the Senate in regard to GMU's literacy crisis.

A Focus on Faculty Development: Search for a Model

Imbued with the NWP philosophy, Don proposed to the Literacy Task Force that, prior to any more drastic and expensive "solution," GMU experiment with a focus on faculty. In early 1978, he received the approval of the Senate to put together for the fall a mini-conference of faculty from across the departments, their objective to take a deeper look at the writing of students and at how their own and colleagues' teaching might be enhanced through reading about and practicing some of the techniques being suggested by new scholars in the teaching of writing.

The Senate also passed at the time a more expensive, student-focused initiative, to be administered by English, to ascertain the writing strengths and weaknesses of all incoming students, and to design and coordinate a tutorial program for new students deemed the most deficient. Named the Composition Tutorial Center (CTC), the service would be staffed by graduate teaching assistants and would certify the competence of its participants through a combination of writing samples and standardized tests (the ETS Test of Standard Written English was chosen for both pre- and post-testing). I mention the CTC here to illustrate both the crisis orientation of the time and the contrast between philosophies that made for tense debate. These two very different responses also characterize what I've come to appreciate over the years as the George Mason attitude: a distinct preference for trying new things over either ignoring problems or trusting to established procedure; a preference for combining and recombining existing entities over business as usual. It's an attitude that makes start-ups, like WAC in 1978, relatively easy to find approval and even a little money for—but that makes sustaining an initiative a particular challenge. The early history of WAC at GMU illustrates this pattern (as has the entire history of GMU WAC, though that's not the focus of this essay). The CTC, on the other hand, though well supported when it began in 1981, closed in 1986, a typical casualty of the GMU philosophy.

The acceptance of Don's proposal for the GMU faculty development experiment, just as we were planning the first NVWP summer institute, meant inevitably that the two entities would be reinforcing. Given Don's intense involvement in the K-12 program, even as both of us were teaching a full load of courses, I took on main responsibility for the GMU conference plans, with help from education professor Robert Gilstrap, another new associate of the NVWP and a veteran GMU faculty member. The GMU program was a much less ambitious undertaking than the NVWP itself, but it lacked the well-articulated model that the Bay Area folks provided the NVWP for its K-12 institutes and courses. We had no models for a college cross-departmental writing workshop. At the time, the only school we had known to do such a thing was Beaver College in Pennsylvania, a private liberal arts school.

What we concocted blended the NVWP structure with the new research just published by the British Schools Council Project and the American scholars Janet Emig and Mina Shaughnessy. The term "writing across the curriculum" we picked up from the new (1976) book by Nancy Martin *et al.*, *Writing and Learning across the Curriculum, 11–16*, but we didn't use it to name our new program. Instead we called ours the "Faculty Inservice Writing Program," a maybe-too-cryptic double entendre to refer to both the writing by the faculty and the faculty's concern for the writing of students. Martin's book and those by James Britton and other British researchers gave us numerous examples of language use in a range of disciplines—none at the college level, however—that we would offer our participants as possible models to adapt to their courses. Emig's 1977 *College Composition and Communication* essay, "Writing as a Mode of Learning," gave us a nice interdisciplinary rationale for the program, while Shaughnessy's groundbreaking *Errors and Expectations,* new in 1977, gave us a productive, writing-centered framework for addressing faculty concerns with "correct English." The NVWP gave us the main structural features for what we would do and how.

The First Workshop, 1978

The first workshop would be an intensive affair, two full November days and one night at the Airlie conference center, some thirty miles from campus, affording full concentration on writing and teaching, with opportunities for brisk walks in the woods and contemplation by the duck pond. To finance the enterprise, we used the Senate's endorsement to secure funds from the Deans of the three colleges, Arts and Sciences, Business, and Education. The money would pay for lodgings, food, and meeting rooms for 20 persons, and allow us to pay an outside consultant and workshop leaders. Adapting part of the NWP summer institute model, we'd devote most of our time to hands-on presentations on aspects of teaching: "Topic Selection," "Audience," "Writing Essay Examinations," and "Correcting and Grading" were among the session titles. In this first conference we set aside no separate time for the personal writing of the participants, but we hoped that the writing they would do during the hands-on presentations would give them some of the same benefits. I also suspect that we didn't want to scare away these college folks by placing too much emphasis on their own prose too soon.

We invited Robert Parker, Janet Emig's colleague at Rutgers and a member of the British Schools council research team that Nancy Martin had headed, as our consultant. On the second morning of the conference he would give a talk on the research and the principles it led to and conduct one workshop. Don and I would also give presentations, mine on survey research I had conducted among faculty and local business folk and that I'd given in the 1978 Summer Institute: "The Writing that Professors and Managers Demand." Perhaps the most ingenious, at least unorthodox, element of the workshop would involve the workshop leaders for the majority of the presentations. Following NWP precedent, we wanted the presenters to be teachers themselves; but we had no obvious faculty from the departments to tap as presenters, and we had no time to identify who might be able to give presentations. So we decided to take the bold step of inviting several of the high school and middle school English faculty who had most impressed us during the NVWP institute to be our presenters. We hoped that their skill and professionalism would allow them to overcome the skepticism of the college faculty; we were banking on the cross-levels philosophy of the NWP to work with this college audience. It did, as it turned out.

Don recently recalled one incident: a middle-school teacher had just finished her presentation, and during the break that followed one of the faculty asked her how often she "consulted." When she replied that she had just been certified by the NVWP and had never spoken to a college audience before, the faculty member was amazed. "Wow," he said, "you mean you don't do this all the time?"

We sent invitations to all full-time faculty and received acceptances from sixteen, representing nine departments. Included, happily, were the most outspoken Senate critics of the English department, who came to take part, not carp. Everyone wrote; everyone contributed to the small groups set up for writing and response in the presentations; everyone talked seriously and positively about teaching; and everyone enjoyed the countryside, the food, the crisp weather. Evidence of our success came through in our follow-up program.

FOLLOW-UP, 1979, AND "AIRLIE II"

Again following the NWP model, we had built into our plan, and into the invitations we'd sent, the responsibility for each participant to attend monthly follow-up meetings during the spring semester. Each person also promised to give a short presentation during these spring meetings on a teaching technique he or she had applied in an actual spring course. As it turned out, these follow-up presentations not only provided continuity and evidence of learning, but they also enabled us to identify our presenters for the next min-conference, to held in Fall 1979; we dubbed it "Airlie II." The success of the first conference made securing funding for the second easier, and we even got a raise that allowed us to add a second night—time that allowed us to form reading/writing groups in which the individual writings of the participants were shared and commented on.

This program was as successful as the first (Elaine Maimon and her colleagues psychologist Barbara Nodine and biologist Gail Hearn were our consultants), and gave us the momentum for what became the next big step in our growth, the summer institutes and the state network of faculty writing programs.

Proposing the Faculty Writing Program, 1980 to 1982, the State Network, and the Writing Research Center

In 1979, an opportunity arose that we were encouraged to pursue by our enterprising President, George Johnson, who was aware of our success with the first two conferences and the NVWP. The Virginia General Assembly had authorized a competitive funding pool, called the Funds for Excellence, for public higher education. Each state institution could propose one or two projects. GMU proposed two initiatives from the NVWP, with the sanction of the English department: an expanded Faculty Writing Program and a cross-disciplinary Writing Research Center. What we felt would make the proposals particularly attractive to our state council of higher education was our cooperation with three other universities: Virginia Tech, Virginia State, and Old Dominion, all of whom were already members of the NWP Virginia network (which Don coordinated) and all of whom promised to develop their own versions of the Faculty Writing Program. In addition, the Writing Research Center we envisioned as a statewide venture: we would solicit proposals from faculty across disciplines and around the state to study any promising aspect of writing in teaching, and we would publish the studies.

The proposal we submitted for the Faculty Writing Program shows how our two years of experience since the complaints by the Faculty Senate had focused our thinking. Objectives included:

1. to train an inter-departmental core of faculty (University Fellows) to become workshop leaders for faculty throughout the university;

2. to increase faculty awareness of writing as a tool of literacy and improve faculty attitudes toward assigning writing within their own teaching fields;

3. to increase the volume and diversity of writing required of students;

4. to evaluate the writing done by students of University Fellows, faculty attending workshops, and faculty "untouched" by the program;

5. to initiate appropriate curriculum changes;

6. to work with other sites of the Virginia Writing Project FWC (Faculty Writing Consortium) to share the growing knowledge of writing across the curriculum. (Draft of "Proposal to the State Council of Higher Education for Virginia," February 20, 1980, from archives of the Northern Virginia Writing Project)

Clearly, we expected any improvement in student writing to be based firmly on faculty development across the disciplines and across schools. Assessment of students would be part of the larger scheme, but would come only after faculty development, as would proposals to change curriculum. The results of the first two workshop series had been sufficiently gratifying to the GMU administrators that there was no objection to this plan and it went forward with no changes. It's noteworthy that in the rationale for the proposal, much more emphasis is placed on the need for faculty development as an antidote to faculty isolation and fear of change than on any charges of insufficiency in student writing; to wit,

> Teachers' reluctance to share teaching methods and writing also stems from lack of an organized community of interest in most universities, including George Mason. Teachers, especially those outside English, often feel inadequate and incompetent both in writing and its evaluation. These fears keep teachers from assigning more than the occasional exam essay in their classes.

It's doubtful that such an appeal would work today, especially to a state education agency, but in 1980, prior to the faculty development model largely provided by WAC in colleges, it was a new and entirely sensible plea. We, and others like us in a few places around the country, were explorers in what at that time was the largely unknown wilderness of college faculty development.

WAC Comes to the NVWP

Just at the time Don and I were writing our proposals to the state, he was embarking on what we didn't foresee would be a rockier adventure in WAC faculty development. Following the first NVWP summer institute in 1978 we had begun teaching in-service courses for K-12 teachers in our home county, Fairfax. The model was working well: we had several full classes (25 students each) in local schools, the newly-certified Teacher/Consultants of the NVWP were giving deft, interactive presentations, and the participants were doing creative, satisfying work in their reading/writing groups, plus earning grad credit for re-certification or toward a master's degree. But our teachers came from high school English departments or wore their "language arts" caps from middle school and elementary school; WAC was not a concern in the K-12 program up to this time.

Then, in 1979, the Fairfax County Public Schools announced a radical curriculum policy change: high school social studies departments, not English departments, would be responsible for teaching students to write research papers. The change came about at least in part as a result of the consciousness-raising by the NVWP: the complexity and importance of the English teacher's job as writing teacher was being recognized and so some of the traditional responsibility was being "shared" with the social studies faculties. But the decision had been utterly top-down, and social studies teachers were angry. How angry Don discovered when he was asked to set up an in-service course for social studies teachers at a local high school, Lake Braddock. Throughout the course Don was the target of the frustration of the teachers over what they saw as a peremptory, disrespectful decision; at one point he asked the county social studies supervisor to come in and listen to what the teachers had to say. The supervisor came, but what the teachers regarded as insensitive response to questions just fueled the fire. Just after the supervisor left and Don had turned his attention to a teacher at one side of the class, he heard a loud BANG behind him. He thought it was a gunshot. But when he turned back, he saw that one of the teachers had taken off his shoe and had fired it off the metal door of a nearby student locker.

LESSONS FROM LAKE BRADDOCK

Despite the hostility, the course was an important development for the NVWP and taught valuable lessons not only for the K-12 program but also for our university WAC endeavor. First, it reinforced our commitment to an invitational structure; we would resist either making top-down decrees in our own programs or accepting responsibility for making the decrees of others palatable to teachers. From its earliest days the BAWP had, unlike most in-service schemes, respected what teachers knew and had not preached a particular way to teach. Instead it identified successful teachers, regardless of approach, and gave them a forum to teach other teachers. Whether in the K-12 program or the GMU program, we'd not tell teachers what to do and how to do it, but through studying teachers we'd identify successful practices and give the teachers an opportunity to teach colleagues. For the GMU faculty program, enacting this philosophy meant such venues as local workshops, team teaching (or linked course) arrangements, conference presentations, and publication in books or newsletters.

A second lesson we learned from the social studies course, coupled with the early success of the GMU program, was the value of a WAC orientation throughout the NVWP. Despite its rough sailing, the course had identified a few teachers who would have as much to teach teachers about writing as a successful English teacher would, just as the Airlie conferences and the follow-up workshops had identified GMU faculty across disciplines who could teach their colleagues in any field about how to work with student writers. The NVWP began to recruit teachers from across disciplines to the Summer Institute. Elementary teachers would be recruited as much for their ability to help students learn science or math or history through writing as by their ability to help students become poets or story writers. By 1983, when the institutes had certified a nucleus of these excellent teachers as consultants, the title of the main in-service course was changed from "The Teaching of Writing" to "Writing and Learning," representing the significant shift from what was usually seen as the province of language arts specialists to WAC's dual theoretical emphasis on learning to write and writing to learn. Today, the name of the course is still "Writing and Learning."

THE FACULTY WRITING PROGRAM SUMMER INSTITUTES, 1980 TO 1981

Our Funds for Excellence proposals were funded for $300,000 in 1980, about half this money supporting two summer institutes, 1980–81, on the NWP model (the other half went to the Writing Research Center, which I don't have space to describe here and that didn't have a deep effect on the growth of the program). We recruited faculty from throughout GMU, especially from our Airlie I and II participants, our primary goal to certify a cadre of what we called "University Fellows"; these would serve, we hoped, as teaching leaders among colleagues and in their professions. We would pay them 15 percent of salary for the five weeks, during which they would develop and give presentations, take part in some sessions with the K-12 institute, and work in small groups on their scholarly or creative projects. The institutes were our most complete adaptation of the NWP model, and they, too, taught us valuable lessons.

In retrospect, the institutes were primarily valuable in furthering the education of several faculty who became outstanding advocates of writing in teaching, though not all at GMU. Several have gone on to important teaching and administrative careers at GMU, where their knowledge of and respect for writing have helped further the aims of WAC. Just two examples: Business Law professor Richard Coffinberger went on to become associate dean of our school of management and recently represented his college on the general education committee that has reinforced the importance of our writing-intensive curriculum. James Sanford of Psychology, where he has served as undergraduate coordinator, has helped build the psych major into a strong, savvy supporter of WAC and, among recent projects, is developing an online Web guide in writing for psych students. Other fellows, given the vagaries of academic culture, took jobs at some point at other schools and so presumably have affected positively the writing climates on other campuses.

Overall, however, if I could turn back the clock, I would have used the money in a different way. While I am a strong advocate of paying faculty for in-service development in teaching, I have seen over the years that less-costly workshops of shorter duration, with frequent opportunities for reinforcement, can be at least as productive as courses like those we ran in 1980 and 1981—and will directly affect many more teachers. The consultant-training model worked for the NVWP because it possessed an in-service course structure that needed well-trained teacher/consultants to give presentations to the many teachers who each year apply for re-certification or who enroll in graduate programs. Indeed, many teacher/consultants have become course coordinators themselves. The same need and a similar population do not exist at the university level. This experience was valuable to me just a year later, in 1982, when the next Funds for Excellence grant implemented WAC in a very different way, one that affected many more faculty in a more profound and, for GMU, a more productive way.

Other manifestations of the 1980–81 Faculty Writing Program grant had other impacts:

1. The money let us begin a newsletter, *Writing*, which gave our teachers a forum for articles on teaching and that kept WAC regularly in the consciousness of faculty across the university. It gave us a level of confidence in the value of newsletters that persists in our WAC program today, as our publication *Writing at Center* (edited by current WAC and Writing Center director Terry Zawacki, herself an NVWP Teacher/Consultant) remains a key element of faculty and administrative outreach;

2. The money enabled us to run a statewide WAC conference at GMU in 1981, one of the very few non-local WAC scholarly gatherings before the Charleston WAC conferences of the next decade. One product of this state networking was the first anthology of WAC program-development essays, *Teaching Writing in all Disciplines,* compiled by Virginia colleague and Virginia Commonwealth professor Bill Griffin for Jossey-Bass in 1982. Bill's collection included pieces by Elaine Maimon, Barbara Walvoord, and John Bean, among other notables, as well as my compilation of examples of successful WAC practices from around the state;

3. Finally, the grant funded time for our University Fellows to write the essays in *Writing to Learn: Essays and Reflections by College Teachers across the Curriculum* (Kendall-Hunt, 1983), one of the early collections of classroom practice essays by WAC faculty.

WAC Changes the Curriculum,
1982–83: PAGE and ENGL 302

This tedious, brief saga will close with years 4 and 5 of WAC at GMU. In 1982, we moved into what Sue McLeod would later elegantly term the "second stage" of WAC, in which the faculty development work would be solidified in real change in the curriculum. Those changes were two: state funding of the design of the Plan for Alternative General Education (PAGE), based on WAC principles, and design of a revamped English composition requirement, with advanced courses in writing in the disciplines (WID).

I said earlier that the Mason philosophy is support of new initiatives and skepticism about the old. PAGE and the revamped comp program both illustrate and belie that generalization. They illustrate it as follows:

PAGE: President Johnson was unwilling to propose renewal of the Faculty Writing Program in 1982, but he was more than happy to support a radically interdisciplinary general education experiment that included WAC as a key element. PAGE was a 12-course 1st and 2nd year program that contained such courses as "Reading Cultural Signs" and "Contemporary Society in Multiple Perspectives." Among other features, writing (and speaking) would be built into every course in appropriate ways, with no separate comp or oral comm. courses. Adapting the NWP model to the University setting, a multi-disciplinary faculty team would design the courses and the program would run through a series of course teams. During subsequent week-long summer workshops (these persisted into the 90's), faculty would teach one another aspects of every course through hands-on lessons like those they'd give the students. These demonstration lessons invariably involved writing-to-learn exercises. Through PAGE workshops, some 150 faculty in its first five years learned WAC principles and practices; even today, faculty who were part of PAGE are among GMU's strongest WAC practitioners and are responsible for its writing-oriented culture. PAGE won the Mitau Award for innovation in higher education from the American Association of State Colleges and Universities in 1986.

But PAGE belies my generalization about Mason's skepticism with the old by lasting in roughly its same form until 1997, when it was translated into the Honors Program in General Education, maintaining today the interdisciplinary and WAC spirit it had in 1982.

English 302 (Advanced Composition): The "Mason attitude" explains at least in part how relatively easy it was to change the University English composition requirement in 1983 from the typical 6-hour freshman composition sequence to a 3-hour first-year course in research and argumentation and a 3-hour junior-level course in "advanced composition." This new course would be taught in three (four by 1986) versions: writing in the arts and humanities, writing in the social sciences, writing in natural science (now natural science/technology), and writing in business.

But this innovation, too, withstood the typical Mason cycle, and 302 remains a key part of WAC at GMU today. Why? Within the mere five years since the Senate Literacy Task Force had announced the "writing crisis" and had blamed the English department, the campus culture had changed to the extent that the only argument needed for the Senate to pass the new structure was that it "reinforced writing across the curriculum": it provided an upper-level course that would supplement teachers' efforts to use writing in major courses in all disciplines. I know that five years of faculty development work in WAC didn't seem to me a short time then, just as it seems impossibly long to those just starting out in faculty development now, but looking back it seems an eye blink. I do have to credit to some extent Mason's innovative spirit for enabling the steady development, the willingness to give support in money and encouragement; I can imagine less hospitable climates and have heard from and worked with many faculty who inhabit them. But I'm also convinced that the NWP model and the people who enacted it with such spirit at GMU in those days deserve much of the credit, too, both for the successful early innovation and for WAC's having become part of the fabric of the GMU community.

NOTE

For more on WAC history at GMU and to see the multiple shapes of the program today, consult our website: http://wac.gmu.edu. For the Northern Virginia Writing Project, consult http://www.nvwp.org/.

WORKS CITED

Britton, James, et al. *Language and Learning.* 1970; 2nd Ed., Portsmouth, NH: Boynton/Cook, 1993.
Elbow, Peter. *Writing without Teachers.* New York: Oxford UP, 1973.

Emig, Janet, "Writing as a Mode of Learning. " *College Composition and Communication* 28 (1977): 122–28.

Gray, James. *Teachers at the Center: A Memoir of the Early Years of the National Writing Project.* Berkeley, CA: National Writing Project, 2000.

Griffin, C. Williams, ed. *Teaching Writing in All Disciplines.* San Francisco: Jossey-Bass, 1982.

Macrorie, Ken. *Uptaught.* Upper Montclair, NJ: Hayden,1968.

Martin, Nancy, et al. *Writing and Learning across the Curriculum, 11–16.* 1976. Portsmouth, NH: Boynton/Cook, 1993.

Moffett, James. *Teaching the Universe of Discourse.* 1968. Portsmouth, NH: Boynton/Cook, 1987.

Murray, Donald. *A Writer Teaches Writing.* Boston: Houghton Mifflin, 1968.

Shaughnessy, Mina. *Errors and Expectations.* New York: Oxford UP, 1977.

"Why Johnny Can't Write," *Newsweek,* December 9, 1975: 58–65.

3 Circles of Interest: The Growth of Research Communities in WAC and WID/WIP

Charles Bazerman and Anne Herrington

Chuck: *The moment of enlightenment occurred in the second floor men's room in Rabb Hall, Brandeis University in April 1971. I had just defended my dissertation and was wondering about what I could do with my life, now that the academic job market was collapsing. Prior to writing my dissertation, I taught first and third grades in Bedford-Stuyvesant Brooklyn for two years, during which I had become more committed to literacy than literature. For want of imagination, however, I had returned to write a dissertation on the poetry occasioned by the death of Queen Elizabeth I. That return had reminded me just how poorly academic writing communicated—or at least the writing I came across in my literary and historical studies. The writing was clever, graceful, and even smart—but it seemed as though nobody was talking with each other. Energy and intellect seemed wasted in minor squabbles or great vessels of imagination passing each other in fogs of their own thought. These ruminations—literacy, doing big things, unemployment, academic obscurity, and narcissistic scholarly communication—were floating around in my head one afternoon when I went to relieve myself of too much coffee. In caffeine-induced grandiosity these thoughts came together over the urinal: I decided my niche in the world would be to somehow improve scholarly communication—and that there was even a living to be had in it. I relieved myself far more easily of the caffeine than of this delusion.*

Anne: *In the inside cover of my copy of* Errors and Expectations, *I have this inscription: "For Anne, My new-found friend from the front lines. Mina Shaughnessy, March 1977." I had asked her to autograph the book after hearing her speak at a conference. That meeting was the bridging point that connected work of my local colleagues and myself to participation in a larger national group of composition scholars and WAC program directors through a FIPSE grant that Mina had encouraged me to submit, a bridging point also between teaching and program development. Research would follow.*

While most of the history of Writing Across the Curriculum is in the programs, workshops, and networks that brought people together around the practices of writing and teaching, research and scholarship has helped inform this practice and has itself become another means by which practitioners of the disciplines have become aware of the importance and character of writing in their fields. Although attributed to individuals or small collaborative teams, this research is as much part of the general climate of concern that fostered the WAC movement and was nurtured by some of the same networks, as well as some others. In the narratives to follow you will find some large differences in the development of the research of the two co-authors, you will also find some major commonalities and points of intersection. We both began our professional careers at the college level in the early 1970s and both of us were teaching academic writing skills in open admissions programs. Our research and program development work arose from interests and questions that arose in our classrooms: what should we be teaching and how can we help our students succeed in college?

Our interests and local situations then took us in somewhat different directions: one more toward the study of the kinds of texts valued in other disciplines, the other more toward pedagogical work with colleagues in other disciplines. One pursued largely historical work transformed by interdisciplinary methods and theories from several social sciences while another drew more on ethnographic research traditions from educational studies. Thus, the plural "research communities" in our title. Still, the story we aim to tell is as much about the intersection of these two circles of interest, a dynamic intersection that has created a research community in WAC/WID. In recreating the stories of our initial moves into research, we also see the importance of published research, of conferences and informal networks of scholars and program developers, and of federal programs that funded the development of many WAC or WAC-related programs, particularly in the 1970s. More broadly, the story we tell together is one of the emergence of a research community/ies with two centers: classrooms and professional sites.

ANNE'S STORY

My association with what I would later learn to call "writing-across-the curriculum" began with teaching for PROVE, a U.S. Dept. of Education Special Services Program for Economically Disadvantaged Students at Johnson State College, VT in 1972. I learned of the position just by happenstance, while looking for a summer job between working on my Masters degree at the University of Vermont. (Note that the Central College Program, directed by Barbara Fassler [now Walvoord] also received some funding from this same Program [Russell 283]). PROVE, the Johnson Program, aimed to provide academic and counseling support to Vermont students who were ill-prepared for college, many with GEDs, many recruited directly from social service agencies. Although the Program's designer was not guided by a WAC perspective, he centered it around a summer program where students took one Communication Skills course and one content course in the Humanities or Social Sciences and where teachers met informally to discuss students' progress: it was only over time working together and gradually learning about other WAC programs and principles that we came to be a WAC program. For the Program's first year, while none of us teaching in it had any special expertise or experience to prepare us for the challenges we would face, we approached them with idealistic energy, excited to be part of a program that aimed to support young adults who for reasons of class and other family circumstances hadn't had the same opportunities of many of us.

Each day before classes, our small group of about eight faculty met over coffee to commiserate over the reality of the challenge we faced. As I try to recall those conversations now, I remember mostly discussions about how individual students were faring, including questions of whether some were doing their work and whether others could do the work. Even the most veteran teachers were unprepared for the difficulties some had understanding the course readings and writing coherent sentences and paragraphs. With little theoretical frame to guide us, in the Communication Skills courses we focused more on these basic skills. And, our morning discussions with colleagues teaching the sociology and economics courses pretty much took what they were assigning for granted and focused on how we, the Communication Skills instructors, and undergraduate tutors could help prepare the PROVE students for those courses. In short, at this point, we were guided more by a one-way service model with a focus on basic skills; there was little shared critical reflection on teaching approaches and the nature of our curricula. Still, these early discussions helped me and others see the value and "naturalness" of working together across disciplines to serve some common learning goals for undergraduate students, and begin to think about some of our teaching challenges as shared, not distinct.

In the mid-'1970s one of our nation's periodic "literacy crises" provided the impetus for new programs and funding support from agencies like NEH and FIPSE. With this sense of crisis, fueled by the 1974 NAEP reports and such press articles as *Newsweek*'s December 9, 1975 "Why Johnny Can't Write," my little school, like others large and small, faced pressures both from without, including our Vermont state college system, and from some faculty within the school to do something to insure that the students entering through open admissions were "literate." Proficiency testing reared its head. (The parallels with the present time do not escape me.) Fortunately, agencies like NEH and FIPSE were also interested in supporting progressive curriculum projects, such as the Beaver College program, funded by NEH. At Johnson, I could see no purpose to a test unless all faculty were involved in the effort to help students develop the skills to be tested and unless writing was being used in meaningful ways for learning across the college.

By this time, I had joined NCTE and was reading *CCC* regularly. In a 1976 issue, I read Mina Shaughnessy's essay "Diving In: An Introduction to Basic Writing," and it resonated with me as describing what our informal group of teachers were trying to learn to do. We had begun at Shaughnessy's second developmental rung for teachers, as missionaries "Converting the Natives" and were now starting to ask the kind of questions about student learning and our teaching that she associated with the third developmental rung, "Sounding the Depths," for instance, what were some of the specific difficulties students were having in our courses? What was working in some classes?

Next I read *Errors and Expectations* and was inspired by her closing chapters regarding the involvement of all faculty in developing students writing and in fostering their success. As pressures for some sort of proficiency test mounted, I read a notice in the *Chronicle of Higher Education* that she was speaking at a conference in March of 1977. I told a colleague we had to go.

After hearing her speak, we asked if we could talk with her a bit about our developing ideas to try to expand our PROVE summer program model and our concerns about the push for proficiency testing. Knowing of the Fund for the Improvement of Post-Secondary Education (FIPSE)'s interest in funding some grants in writing, she encouraged me to submit a proposal to them. Since one of FIPSE's stated funding interests was assessment, I piggy-backed development of WAC workshops for faculty with development of a proficiency exam. I realized we already had a nascent WAC group at Johnson—the ones of us who had been involved in the PROVE program.

FIPSE funded seven grants in writing for the two-year period 1977–79, including two other WAC ones, one directed by Joan Graham at the University of Washington; another by Carolyn Kirkpatrick and Mary Epes at York College, CUNY. It also funded a research project co-directed by Sondra Perl, Richard Sterling, and John Brereton, also from CUNY. During the two years of the grants, FIPSE provided the funds to bring the directors of those seven grants, often with outside consultants, together twice per year ostensibly to encourage sharing ideas across our grants. It was through participation in this group that I came to have a name for what my colleagues and I were about: writing across the curriculum. Equally important, those gatherings served as an entry to scholarship and to a wider national network of composition scholars and WAC program directors. At our first gathering in 1977, the consultants that FIPSE brought in included Linda Flower and Lee Odell. David Russell's history reminds me that 1977 was also the year of the Rutgers NEH seminar on writing across the curriculum where Lee Odell was also a consultant along with Toby Fulwiler and others. NEH and FIPSE sponsorship of WAC programs and conferences, including the collaboration between these two agencies, proved central to the growth of WAC programs and a scholarly community across institutions.

I invited Lee to lead two workshops at Johnson State, and he was tremendously influential in shaping our work as teachers, introducing the notion of writing to learn and teaching approaches as well as an analytic frame for planning writing assignments. It also during this two-year period, that I met Elaine Maimon at a jointly sponsored meeting of FIPSE and NEH-funded writing projects. In other words, my circle was beginning to expand beyond Johnson and to include not only teachers, but program directors and scholars. I recall that period as one of intense excitement: for us at Johnson, excitement about our teaching and our students' accomplishments, and excitement that we were part of a small, but energetic and growing national movement.

Having the grant also required me to evaluate grant activities and that marked my first steps into research. With advice from Lee Odell and another expert on program evaluation, I began a number of activities to evaluate our work. For our WAC project, that included surveying faculty and students about their experiences, as well as collecting samples of assignments and students' writings.

The first article I wrote, "Writing to Learn: Writing across the Disciplines," draws on that data. I wrote it out of an impulse to signify the worth of our enterprise and, implicitly, make a case for it to others. In other words, I was writing as an *interested* participant, both teacher and program developer. My focus was on teaching strategies assumed to effective across disciplines, not on particulars of writing within a given discipline. The scholarly work that influenced me in shaping my ideas included two early WAC-related articles: Janet Emig's "Writing as a Mode of Learning" and Lee Odell's "Teaching Writing by Teaching the Process of Discovery." I note now that I also cite an article written by Don Tobey, a resource economist and one of my Johnson colleagues, on "Writing Instruction in Economics Courses," and an interview by Lois Rosen with James Britton.

Through the grant—largely through attending conferences—I became more and more aware of wanting to read more and develop scholarly research skills. (My c.v. reminds me that my first national conference paper on WAC was in 1980, "Across the Disciplines: Writing as a Way of Learning," at CCCC's.) So, I began doctoral studies, working primarily with Lee Odell and also studying rhetoric with Michael Halloran. When I entered graduate school, I knew that I wanted to pursue studies related to writing across the curriculum. I was convinced by the arguments made by Lee Odell and Janet Emig that writing is a powerful way of learning, convinced that that learning included more than solely cognitive skills, really interested to know about what shaped the nature of that learning for students. As a graduate student, my reading expanded to include scholarship associated with Composition Studies, particularly with cognitive and personal growth approaches (for example, Britton, Nancy Martin et al.'s *Writing and Learning across the Curriculum 11–16,* Fulwiler and Young, all ones I would associate with WAC) as well as scholarship in rhetoric, argumentation theory, and sociolinguistics (from Aristotle to Toulmin to Hymes). I also read a piece by Charles Bazerman, "What Written Knowledge Does: Three Examples of Academic Prose" (1981) that was influential in helping me conceptualize writing in specific disciplines and think about distinct ways of creating knowledge within specific disciplines. In 1982, I sought him out at MLA, hearing him deliver a paper and speaking with him afterward; at my request, he sent me a copy of his paper, "Discourse Paths of Different Disciplines," (I still have that yellowed mimeographed copy in my files.) These areas of scholarship combined fit with my sense that there were pedagogical issues that cut across disciplines, that writing did play a profound role for learning, and that the nature of that learning varied with disciplinary genres and contexts.

Thus, my study of writing in two college chemical engineering classes, a study shaped by the emerging scholarship that has contributed to WAC and WID, although at the time, I would not have cited that distinction. Both circles of scholarship enabled me to answer the questions I wanted to get at about what I sensed as distinct kinds of learning that were furthered by the writing students were doing in distinct courses within chemical engineering and about classroom situations conducive to that learning ("Writing"). I see that study as centered at the intersection of WAC and WID: looking at writing as shaped by and embodying the purposes, social roles, ways of reasoning of not only a given discipline/profession, but distinct forums within a given discipline/profession; and at looking at classroom situations conducive to learning. These were questions of a researcher, not a teacher-researcher or a program developer.

For me, the informal network of researchers grew during the early to mid-1980s through participation in smaller conferences that lend themselves more to informal consultation. Not surprisingly since I was at Penn State during this time, the Penn State Conferences on Rhetoric and Composition between 1984 and 1986 come to mind. I recall finally meeting Barbara Walvoord there and spending time talking with her and Virginia Anderson regarding research projects they were launching related to their WAC program, subsequently published in *Thinking and Writing in College*. That conference also provided the venue for further conversations with Chuck, also with Lucille McCarthy and Steve Fishman, and Carolyn Miller. While I can imagine that someone doing a review of research would sort us and even different work any one of us has done into WAC or WID groupings or even other groupings (e.g., sociology of science), I resist thinking of those groupings as fixed or distinct.

My work as a teacher and researcher has been and remains stimulated by what Chuck terms the boundary dialogues that occur across groupings and the blurring of boundaries that ensues. We prompt such at our own schools by creating occasions to work with a cross-disciplinary groups of faculty to reflect on our teaching and students' learning. For instance, sitting with colleagues at UMass to try to identify learning objectives for our WAC Program became an opportunity to discuss teaching approaches that could be used across disciplines as well as to try to understand the different genres and functions of argument in, say, English and Management. Such discussions are also prompted by conferences, other scholarly exchanges, and collaboration across institutions, specifically ones that bring together various perspectives and scholars with somewhat different research focuses. In more recent years, the National Conference on Writing across the Curriculum has fostered such exchanges. For me, collaboration with colleagues in the Language Development Programme at the University of Cape Town has also spurred my reading of Critical Discourse Theory and brought it into my own research as a way to address questions of power and identity as we seek to understand the dynamics of language learning and writing in all our courses across the curriculum (Herrington and Curtis). In short, both now and in my formative years, standing within the intersections and moving among circles has been generative for my scholarly work as well as teaching and WAC program development.

CHUCK'S STORY

Although I may have thought in 1971 that one could earn a living by improving academic writing, the world did not confirm my illusion. Upon finishing my dissertation, I went back to New York without a job. After posting my services on bulletin boards around the many universities in the city, I got all of one response, from a foreign student who wanted me to edit his dissertation. Then I went to an employment agency that offered me the opportunity to ghost write a dissertation in psychology. Keeping my eye on the prize, I let both opportunities pass.

After a term of piecing together jobs on several campuses in and around New York, I landed a full-time position teaching writing to open-admission students at Baruch College of the City University of New York. Open Admissions was initiated just a year before and many of my colleagues were shell-shocked by nontraditional students. I recognized in these students, however, the more successful older siblings of the elementary students I had recently taught—the ones who hadn't dropped out, who weren't in gangs, who hadn't over-dosed, who survived deeply troubled schools with a residual belief in education and literacy. They were motivated and willing, despite the schools failing to provide them the resources to do well in the university. To figure out what they needed in order to meet the writing demands of college (this was in the prehistoric days before graduate training in composition), I began to look at the kind of writing students were doing in their other courses. What I found was that writing assignments were closely linked to reading assignments. And I worried a lot about the research paper, because students who had done well in the first term course based on personal and argumentative writing seemed to have much greater difficulty with the research paper, which was the central assignment of our second term course. What a research paper entailed was vague to me other than it required technically correct footnotes and bibliographies. Although it seemed to bear some resemblances to equally vaguely described term paper in other courses, I was able to gain no clear definition from colleagues, professional materials, or textbooks of what a research paper was or what skills were useful to accomplish it well.

Fortunately, I wasn't alone in this journey of understanding the needs of the nontraditional student. The early years of open admissions evoked a legendary response by teachers on each of the 18 campuses of the City University, and these were gathered together citywide under the leadership of Mina Shaughnessy, Bob Lyons, Harvey Wiener, Ken Bruffee and others. A new term "Basic Writing" reframed how we understood students who were only late in their educations being introduced into the power and struggle of writing. The newly formed organizations of the CUNY Association of Writing Supervisors (CAWS) and the Instructional Resource Center brought together writing instructors from across the city committed to teaching, program development, and research and in writing. We first characterized the literacy tools for academic success in general terms of academic registers and discourse, as eventually spelled out in the later chapters of Mina Shaughnessy's *Errors and Expectations.*

As I struggled with teaching the research paper, I began to focus on the challenges of writing about reading, which I then came to see as central to academic writing. A few years later, literary theory invoked the term intertextuality to address some issues surrounding authorship and textual integrity; that term came to encompass the concerns I was addressing, although I believe composition's use for the term raises broader and more fundamental issues than the literary usage (see Bazerman, "Intertextualities"). Moreover, as I explored the research paper's relation to writing assigned elsewhere on campus, I found there were substantial differences in the structure and expectations of the assignments from one class to another, as well as the intertextual and skill resources they needed to draw on to write those papers. In order to explore these issues I did some faculty surveys in 1976 through 1978 which resulted in some institutional reports and a several unpublished regional conference papers on such topics as "English and the Other Departments," "The Role of Reading in the Kinds of Writing Students do in College," and "The Importance of the Literature in Writing in the Social Sciences." However, when first doing this work, I had not yet linked up with contemporaries with similar interests, and I found my sources and inspiration in prior generations of literacy educators such as I. A. Richards, Mortimer Adler, and Richard Altick.

Only with the last of these papers, presented at the Delaware Valley Writing Conference, held at Beaver College outside Philadelphia in October, 1978, did I become aware of the Writing Across the Curriculum movement. It was with great excitement I found out about the WAC program at Beaver, the collaborative work of workshops on that campus, and the research and textbooks being carried out by the Beaver faculty. Outside the conference meetings I met with Elaine Maimon, Barbara Nodine, Finbarr O'Connor and other Beaver colleagues to share what we had been finding about disciplinary differences in writing and our plans for textbooks (theirs to be *Writing in the Arts and Sciences* and mine to be the *Informed Writer,* both appearing

with 1981 copyrights). Later that academic year I visited Beaver again
to see their workshops in action. While much of the early WAC movement was directed by writing to learn pedagogy and writing reinforcement across the curriculum, we agreed that these needed to be carried
out in a discipline-sensitive way through dialogue with disciplinary
faculty and research on writing in the disciplines.

At the same time as I was finding the WAC movement I was also
finding the value of sociological thought and research for understanding writing. In composition the psychologically-based process movement was already becoming a major positive force; I was, however,
looking at the social organization of disciplinary activities rather than
at internal processes of individuals, although ultimately disciplinary practices and standards become embedded in each practitioner's
thought and habit. In the spring of 1978, a colleague directed me towards the sociology of science seminar at Columbia University run
by the eminent sociologists Robert Merton and Harriet Zuckerman.
During my sabbatical year of 1978–1979 devoted to finishing the *Informed Writer,* I attended the seminar regularly and was to continue to
participate as my teaching schedule allowed for the next several years.
Coincidentally at that time within the sociology of science, a strong
interest was emerging in the rhetoric of science and the discursive con-
struction of scientific knowledge, with scholars such as Susan Coz-
zens, Bruno Latour, Steve Woolgar, Karin Knorr, Nigel Gilbert, and
Michael Mulkay beginning to publish in this area. In the fall of 1979
I began attending the meetings of the Society for the Social Studies
of Science, and immediately attempted to draw composition folk into
the exciting knowledge being presented there; for over a decade writing people formed a small but continuing constituency of that interdisciplinary society. My own publications and talks became explicitly
sociological as I presented a papers at the C's in 1979 on "Written Language Communities" attempting to introduce that term to composition, but composition did not yet seem ready for sociology as I could
not get it published. One rejection letter from a then eminent leader of
the composition profession observed that all this was old hat to rhetoricians. This is just as well, because I soon found the term "community" too broad and undifferentiated: I moved to more concrete ways of
talking about communicative forums, text circulation networks, and
social roles mediated by texts. In a 1983 article "Scientific Writing as a

Social Act" I found some more satisfactory ways of applying the sociology of science literature to writing.

In the summer of 1979 by attending Richard Young's NEH Summer seminar I also linked up with the national composition and rhetoric research community that was forming as it clustered around Carnegie Mellon. Based on general models of invention, writing process, and rhetorical argument, this world had not yet addressed discipline specific issues raised by the WAC movement or research into disciplinary writing practices. As part of that seminar I stretched the bounds a bit by presenting a paper on composing processes of sociologists, based on an analysis of the accounts reported in the volume *Sociologists at Work.* The relation between general and situated discipline specific models of process and argument has remained a continuing issue defining WAC's relation to general composition teaching and practice. This boundary dialogue with general composition and rhetorical studies has been as important in shaping WAC as the internal dialogue among WAC practitioners and the external dialogue with social studies of disciplinary cultures, knowledge, language, and practice. Other important boundary dialogues for WAC are with scientific and technical writing as well as business communication.

As genre became an organizing concept for myself and others working with specialized writing practices, I became interested in the historical development of forms of writing in relation to the histories of science and technology. This connection was facilitated by the joint meetings in the 1980s of the various science studies societies (Society for the Social Studies of Science, History of Science Society, Society for the History of Technology, and the Philosophy of Science Association). As I pursued this work I found the extensive archives of scientific writing continuingly useful, such as the American Institute of Physics, the Dibner Collection and the Burndy Institute, the Bakken Collection, and the Edison papers. The archivists of these and other collections were extremely helpful, as they understood the importance of the textual manifestation of science and technology. The work of historians of the sciences, technologies, and other disciplines provides a rich source for understanding writing practices which I believe writing studies should draw on more fully. A number of historians have also done work directly relevant to rhetoric and writing—including Jan Golinski, Ted Porter, Peter Dear, Larry Stewart, Adrian Johns, Steven Shapin and Simon Schaffer.

The importance WID researchers attributed to the concept genre also gave us common cause with applied linguistics, particularly the ESL specialty then known as English for Special Purposes and now known as English for Specific Purposes. While I only first became aware of this field in 1982 when meeting John Swales in Singapore, in the U.S. there were already many people who regularly worked at the border of composition and ESL and were quite familiar with the value of ESP approaches for WAC. Over the years this point of connection has become increasingly important, connecting WAC up with both linguistically informed practitioners in the U.S. (such as Dwight Atkinson, Ann Johns, Ulla Connor, and John Swales who had moved to the U.S.) and to people who do similar work to ours in the rest of world (such as Vijay Bhatia, Ken Hyland, Aviva Freedman, Britt Luise Gunnarson, and Anna Trosberg). In much of the world teaching of first and second language writing in higher education is the domain of applied linguistics rather than literature departments. Moreover, these applied linguists tend to take a specific purposes approach, in line with the tendency of the undergraduate curriculum in most of the world to be more closely tied to disciplinary tracks than the U.S. system of majors. At the same time we recognize that ESP applied linguists are our counterparts, it is also worth recognizing that WAC has the potential of being a major contact point with burgeoning higher education writing programs throughout the world.

One final simultaneously developing network of scholars has been of importance to WAC has been the Rhetoric of Inquiry movement. Founded in the early 1980s at the University of Iowa—by economist Donald (now Deirdre) McCloskey, political scientist John Nelson, and historian Allan Megill—it engaged an interdisciplinary group of scholars into reflexively understanding the rhetoric of their own disciplines in order to increase the clarity, focus, and purposefulness of disciplinary inquiries. In 1984 the group sponsored a major conference on the Rhetoric of the Human Sciences, which resulted in a major volume of the same name in 1987, that brought rhetoricians together with disciplinary practitioners examining the rhetorics of their field. The continuing work of the Project on Rhetoric of Inquiry (POROI), has advanced knowledge of disciplinary rhetorics and has sponsored numerous opportunities for WAC scholars to interact with disciplinary specialists. The ongoing work of the center can be sampled at http://www.uiowa.edu/~poroi/

Perhaps because Baruch College never developed a WAC Program during the years I was there (1971–1990), despite some attempts to get one going, I devoted my attention mostly to research. While I remained committed to the project of WAC, I understood that the research and pedagogy I was developing was looking more to practices in the disciplines than to the immediate design and operations of WAC programs. Even though I believed and continue to believe that WAC programs should be informed by writing practices in the disciplines, I recognized that WAC had a different programmatic interest, and research into WAC was not the same as research into writing in the disciplines. This recognition led to my giving a subtitle *Using Sources in the Disciplines* to the second edition of *The Informed Writer* appearing in 1985.

I also came into contact with other writing researchers beginning to take an interest in scientific and other disciplinary writing. At the 1979 4C's I remember being delighted to meet Carolyn Miller and Jim Zappen who were also presenting papers on writing in science. Carolyn Miller was in presenting an early version of her paper on genre that was to influence so many of us so deeply. Other good friends I met in those early years who were to form a nucleus of WAC researchers included Carol Berkenkotter (at Richard Young's NEH seminar), Anne Herrington, David Kaufer, Lucille McCarthy, Marie Secor, and Jeanne Fahnestock. As a group formed, with several collaborators I helped bring together conference panels and symposia throughout the 1980s, and then developed publication opportunities to support the production of more research on disciplinary writing, including the symposia on "Rhetoricians on the Rhetoric of Science" and "What are We Doing as a Research Community?" and the edited volume (with Jim Paradis) *Textual Dynamics of the Profession.* My awareness of the role of texts in disciplinary formation gave impetus to discipline building activities: at the 1988 CCCC, Cheryl Geisler and I started the Research Network Forum and at the 1991 CCCC, Janice Lauer and I began the Consortium of Graduate Programs in Composition. Since the 1980s this cluster of WAC and WID scholars has grown and I have done my best to support the communication networks that bring them together. Another important aspect of communal discipline and knowledge building is the writing of reviews of literature, which I began with "Scientific Writing as a Social Act" (1983) and "Studies of Scientific Writing: E Pluribus Unum" (1985) and have continued to this day along with more extended reference and summative volumes. This is a work others have shared, particularly David Russell with his history and review articles and our shared editing of *Landmark Essays in Writing Across the Curriculum;* Randy Harris has also edited a volume of *Landmark Essays in the Rhetoric of Science.* The research literature provides an important intellectual infrastructure for any profession, and it is important that we all contribute to maintaining and making that network for each other.

These support networks also helped me carry forward and give focus to my own research in this period of the early and mid-1980s, which was building towards *Shaping Written Knowledge,* which appeared in 1988. But the story of those studies is beyond the scope of this movement-oriented essay, and I have described it elsewhere (see particularly the introduction to *Constructing Experience* and "Looking at Writing; Writing What I See.")

This research role and the networks developing around it have often been at some distance from the practical work of developing Writing Across the Curriculum programs, but I would like to think it has provided some support and direction for WAC. At the very least I know the work of the researchers has provided reading materials for seminars and served as fodder for legitimation of the field. I know I have often enough spoken for just such purposes of getting dialogue going at WAC seminars and/or providing academic warrant for WAC programs just starting up. But I am afraid that still by the later 1980s, where we break off this narrative, to some in the composition field and even some engaged in WAC programs this research remained arcane and specialized. As WAC programs brought writing specialists more and more in dialogue with faculty in other disciplines, writing specialists came to take seriously the particularities of disciplinary practices, and WAC programs evolve informed by this knowledge. Research into disciplinary practices is simply a way of helping along this process of learning about the differences of writing practices in different domains at the same time as pointing out that writing is extremely important to them all.

CHUCK AND ANNE

The divergence of the narratives of our networks reflects the divergent experience of a number of our colleagues as well. Some, such as David Russell, Carol Berkenkotter, Paul Prior, Cheryl Geisler, Tom

Huckin, Anthony Pare, Graham Smart, and Anne Blakeslee, have hewed more to researching writing practices in disciplines and professions—and have headed into interdisicplinarity, while others such as Lucille McCarthy, Steve Fishman, Lee Odell, and Barbara Walvoord have kept their reseachers' eyes on classroom and programmatic developments—staying much closer to the field of composition. Yet we all remain in contact, reading each others work, publishing in similar venues, seeing each other at conferences. And we provide each other rationale and resources for each other's work.

In this we remain a cluster that stands between English departments and regular composition on one side and other disciplines on the other. On the humanities border we extend understanding and practical and critical engagement with the powerful discursive practices of the disciplines and professions, where knowledge, power, and social decision making are forged and in which our students will participate in creating a future for all of us. On the social science and sciences border we help make visible the important role writing, communication, and discursive skills play in disciplinary work and we provide means for improving and making more reflective the discourses that are so shaping of our world. As well we provide means for more democratic and diverse access so that these discourses of power are open to influence by all who have a stake in the consequences of disciplinary and professional actions. Our continuing research in writing in the disciplines and in disciplinary classrooms across the curriculum will help clarify what writing does in the world, how it does it, and how people can come to learn to wield that power. In this work is realized important intersections of the humanities and the other disciplines, and continuing value humanities approaches to human creation can have in the world. After all, if disciplinary and professional knowledge and decisions are created in the writing of individuals participating together, then it is no stretch to see all of the disciplines as humanistic endeavors. But we need the research to show this and the important gains to be made by taking this perspective.

Works Cited

Anderson, Virginia, and Barbara Walvoord. "Conducting and Reporting Original Scientific Research: Anderson's Biology Class." *Thinking and Writing in College: A Naturalistic Study of Students in Four Disciplines*. Ed.

Barbara Walvoord and Lucille P. McCarthy. Urbana, IL: NCTE, 1990. 177–227.

Bazerman, Charles. *Constructing Experience*. Southern Illinois UP, 1994.

—. "Discourse Paths of Different Disciplines." MLA Convention. Los Angeles, 30 Dec. 1982.

—. "English and the Other Departments," Conference Paper. Rutgers-Newark Writing Conference, April 1977.

—. "The Importance of the Literature in Writing in the Social Sciences," Conference Paper. Delaware Valley Writing Conference, Philadelphia, October 1978.

—. *The Informed Writer*. 1st ed. Boston: Houghton Mifflin, 1981.

—. *The Informed Writer: Using Sources in the Disciplines*. 2nd ed. Boston: Houghton Mifflin, 1985.

—. "Intertextualities: Volosinov, Bakhtin, Literary Theory, and Literacy Studies *Bakhtinian Perspectives on Language, Literacy, and Learning*. Ed. Arnetha F. Ball and Sarah Warshauer Freedman. Cambridge, UK:. Cambridge UP, 2004.

—. "Looking at Writing; Writing What I See." *Living Rhetoric and Composition*. Ed. Theresa Enos and Duane Roen. Mahwah NJ: Erlbaum, 1998: 15–24.

—. "Response Grows from Understanding," Conference Paper. Rutgers-Newark Writing Conference, April 1978.

—. "Rhetoricians on the Rhetoric of Science" (Symposium). *Science Technology and Human Values* 14.1 (Winter 1989): 3-6.

—. "The Role of Reading in the Kinds of Writing Students Do in College," CUNY Writing Conference, New York, April 1978.

—. "Scientific Writing as a Social Act: A Review of the Literature of the Sociology of Science." *New Essays in Technical Writing and Communication*. Ed. Paul V. Anderson, R. John Brockmann, and Carolyn R. Miller. Farmingdale: Baywood, 1983: 156–84.

—. *Shaping Written Knowledge: The Genre and Activity of the Experimental Article in Science*. Madison: U of Wisconsin P, 1988.

—. "Studies of Scientific Writing: *E Pluribus Unum*." *4S Review* 3.2 (1985) 13-20.

—. "What Are We Doing As a Research Community?" (Symposium). *Rhetoric Review*, March 1989.

—. "What Written Knowledge Does: Three Examples of Academic Prose." *Philosophy of Social Science*. 11 (1981): 361–87.

—. "Written Language Communities," Conference Paper. Conference on College Composition and Communication, Minneapolis, April 1979.

—and James Paradis (eds.). *Textual Dynamics of the Professions*. Madison: University of Wisconsin Press, 1991.

—, and DavidRussell (eds.). *Landmark Essays in Writing Across the Curriculum*. Davis, CA: Hermagoras Press, 1994.

Britton, James, Tony Burgess, Nancy Martin, Alex McLeod, and Harold Rosen. *The Development of Writing Abilities (11–18)*. London: Macmillan, 1975.

Emig, Janet. "Writing as a Mode of Learning." *College Composition and Communication* 28 (1977): 122–28.

Fulwiler, Toby and Art Young, ed. *Language Connections: Writing and Reading across the Curriculum*. Urbana, IL: NCTE, 1982.

Harris, Randy (ed.) *Landmark Essays in the Rhetoric of Science*. Erlbaum 1996.

Herrington, Anne. "Writing in Academic Settings: A Study of the Contexts for Writing in Two College Chemical Engineering Courses." *Research in the Teaching of English* 19 (December 1985): 331–361.

—. "Writing To Learn: Writing Across the Disciplines." *College English,* 43 (April 1981): 379–87.

—, and Marcia Curtis. *Persons in Process: Four Stories of Writing and Personal Development in College.* Urbana, IL: NCTE, 2000.

Maimon, Elaine P., et al. *Writing in the Arts and Sciences*. Cambridge, MA : Winthrop Publishers, 1981.

Odell, Lee. "Teaching Writing by Teaching the Process of Discovery: An Interdisciplinary Enterprise." In *Cognitive Processes in Writing: An Interdisciplinary Approach.* Ed. Lee Gregg and Erwin Steinberg. Hillsdale, NJ: Lawrence Erlbaum, 1980.

Rosen, Lois. "An Interview with James Britton, Tony Burgess, and Harold Rosen." *English Journal* 67 (November 1970): 55.

Russell, David. *Writing in the Academic Disciplines, 1870–1990: A Curricular History.* Carbondale: Southern Illinois UP, 1991.

Shaughnessy, Mina. "Diving In: An Introduction to Basic Writing." *College Composition and Communication.* 27 (1976): 2234–39.

—. *Errors and Expectations:* A Guide for the Teacher of Basic Writing. New York: Oxford UP, 1977.

Tobey, Don. "Writing Instruction in Economics Courses: Experimentation across Disciplines." *Journal of the Northeastern Agricultural Council.* 8.2 (1979): 159–64.

"Why Johnny Can't Write." *Newsweek* 9 Dec. 1975: 58–65.

4 The Start of Writing in the Disciplines/Writing Across the Curriculum in the California State University System

Carol R. Holder and Susan H. McLeod

Carol: *In 1979, when Fall Quarter was about to begin at California State Polytechnic University Pomona, Harold Levitt, Chair of English and Foreign Languages, asked me if I'd take on the job of coordinating the department's composition program. I had recently returned to campus having completed requirements for a PhD from Claremont Graduate School and thus had just begun enjoying my stature as an associate professor, ten years after starting out at Cal Poly Pomona as a part-time lecturer and then as an assistant professor. I had many years' experience teaching freshman English, basic writing, upper-division writing, and writing in accounting, but language acquisition and language use, not composition and rhetoric, had been the focus of my graduate work. Nonetheless, I took on the position Harold offered, thinking I was signing on for a big dose of class scheduling, hiring and supervising the growing numbers of temporary faculty, and overseeing the selection of a few textbooks from which everyone teaching comp would choose. I had no vision of planning a writing across the curriculum program. I can't swear to it now, but I don't think I was even aware of the development of "writing across the curriculum" programs anywhere, having focused during the '70s on teaching lots of classes, developing a new course on writing in accounting, struggling to keep up with the paper load, commuting from a sleepy surfing commu-*

nity in south Orange County, playing percussion with the Hula Buckeroos, and getting the PhD that would make me eligible for promotion.

Sue: *"Have you heard about writing across the curriculum?" The year was 1979, and the speaker was an old friend from Peace Corps days a decade earlier who was now a historian teaching at SUNY Brockport. He was visiting us in Bethesda, MD, and was enthusing over our kitchen table, telling me, the teacher of writing, something he assumed I should know about, something he said had transformed his teaching. I had not heard of it. Later that year I enrolled in a seminar offered by the Washington Center for Learning Alternatives (which later shortened its 1960s title to "Washington Center"); the seminar was led by Chris Thaiss. From Chris I learned more about what had made my friend in history so enthusiastic. It did not occur to me, though, that WAC would become part of my own professional development—indeed, my life's work—thanks in large part to Carol Holder, the Jane Appleseed of WAC/WID in California.*

Carol's Story

Background: Writing and Standards in the CSU in the 1970s

As was true elsewhere in the country during the 1970s, faculty in California schools began to be concerned about student writing. In response to this concern, the California State University, a large multi-campus system of which Cal Poly Pomona is a part, instituted several system wide testing programs, focused on writing. We (mostly English faculty—see White) developed the CSU English Placement Test required for all admitted students and used to place students in freshman or pre-baccalaureate (no-credit, remedial) writing courses. The CSU English Equivalency Examination was an optional challenge exam, and students who passed that earned eight semester units of composition at any CSU. And finally, the CSU Board of Trustees mandated an upper-division Graduation Writing Assessment Requirement, to be designed and implemented locally on each campus, to assure that no degrees be awarded to students who lacked minimal basic writing skills. Because of these three testing programs, faculty in many disciplines, not just English, became familiar with means for assessing writing proficiency, and the advantages and disadvantages of a variety of tests and scoring practices. Also, as we learned in holistic scoring sessions of the Graduation Writing Test (GWT) at Pomona, faculty in different disciplines valued different features, forms, and functions of writing. What was also abundantly clear: Most of our freshmen did not do well on the English Placement Test, and a good fraction of our upper-division students, the majority of whom were and are transfers from community colleges, would fail the GWT repeatedly (see Johns for a case study of such a student). We didn't need "Why Johnny Can't Write" articles in national news magazines to fuel faculty talk about student skills, writing standards, and changes needed in courses and instruction.

At this same time (1975–1980), faculty in the Cal Poly Pomona Accounting Department were hearing demands from their industry advisory board (representatives from businesses and accounting firms employing Cal Poly graduates—similar to advisory boards found in most pre-professional programs) for more focus on developing writing skills in graduates. In response, the department experimented several years with a senior-level writing seminar, team-taught by English and accounting faculty. In the mid '70s, Alan Senn in accounting and I developed the writing seminar and taught in and coordinated multiple sections for a number of quarters. Most of the writing assignments were modeled on professional writing tasks students would face after graduation. Our inspiration was not the work of WAC programs starting around the nation but the case approach to instruction in business. However, what we learned in this experimental discipline-based writing course later inspired the design of much of our Writing in the Disciplines program.

In these accounting writing seminars, I learned the power of learning writing in the context of a particular discipline. (I was also lucky to learn some tax law that would help me with the IRS.) With team-teaching, I experienced the full range of attitudes about writing instruction held by faculty who do not teach writing courses. One refused to read any papers, or to meet with the students; whatever I did was fine with him. Others were more cooperative, if not completely enthusiastic. And one, a lecturer, Gail Fults, who later took a tenure-track position at Humboldt State University, embraced the opportunity to learn about writing; convinced of the necessity for students to have frequent opportunities if they were to develop confidence and competence as writers, she developed new writing assignments for every course she taught. Several years later, through her testimonials about writing in her accounting courses, Gail would become instrumental in the spread of fledgling writing across the curriculum programs in the CSU.

"Beyond Freshman Composition" Proposed:
Academic Year 1979–1980

During my first year as composition coordinator, probably winter 1980, colleague Ted Humphrey noticed a call for proposals for campus-based projects to improve basic skills—reading, writing, critical thinking, and quantitative skills—issued by the CSU Office of the Chancellor "Fund for Innovation and Improvement in Education" (renamed Academic Program Improvement in 1981). A group of us representing five or six different departments cooked up a response to the RFP, seeking funds to stimulate the addition of writing assignments in upper division courses in the majors. We were not proposing writing *intensive* courses, or additional composition courses, but the incorporation of frequent, short writing assignments in *any* course. We had seen student writing on our GWT, and we had several years of test results showing 40 percent of the students failing the GWT every quarter, with proportions much higher in pre-professional disciplines. Every time I taught our second-quarter composition course, my students—80 percent of them upper-division, not freshmen—claimed to have little or no writing in other courses. We called our proposed project "Beyond Freshman Composition," meaning we wanted to focus on writing assignments appropriate in courses that would *follow* freshman English.

We believed that improving basic skills, writing in this case, would require the collaboration of the entire faculty, not the refinement of a few courses taught by faculty in English. When I look now at the proposal, I see a focus on teaching composing, revising, and editing skills in the context of courses in the major: "Students must be given the opportunity to apply the skills and techniques presented in freshman composition in courses offered by their departments. All teachers must assume some degree of responsibility if students are to be competent writers at graduation." The plan was to work in cross-disciplinary faculty teams to develop writing assignments tailored to specific courses and to conduct faculty workshops on grading and responding to writing. Nowhere is there a mention of "writing across the curriculum" or "writing to learn."

The response to our proposal was positive but required that we make major modifications to our project design to work within an award amount far below what we had requested. After a brief period of negotiations with a very supportive administrator in the Chancellor's Office—Linda Bunnell Jones, who several years later left the CSU for the Wisconsin system, and later Colorado State—we were funded in the spring of 1980 for a project, Beyond Freshman Composition, which would start in Fall 1980. Other Cal States funded by the CSU Chancellor's Office at the same time for writing projects were Dominguez Hills (Writing in Natural Sciences), Sacramento (Writing in General Education), and Northridge (Outwrite Program).

CSU San Bernardino NEH-sponsored Writing Reinforcement Program: Summer 1980

Before we could actually start our Beyond Freshman Composition program, a new opportunity surfaced that would be a major influence on the Cal Poly Pomona program. In the summer of 1980, I received an invitation from Helene Koon to conduct a four-day faculty workshop at a neighboring Cal State campus in San Bernardino. Two years earlier, the campus had received a four-year award from the National Endowment for the Humanities to develop a university-wide "Writing Reinforcement Program," including faculty development focused on improving writing in all courses. Each summer for four years, one fourth of the faculty was to participate in a four-day workshop on assigning writing and grading papers. Summer of 1980 was the third year of the four; the project directors felt that all the "early adopters" (see Rogers) had already participated, and that those who had not yet taken part were the most skeptical, reluctant and unconvinced of the value or need for a week-long workshop.

I don't recall why the invitation came to me, since at that point I had zero experience conducting faculty workshops. I asked Andrew Moss, who had just been hired in a new faculty position at Cal Poly Pomona as director of our basic writing program, to be my partner in the San Bernardino venture. At least, that *might* be the way it worked, and is, as Andy recalls. However, I think it may have been that Andy received the invitation from San Bernardino, and asked *me* to join *him* in leading the workshops. Memory and record-keeping fail on this point, but no matter: We had the good fortune of two full months working together to plan the four days, learning from each other and inventing our brand of writing across the curriculum at his Santa Monica kitchen table. Andy brought years of teaching and research on writing in the disciplines from his former institutions, UCLA and UC Riverside, and extensive and thorough knowledge of relevant books and articles. Together we broadened the assignment design workshops to incorporate writing-to-learn exercises and examples, and the evaluating writing sessions to include peer review and student work on paper in groups. The San Bernardino workshop we constructed and delivered was a success, based on faculty response and the new assignments they developed. That summer work proved invaluable in my preparation for our own Beyond Freshman Composition project.

1980–81: Beyond Freshman Composition
Launched at Cal Poly Pomona

At Pomona, our project plan included support for me as the project director to assemble materials to support writing in different disciplines, to consult with campus faculty and deans, and to travel to consult with faculty and project directors at several other campuses in the state. My travels in the fall of 1980 included trips to UC Davis (writing in science), CSU Sacramento (consultation with Betty Reveley, who was conducting faculty workshops on student writing, plus Charles Moore and Bob Miendl), Sonoma State (Eugene Soules and Helen Dunn), Stanford (consultation with Arthur Applebee in English Education), and UC Berkeley (consultation with James Gray and Mary K. Healy of the Bay Area Writing Project). My meetings with the BAWP team led me to the work of James Britton, Nancy Martin, and the London Schools Council Project, as well as to the support for writing across the curriculum at many of California schools, spinning off the work of BAWP. At Sacramento State, Betty Reveley shared her favorite student paper for a workshop on responding to and evaluating writing, an error-riddled research effort entitled "Frank Lloyd Wright and the Praie House" [sic]. Betty would again in 1982 at a CSU conference share that paper and her use of it to generate discussion of styles of responding to student writing, leading into a discussion of the issues raised in

Mina Shaughnessy's *Errors and Expectations* and focusing on the futility of editing students' work for them.

After a call for participants in the fall, we had twenty faculty signed up for two Saturday workshops in the winter or spring quarters. I had hoped for at least twice that many. My consultation on campus in the fall revealed among faculty not just complaints about poor student writing but concern about their students' abilities to write as professionals after graduating, yet they admitted that they had been gradually assigning less writing and offered several reasons: because of the poor quality of student work, their reluctance to spend the time required to grade written work, and/or fears that students would drop their classes or give them lower evaluations as instructors if they assigned more writing than did their department colleagues. My goal was to test an approach to reversing that trend, in two four-hour Saturday faculty workshops followed by one-on-one consultation. As I wrote in my final report on the project, the goals of the activities were to encourage participating faculty to

1. assign more writing in some, if not all, of their classes;

2. assign shorter, more frequent papers starting at the beginning of the quarter;

3. assign a greater variety of types of writing in each class and make greater use of writing as a means of learning;

4. have a better understanding of the writing process and devise assignments that help students with all stages of that process, including revision; and

5. feel more confident about evaluating student papers and handling the increased paper load.

The winter quarter workshops were built around materials that Andy Moss and I had developed for the San Bernardino faculty workshop, but between winter and spring quarters, in late March 1981, I attended the Conference on College Composition and Communication in Dallas, and, most importantly, a one-day pre-conference workshop on conducting faculty workshops, led by Toby Fulwiler and Bob Jones of Michigan Tech. (See the chapter by Fulwiler and Young in this volume.) As a result of that workshop, I made some major changes in methods of presentation in the spring quarter workshops, increasing the level of participation and involvement of the faculty. Also, what I learned from them (and from Betty Reveley) on the use of overhead projectors to coordinate participants' contributions and pace the workshop sessions proved invaluable. In the "lessons learned" section of my final report, I wrote:

> Leaders should keep lecture-type presentations to a minimum. . . . I found with the winter quarter group that so many questions followed what were to be very short lectures that there was little time left for the activities that followed, activities that would encourage the participants to apply the ideas to their own classes. In the Spring (after attending the Fulwiler-Jones workshop at the Dallas conference), I started all sessions with activities; these and the discussions that followed drew more response and from all participants. Many of the ideas I used are explained in Fulwiler's article "Showing, Not Telling."

Cal Poly Pomona and Writing in the Disciplines (1981–82)

Although the faculty workshops in our Beyond Freshman Composition project resulted in changes in instruction and assignments, for the second year we abandoned the during-the-quarter Saturday workshop plan and adopted the San Bernardino plan of offering a four-day workshop the week before classes begin. The Office of the Chancellor provided second-year funding for the project, with increased campus contribution, but insisted that we drop the Beyond Freshman Composition name and use instead "writing across the curriculum." I resisted. Words like "curriculum" had always made me squirm, and, forgive me, "across the curriculum" seemed nowhere, and fleeting at best. We settled on Writing in the Disciplines.

In the second year of our project, we made many changes: 29 hours of workshop time instead of 8, workshops prior to the start of the academic quarters, 36 participants instead of 20, two workshop leaders instead of one, individual follow-up meetings and a reinforcement workshop mid-year, and more investigation and documentation of the results of the project. We started building our collection of Assignments That Work, new writing assignments that had succeeded in engaging and challenging students in different disciplines, at different levels. Many of these assignments have served as models or examples for faculty in later workshops, at Cal Poly Pomona, on most other Cal State campuses, and at colleges and universities around the country.

We learned we had a model that worked on our campus, for our faculty, and this proved to be a durable structure and the basis for the Writing in the Disciplines program that continues to the present. More than 500 faculty have participated in the project one year or another, and occasional inquiries reveal that most who participated continue to assign and use writing in the classes they teach. After the first two years of grant support, the program continued with support from the Vice President for Academic Affairs (Paul Weller, followed by Bruce Grube). It became part of the offerings of the Faculty Center for Professional Development when that program started in 1990, in part because I continued to direct Writing in the Disciplines after taking on the new assignment directing the Faculty Center.

Research and Dissemination

From the start, those of us involved in Beyond Freshman Composition/ Writing in the Disciples at Cal Poly joined a national conversation, coming into discussions that had been on-going for several years. Although not as active as many leaders in the WAC movement, we shared our work in presentations, consultations, and publications, both to make our discoveries available to others and to benefit from the perspectives of those with different ideas of what works best in WAC. In the spring of 1981, Andrew Moss and I made presentations at the Conference on English Education, sharing what we developed for the San Bernardino Writing Reinforcement Program faculty workshops.

Also, our work in writing across the curriculum led us in new directions in our research. In the summer of 1981, we investigated writing on-the-job, visiting businesses, labs, schools, and other organizations, often interviewing graduates of Cal Poly Pomona. What we learned from scientists, architects, engineers, teachers, and business managers helped us appreciate the importance of writing in different careers, and see the skills our students would need to have successful careers in different professions. Also we gained insight into what had made a difference for professionals, while they were in college, in their preparation for reading and writing at work. We learned how writing forms the backbone of engineering projects, how environmental impact reports impact contracts and careers of architects, and how a manager learned how to write from a history professor who had insisted on a paper being rewritten four times. This research improved our work with faculty on developing new writing assignments, especially those that would simulate professional writing tasks that students could expect to encounter after graduation.

The materials that Andy and I developed for faculty workshops, and the results of our research on writing in professional contexts, form the basis for a handbook that we wrote for faculty, *Improving Student Writing: A Guidebook for Faculty in All Disciplines*. This 60-page book was first printed and distributed using grant funds from the CSU Office of the Chancellor, but after a few years, realizing that we didn't have time to be in the publishing business, we contracted with Kendall-Hunt to distribute the book, with a much-improved cover. The first Kendall-Hunt printing was 1988; the book is currently in its tenth printing.

In 1982, we presented our work on a panel we proposed for 4Cs, "Making Connections: Relating the Curriculum to Professional Writing Contexts" and in an article published in *Inside English* (the journal of the California Association of Teachers of English). The 4Cs conference for the next five years would be crucial for sharing the work we were doing and connecting with project directors elsewhere. Unlike the culture of hiding work in progress so as to publish something before others can, the writing across the curriculum researchers and practitioners were in the habit of sharing openly and broadly, allowing projects and their directors everywhere to benefit from best practices and progress quickly. In 1983, a one-week course at NYU with Dixie Goswami introduced many of us to classroom research, and from there I went to writing conferences at Beaver College and Penn State (see the essays by Maimon and by Kuriloff and Peterson, this volume). In 1984, I was invited to be one of four institute "teachers" at a conference at Rice University, organized by Linda Driskill. Lee Odell was the primary teacher, and I learned more about writing and about conducting faculty workshops from the conference itself and from watching Lee in action.

More on WAC in the Cal State University

Meanwhile, the California State University Office of the Chancellor was interested in seeing more campuses start writing across the curriculum programs. Linda Jones's office funded two dissemination conferences in the spring of 1982, one in the north part of the state at

CSU Chico, organized by Victor Lams and Brooks Thorlaksson, and the southern one at Cal Poly Pomona, organized by Andrew Moss and me. Following these dissemination programs, the Office of the Chancellor issued a call for proposals for replication projects, inviting Cal State campuses not yet funded to launch writing projects of their own, adapting features of successful projects elsewhere and consulting with those project directors. In 1982–83, I worked with two new project directors, Susan McLeod at San Diego State University and Kim Flachmann at Cal State Bakersfield, both of whom designed and directed very successful projects, taking materials and approaches from the Pomona project and adapting them and adding to them in ways compatible with their own approaches and suitable for their campuses, both different from each other and from Cal Poly Pomona. Susan went on to develop more connections and become a catalyst herself nationally, through her publications, presentations, and consulting, moving from SDSU to Washington State University, and then recently to UC Santa Barbara, to direct their writing program, while continuing her research and writing projects, like organizing this volume.

Other CSU campuses also adapted materials and approaches from the Pomona Writing in the Disciplines project, and brought, through faculty expertise, a wealth of new ideas to engage faculty in thinking about writing and reading, and teaching and learning. I worked with Tom Klammer leading workshops at Cal State Fullerton for many years, and with Priscilla Chaffe-Stengel and Ethelynda Harding at Cal State Fresno.

The story of the development of Chico's Writing Across the Disciplines program makes for a lively chapter in Fulwiler and Young's *Programs That Work* and won't be recounted here. Stephen BeMiller serves as narrator, with seven others contributing. The story of that chapter fits well in this volume, with its revelations on the power of collaboration among faculty—writing as a team, working as a team.

In all, I visited most of the Cal State campuses, plus another 30 or so elsewhere around the country, making connections with faculty, writing program administrators, and, indirectly, other WAC consultants who had preceded me (e.g., John Bean, Toby Fulwiler, Lee Odell, Sue McLeod, Chris Thaiss, Barbara Walvoord, and many others). Conferences like 4Cs and the National Writing Across the Curriculum Conference, as well as email, listservs, websites, and publishing projects—have been opportunities for WAC directors old and new to maintain contacts and to keep learning from each other. Just as our own circle of contacts, or set of links, have developed among faculty on each of our campuses, our campus programs have benefited from the work of WAC leaders and faculty elsewhere in the country. The Web (especially the WAC Clearinghouse based at Colorado State University) has made it easy for faculty to publish their writing assignments and share ways that writing works in their classes, and for project directors to share ways that WAC programs are evolving, impacted by changes that affect everything in higher education: funding cuts, accountability demands, new technologies, changes in the faculty workforce, and changes in our students and their values. Many WAC pioneers are still WAC leaders, on their campus if not nationally. Others are now college and university administrators, faculty development directors, English professors, independent scholars, and retirees—wealthy and mellow, I hope. My hunch, based on a small non-random sample, is that most are still conducting faculty workshops and still view writing across the curriculum as the most effective faculty development program in colleges during the past century, one that is needed just as much now as it was in the 1970s.

Sue's Story

Background: the Context for WAC in the 1970s

The 1970s was a decade when many of us who got our degrees in something called English (usually literature) were trying to figure out how our involvement in the social activism of that period of time—the civil rights movement, the women's liberation movement, the anti-war movement—could be translated into our professional lives. We were out to change the world, trying to figure out how to do that within existing institutions ("work within the system for change" was our mantra). In my own case, after a year teaching at a Historically Black College and spending two years with the Peace Corps in Ethiopia, I plunged back into graduate school at the University of Wisconsin. It was the height of the Viet Nam war. As a TA I taught writing classes that had in them young men of draft age; trying to make sure these students in particular could write well enough to stay in school and not be sent off to war became a driving force for most of the TAs (Ira Shor, now known for his work in critical pedagogy, was perhaps the most vocal among us). The world of literary criticism, which we had thought we wanted to enter when we began our graduate study, seemed increasingly irrelevant to the social forces around us. Teaching people to find and use their own voices to bring about social change—or just to save themselves from being cannon fodder—seemed much more important.

Getting Started at San Diego State

During the decade after finishing my degree I taught writing as a part-time lecturer (for most of that time at San Diego State University, part of the same multi-campus system as Cal Poly Pomona), learning all I could by reading and by talking with other lecturers like myself—first in San Diego, then in Washington D.C., following my husband as his career developed. In 1981, when we returned to San Diego, I attended a local conference at which I met Andy Moss; as we were chatting during one of the breaks, I learned of the program he and Carol were developing at Pomona, and—more importantly—that the Chancellor's Office of the California State University System had a call for proposals for inter-campus grants to replicate successful programs from one CSU campus on another. He gave me his card and Carol's number, encouraging me to think about starting such a program at San Diego State.

I called Carol as soon as I got home, and she offered to help me write the grant; we spent one Saturday afternoon at her beach house in San Clemente going over her materials, including those that later became the book that she and Andy published (as well as the "Praie House" student paper she mentioned above, which I still use in faculty workshops). I asked for, and she gave me, copies of everything. I used most of what she gave me in my proposal, and I got the grant.[1]

After the euphoria wore off, panic set in. What had I gotten myself into? Like Carol at the beginning, I knew zero about running faculty workshops. I called Chris Thaiss, since I had learned about WAC originally from him. Although I did not know it at the time, Chris had taken over and was expanding the WAC National Network (see his "Still a Good Place to Be," this volume) and was exactly the right person to call as I was searching for connections and colleagues. Chris made soothing noises and gave me advice, as well as Toby Fulwiler's phone number. Toby was likewise incredibly generous and helpful to the hyperventilating stranger on the other end of the line. Carol contacted me with more advice, and offered to come down to San Diego to run one day of the four-day faculty workshop I had proposed. My husband took the kids to the beach. My mother-in-law made cinnamon rolls for participants to have with coffee in the mornings. I was ready.

Four days later, I was exhausted, but elated. It had gone better than I could have imagined, but even more, I now found that I was in demand all over campus for similar workshops; my faculty colleagues in the disciplines were enormously enthusiastic about the techniques they had learned for assigning and grading papers, but even more, for the understanding of writing as a mode of learning.

The First Faculty Workshop

As I look at the agenda for that first ambitious workshop, I am struck by three things. First, as a result of the WAC community that was just beginning to form, I had an enviable level of support—I was using proven workshop materials and techniques from Carol, Andy, Toby, and Chris, and although I had not yet met them, from Chuck Bazerman ("What Written Knowledge Does" and the textbook *The Informed Writer,* which I was using to teach my composition classes) and Anne Herrington, whose article "Writing to Learn" was enormously helpful as I planned the workshop. I had to invent very little myself during my rookie year. Second, my training and experience in the Peace Corps was key to my own success as a workshop leader and eventually as a WAC director. Among the tenets of the Peace Corps are understanding of and respect for the host country culture, including immersing oneself in the language of that culture, while at the same time acting as an agent of change—working at the grassroots level on issues having to do with the greater good of the community.

I had my first lesson in respect for disciplinary discourse in that first workshop. I had included a short exercise taken from Richard Lanham's book *Revising Prose* as a way of helping faculty think about how to help students revise. The psychology professor took issue with the notion of always using active voice, that in fact passive voice was perfectly appropriate for her discipline. She was quite articulate, and others joined in, taking sides in the active vs. passive voice debate. It was clear from the way the discussion sorted itself out that my notions of voice and style were based on my background in humanities, but that the social sciences and the sciences thought very differently. In fact, in their view, their own discourse was "objective" while that of the humanities was "flowery." It was a good-natured discussion, but one in which we all learned that when faculty say "students can't write," what they sometimes mean is "students can't write the way I do." I designed a way to deliberately bring about a discussion of the differences in disciplinary discourse for future workshops, since I found it to be such a provocative and productive conversation. (I do this by passing out a very short but well-written student essay with no other instructions other than asking faculty to grade it; the scientists and social scientists invariably give it a high grade, since it is concise; those in the humanities usually give it a low grade, since it "lacks development.") As others in this volume have indicated, faculty conversations like these are the heart of WAC programs across the country.

Finally, I am struck by the differences between this workshop and later ones, differences due in large part to becoming involved with the San Diego Writing Project. My involvement started after a chance meeting with Mary Barr, who was involved in the Writing Project and was working for the San Diego School District. She had been trying for several years to interest someone in the San Diego State English department in cooperative workshops, but had not been successful. I jumped at the chance. From 1983–86 Mary and I worked to set up joint workshops (Jim Moffett and Mary K. Healy came for one memorable one), and I became involved in workshops at the secondary level, the most interesting of which was at San Diego High School as it was being transformed into the Writing Magnet and International Baccalaureate high school. I learned much from my colleagues in the San Diego Writing Project and in the secondary schools; this experience enabled me to speak with more authority with my university colleagues about writing preparation at the high school level, and it also provided a model of the faculty workshop (teachers teaching other teachers) that I adapted for my own workshops. Again, as others in this volume have mentioned, the National Writing Project was an important model for our faculty workshops, teachers talking to other teachers about teaching.

WAC and the Dissemination of Innovation

I had attended the dissemination conference that Carol had organized at Pomona the spring of 1982 (described in her section of this essay), just before I held my first faculty workshop. There I met Ed White, from Cal State San Bernardino, who during one of the evening happy hours outlined what I recognized as the theory of the dissemination of innovation (Rogers)—a theory I knew from Peace Corps days from the practitioner's point of view.[2] Briefly, Rogers tells us that innovations are accepted first by the "innovators" in any group, then the "early adopters" (who wait to see how it has gone with the innovators), then the "early majority," who are more conservative than the early adopters, and finally the "late majority." There is also a group of "laggards" who adopt innovation when it is no longer innovative, or who simply will not adopt innovation. Rogers defines dissemination as the process by which an innovation is communicated through certain channels over time among the members of a social system. The adoption process is individual; diffusion is a group process. Stephanie Vanderslice has pointed out the relationship between Rogers's theory and the early WAC movement. It is true, as she states, that until the publication of *In the Long Run* (Walvoord et al.), no WAC research had explicitly linked this theory to WAC. However, at the practitioner level, we were all aware of how to bring about change and aware of the theory, if not always the theorist (recall that we were also children of the 1960s and 70s who were out to change the world). Carol certainly understood it, since the conferences she mounted were specifically aimed at dissemination, the diffusion of innovation as Rogers describes it, as were her visits to the Cal State campuses. Without her efforts, WAC would not have spread as it did, or spread as quickly, throughout the entire CSU system.

Key to the dissemination of innovation of WAC innovation were The Chicago Conferences as Margot Soven describes them (this volume); these conferences also played an important part of the creation of the social system we now think of as the WAC community of scholars and practitioners. The Academic Vice President of San Diego State was so impressed with the results of that first faculty seminar that he sent me to the 1983 Chicago Conference on Writing and Higher Order Reasoning (held in May of that year) to meet Elaine Maimon and, as he put it, "pick her brain" about how best to continue the program. Elaine very graciously met with me (the only time she had was just before she left, so I sat in her hotel room while she finished her breakfast and packed her bags); she advised me to establish an Advisory Board for the program and start them thinking about curricular requirements. It was at this conference that I also met Margot Soven, who has become a good friend and collaborator on many WAC projects. Later that same year I attended my first National Network of WAC programs at the NCTE Conference in Denver, at the invitation of Chris Thaiss. A year later he invited me to serve on the Board of Consultants, a group that has been key to the dissemination process of WAC innovations (see "Still a Good Place to Be," this volume).[3] I went from being part of a state-wide community of WAC directors, established so effectively by Carol, to a growing WAC community at the national level.

The National Network group, together with other members of the WAC community, have now published four collaborative books, including this one.[4] When the first two books went out of print, we arranged with Mike Palmquist and the WAC Clearinghouse to have them put on-line, so that others in the WAC community might still be able to use them (http://wac.colostate.edu/index.cfm). The WAC Clearinghouse is just the latest development in the dissemination of WAC ideas in the social system we call the WAC community. It is clear that this dissemination continues, via technology as well as conferences, consulting visits, networks, professional articles and books. Given the staying power that WAC has demonstrated, as evidenced most recently by the attendance at WAC sessions at the Conference on College Composition and Communication, my assumption is that this dissemination of WAC ideas and concepts will continue as long as developing students' writing and critical thinking skills are deemed important at the college level.

NOTES

[1] A note on the politics of part-time employment: because I was a lecturer, I was not eligible to write such a grant, but no one else in the English department was interested. (In fact, the full-time faculty were actively hostile toward the idea, which created some drama—the finale of which was the creation of a separate department of Rhetoric and Writing Studies at San Diego State some years later.) I wrote the grant proposal, but the department chair was the one whose name was on it as the one who could then technically receive the grant.

[2] Although Rogers is the person most identified with this theory, he developed it using the work of earlier researchers who studied the diffusion of hybrid seed among Iowa farmers

[3] I also had the good fortune to attend one of the earliest WPA Workshops, led by Maxine Hairston, in the summer of 1984. Although the topic was writing program administration rather than WAC, several of us involved

were also administering WAC programs and have kept in touch since that time.

⁴ The first three are *Strengthening Programs for Writing Across the Curriculum* (Jossey-Bass, 1988), *Writing Across the Curriculum: A Guide to Developing Programs* (Sage, 1992), and *WAC for the New Millennium: Strategies for Continuing Writing Across the Curriculum Programs* (NCTE, 2001).

Works Cited

Bazerman, Charles. "What Written Knowledge Does: Three Examples of Academic Discourse." *Philosophy of the Social Sciences* 11 (1981): 361–87.

Fulwiler, Toby. "Showing, Not Telling, at a Writing Workshop." *College English* 43 (January 1981): 55–63.

Herrington, Anne. "Writing to Learn: Writing Across the Disciplines." *College English* 43 (1981): 379–87.

Johns, Ann M. "Interpreting an English Competency Examination: The Frustrations of an ESL Science Student." *Written Communication* 8.3 (1991): 379–401.

BeMiller, Stephen, et al. "California State University, Chico." In *Programs That Work: Models and Methods for Writing Across the Curriculum.* Ed. Toby Fulwiler and Art Young. Upper Montclair, NJ: Boynton/Cook, 1990. 115–36.

Lanham, Richard. *Revising Prose.* 1979 4th ed. New York: Pearson Longman, 1999.

Moss, Andrew, and Carol Holder. *Improving Student Writing: A Guidebook for Faculty in All Disciplines.* Dubuque, IA: Kendall-Hunt, 1988.

Rogers, Everett. *Diffusion of Innovations.* 1962. 5th ed. New York: Free Press, 2003.

Vanderslice, Stephanie. "Listening to Everett Rogers: Diffusion of Innovations and WAC." *Language and Learning Across the Disciplines* 4 (May 2000): 22–29.

Walvoord, Barbara F., et al. *In the Long Run: A Study of Faculty in Three Writing Across the Curriculum Programs.* Urbana, IL: NCTE, 1997.

White, Edward M. "The Opening of the Modern Era of Writing Assessment: A Narrative." *College English* 63.3 (January 2001): 306–20.

5 WAC Becomes Respectable: The University of Chicago Institutes on Writing and Higher Order Reasoning

Margot Soven

Wow, those Conferences were a while ago! They were amazing—I remember being inspired by them. At the time I was working on my doctoral dissertation proposal, and I remember defining my topic as a result of those meetings. [I was] essentially looking at how student cognitive development was linked to writing, using the Perry model. Personally, the conferences had a strong impact on my professional decisions, and the direction of my work.

—Nancy Shapiro, University of Maryland

In terms of influences, of course the big one was meeting with Elaine and getting excellent advice on how to build on the success of my first faculty seminar . . . I also remember hearing Reed Larson, a student of Mihaly Csikzentmihalyi, talk about experiments with high school students writing and emotion, a talk that helped inspire my own interest in emotions and writing. All in all, it was a rich experience, in that it helped me make connections with folks in WAC and NCTE, but also helped give me some grounding in what we meant by "critical thinking" and inspired me to learn more about developmental and cognitive psychology in order to be a better teacher myself. I was eager to learn as much as I could, and I think that described many of us who attended.

—Susan McLeod, University of California, Santa Barbara

As I peruse my old, fat notebook, I realize that many/most/all of the concepts presented at the conference are ones that have influenced me throughout my entire career. It was an excellent learning experience.

—Martha Townsend, Director Campus Writing
Program, University of Missouri

I always learned a great deal from each of the Chicago Conferences!

—Elaine Maimon, University of Alaska, Anchorage

Introduction

From 1983 to 1993, the University of Chicago, through its Continuing Education Programs Department, sponsored a series of three-day institutes (Thursday evening through Sunday afternoon) on the relationships between intellectual development, critical thinking, and writing at the college level. The programs changed during the ten years, expanding to include such subjects as general education, world cultures, and student diversity. However, all of the conferences continued to be concerned about the subjects which inspired the conferences originally: intellectual development, critical thinking, and writing.

What was so special about the University of Chicago Institutes on Writing and Higher Order Reasoning? Why, when I was doing my research for this chapter, did people thank me for reminding them about Chicago? As the comments preceding the chapter reveal, for those of us who attended the conferences at Chicago they were an extraordinary—in many cases a defining—experience for years to come. My purpose in this chapter is to explain why this was the case, and to assess the impact of the conferences on the Writing Across the Curriculum (WAC) community. But I hope I can do more than that. I want to project some of the "electricity" of those years, to tell about the "intellectual high" we experienced in Chicago. Apart from my own recollections, use the memories of some former conferees, the Chicago "groupies" who were kind enough to stop the clock and "return to Chicago."

Let's begin with two questions:

1. Why were the conferences so successful as conferences? What made them so engaging? Can we use them as models for future conferences in higher education, not just about WAC, but also about other issues?

2. How did the conferences contribute to WAC as a national movement? How did they enrich WAC's theoretical framework, and how did they expand and strengthen the WAC community?

The Chicago Conferences were successful for five reasons:

1. *Program Excellence:* Every program included top scholars from a variety of fields who presented new and cutting edge ideas and theories in the plenary sessions. The list of scholars who gave major presentations is an impressive one. For example, speakers on writing and rhetoric included Wayne Booth, Joseph Williams, Elaine Maimon, Andrea Lunsford, David Bartholomae, Kenneth Bruffee, and many others. The workshop sessions were conducted by program administrators (like myself) who were experimenting with alternative models for writing programs and faculty development at their home institutions. These people were also leaders in a field of a different kind. They were on the front lines, teaching writing themselves and training other faculty to teach writing. In future years this group would author many texts for both students and instructors on the subject of writing and WAC.

2. *Timing:* It was the 1980s. Writing Across the Curriculum was coming of age on many campuses. Colleges were busy reevaluating general education programs and the core curriculum. A sense of urgency was in the air. The subjects of the conferences, critical thinking, writing, and students' intellectual development, were hot. As Elaine Maimon says, "After worrying in the 1960s and 1970s that Johnny and Janey can't read or write, educator in the 1980s concluded that the real problem is that

students can't think" (xv). Many of us felt we needed to know more (immediately!) about the relationship of thinking and writing to become better teachers and better program administrators.

3. *Format:* The Conferences were interactive. You came to each conference prepared to participate actively. A packet of readings on the conference topics had been distributed several weeks earlier. And, in addition, you were asked to bring materials from your own programs or classrooms. You left the conference with new writing assignments, new ideas for developing programs at home, and in many cases, ideas for research projects. Plenary sessions and concurrent panels alternated with participant discussion groups that often focused on the materials people brought from their schools. I was a discussion leader at the first conference I attended in 1983. After the conference, I received a letter from one of the participants, Barbara Olds, of the Colorado School of Mines, saying that the participant discussions were the most valuable part of the conference.

4. *The Participants:* Much of the excitement came from the unusual mix of participants. Experts and novices, writing program administrators and doctoral students, literary scholars and philosophers, scientists, psychologists and anthropologists, theologians, rhetoricians, and linguists—all came together at the historic Blackstone Hotel on Michigan Avenue in Chicago to talk about thinking and writing. It was quite a party, and it lasted for ten years. Many of the conferees, like me, were new faculty. "Chicago" gave us the chance to meet informally with experts in many fields, a rare opportunity, and virtually impossible at large professional conferences. Because of the conference was limited to two hundred participants, and many of us attended several times, the conferences marked the beginning of lasting friendships and professional collaborations that often led to joint research projects, new books, and a host of other activities. In some cases, these collaborations are still alive and well. Susan McLeod and I met in Chicago; our mutual interests ignited a twenty year friendship that has been both professionally and personally rewarding.

5. *Prestige:* "If the University of Chicago is sponsoring these conferences, they must be good." Everyone was impressed, including my department chair, who brought the conferences to my attention. (He also noticed that the Program Consultant of the second conference, Michael Ditchkofsky, was a La Salle graduate. What could be better?) I was the new writing specialist on campus, and he wanted me to attend. The University of Chicago was the first prestigious school to acknowledge the legitimacy of the teaching of writing as a field worthy of study and scholarship. Both presenters and participants were eager to attend meetings sponsored by one of the most respected universities in the country.

Although all of these reasons were vital to the success of the conferences, it was the conference programs that drew the estimated 3,000 attendees over the ten years and induced many of us to return year after year. Elizabeth O'Connor Chandler, the Director of the Teaching and Learning Center at the University of Chicago, estimates that eighty to one hundred institutions eventually took part in the conferences, a large number of them sending teams of faculty several years in a row. In a recent email, she said, "Rarely am I surprised by the discovery of a four year institution in the United States that I have not heard of, given the popularity of the Institutes." A glance at any one of the lists of participants convinces me that no other set of conferences during the last twenty years attracted faculty from as many schools from coast to coast For example, at the conference held in November, 1986, the participant list includes faculty and administrators from four year liberal arts colleges and large state universities such as Ithaca College, University of California, Kansas State University, the U.S. Air Force Academy, Ohio University, Fairleigh Dickinson University, and the University of Pennsylvania.

THE GENESIS OF THE CONFERENCES

The Institute programs started as programs only occasionally do, with just the right mix of people coming together at just the right time. How lucky we are that Carol Schneider, the Director for Academic Programs at the University of Chicago, Elaine Maimon, at that time the Director of Composition at Beaver College (now Arcadia University) and Joseph Williams, Professor of English and Linguistics, also at the University of Chicago, crossed paths in the early 1980s.

Elaine Maimon had just completed the now famous NEH (National Endowment for the Humanities) funded seminars on writing at Beaver College and had launched a project on thinking and writing funded by FIPSE, the Fund for the Improvement of Post Secondary Education (see Maimon, this volume). At a meeting of FIPSE project directors in Chicago, Elaine heard that Carol Schneider was organizing conferences on cognitive issues involved with adult education. It soon became clear to Elaine that the "writing world was working on similar issues, especially the emphasis on the relationships between thinking, reasoning and writing, even though we might be reading different books and articles and talking to different people."[1] Elaine suggested that it would be fruitful to bring the two groups together, and subsequently found herself invited to the first conference. Carol Schneider said, "Writing people became the catalysts for the conference. Writing was and still is a primary issue in both general education. In the early years of the conference many people came because of their concern about general education and writing." However, both Elaine and Joe credit Carol with "making the conferences happen." Joe said, "Carol was a terrific organizer and planner. She made them happen and deserves the credit."

Joe remembers that when Carol asked him to help plan the early conferences, he had already been thinking about the inadequacy of current approaches to writing instruction. He remembers that "experience up to that time had convinced me that people performed intellectually and in writing inconsistently, depending where they were in their understanding of what they were writing about and being asked to think about. It also seemed that there was a one size fits all approach to writing that didn't match the experiences people had when they moved from field to field."

Joseph Williams saw the Institutes as a great opportunity to "plan a really great party. I'd invite all the people whose work I had read and admired who would make really great conversationalists and who probably had not had the chance to talk to one another. I had been ranging fairly broadly in cognitive psychology, critical thinking, rhetoric, and writing and so on, and the connections among the various fields seemed to me obvious, but not too many people in rhetoric or composition were cashing in on what people in other fields were doing, much less even knowing they existed. So these conferences were an opportunity to create a kind of yeasty few days where people who don't talk to one another, could."

Unlike most professional conferences, where the conference chairs change annually, and the effort is to create variety in the programs rather than continuity, the same core group, Elaine, Joe, and Carol, continued to plan the Institutes around the same issues, critical thinking, intellectual development, and writing. New people were gradually added to the planning group. But having a core group of conference planners assured the continuity between the programs. Joe says, "As I look back on them [the conferences], I have very good memories of sitting around with Carol and others, planning the next ones. Those chats were first rate conversations."

These "chats" produced intellectually rigorous conference agendas which reflected discursive nature of the conferences. New issues grew out of the conference debates. The conferences were a "work in progress." In character they adhered to the philosophy announced in the early programs. All of them were about, "problem structuring, exploration, and discovery." They never promised "answers" but they offered alternative ways of defining educational problems and suggested alternative approaches to solving them. If you were looking for a WAC "formula" you needn't have come to Chicago.

THE PROGRAMS

At the heart of the conference debates were several questions:
- What is critical thinking?
- What do we know about our students? How can we "understand them?"
  o How are thinking and writing related?
  o How do we teach students the conventions of thinking and writing, which define the academy?

In the early conferences "thinking and writing critically" was defined as the ability to solve the increasingly complex problems that students confront as they progress from introductory to advanced courses. "Understanding our students" was defined as becoming acquainted with the implications of research on students' cognitive and ethical development during the college years, two subjects most of us who attended the conferences knew little about. Most of the research at that time on the development of writing ability had been conducted with elementary and high school students. Composition specialists were familiar with Piaget, because of James Moffett's sequence of writing assignments based on a Piagetian model of intellectual growth, but Moffett's curriculum stopped at Grade 12. We also knew about James Britton's theory "that children develop writing ability by moving from personal forms of writing (what he calls expressive to poetic) to more public, workaday forms which communicate information (what he calls transactional)" (Russell 276). But Britton's research applies only to junior high and high school students.

In the cover letter for the May 1984 conference, entitled "Writing, Meaning, and Higher Order Reasoning," Joseph Williams framed the agenda for the early conferences, "In the last decade we have witnessed the emergence of three lines of research into the ways students develop intellectually, research that could significantly change the way we think about our approaches to teaching writing and invention:

- Contrary to what has often been assumed, young adults do not finish their cognitive development by the time they leave adolescence. If research by Lawrence Kohlberg, William Perry, and those extending the work of Piaget is correct, students continue to change and grow in ways which profoundly affect their approaches to complexity, problem structuring, and the making of meaning.
- Creative problem solving and higher order reasoning are not mysterious capacities that some students are born with, others not. They are intellectual abilities that can be developed in systematic ways.
- Writing is an activity that contributes simultaneously to the solution of a problem and to the way a problem is posed. The way a teacher uses instruction will strongly influence how his or her students approach the task of finding and solving significant problems."

The early conferences defined mature intelligence as a holistic generic competence, mostly independent of subject matter and explained cognitive growth as a progression from less abstract to more abstract forms of thinking. The 1984 conference featured presentations on William Perry's model of cognitive development during the college years and other research on intellectual development of college students such as Michael Basseche's work on the development of the capacity for dialectical thinking from the freshman to the senior year in college. I remember thinking that this research would be enormously helpful in our efforts to understand student writing.

The design of writing assignments became the pedagogical focus of the conference Workshops, representing " the "theory into practice" part of the conferences. To quote from the program, "The following Workshops represent a range of innovative campus models for teaching writing in ways that intentionally expand the student's competence in modes of inquiry and invention." The six workshops in this strand presented six different models for sequencing assignments, but the underlying assumption in each case was the same: Students will be nudged forward along the ladder of cognitive complexity if you just give them the right tasks. Illustrative workshops talks include "Designing Writing Assignments to Improve Critical Thinking in the Academic Disciplines" (Lucy Cromwell and Joyce Fey, Alverno College); "Structuring Writing Assignments to Foster Intellectual Development" (Faith Gabelnick and John Howarth, University of Maryland).

The "Participant Working Groups" which followed these workshops gave us the opportunity to apply what we had learned from the psychologists by examining sample student writing for evidence of the intellectual development. We also discussed ways of responding to and devising writing assignments appropriate to different students.

Concern about the role of affect and attitude on thinking was also part of the early conference programs. Reed Larson, then Assistant Professor in Psychiatry at Michael Reese Hospital of the University of Chicago, gave one of the most eye-opening talks on affect at the May 1984 conference. In his presentation, "Student Involvement in Writing Assignments and the Quality of Writing, A Research Report, " Larson demonstrated the strong correlation between affective responses to writing a research paper and the quality of the writing in the papers. Although many of us were familiar with Daly and Miller's work on students' attitudes towards writing in general, Larson challenged us to think about students' emotional states while they complete a specific writing assignment. Susan McLeod tells me that this talk inspired her own strand of scholarship about the affective domain and the writing classroom.

Larson's talk was representative of the trend at the conferences to move from general to specific contexts on all the conference topics. For example, at the next conference in November, 1985, the emphasis of the conference shifted from defining critical thinking in generic terms to defining it in terms of the "requirements of specific domains of discourse" and the teaching of critical thinking was explored in terms of introducing students "into the implicit values and assumptions that determine the form of critical thinking in different discourses." As Carol Schneider told me, "critical thinking" rapidly became a moving target.

By 1986, the connection between thinking and the disciplines was made even more explicit. The concept of "interpretive communities" was introduced for the first time at the conferences. Williams writes in the introduction to the program, "It is misleading to think of ourselves as teaching general thinking skills or mental abilities. In teaching students, in reading their written work, we are inevitably drawn into the cognitive frameworks, knowledge bases, and inquiry strategies of particular interpretive communities. As teachers we need to be self-conscious about the interplay between our own interpretive and evaluative schema and those the student brings to the learning situation. As members of a community committed to critical self scrutiny we need to develop more effective ways of helping students mediate and integrate competing claims of disparate interpretive communities." The writing assignment was still featured as the key to developing critical thinking skills. At our presentation, William Sullivan, a member of the Philosophy Department at La Salle University, and I discussed a sequence of writing assignments which might help students see the connection between core courses and the major. We defined "interpretive community" in yet another way, as we distinguished between the goals of courses in the major in contrast to the goals of humanities courses in the core.

The 1987 May conference marks a watershed in the Institute programs. At the May Institute, "Interpretive Communities and the Undergraduate Writer," the program took a major turn. In my recent correspondence with him, Joseph Williams describes the nature of the transition: "As the conferences went on, I began to see more clearly how socially based the act of writing is, but not in the ways the folks at Carnegie Mellon had been claiming. Their social view of writing had (to me) degenerated into a kind of descriptive 'boxology' that had little or nothing to do with the feel of reading and writing on the hoof. What became especially clear, I think, was that everyone behaves like a beginner when they write in a new field for a new audience regardless of their previous experience." In Williams' chapter, "Two Ways of

Thinking About Growth," in *Thinking, Reasoning and Writing*, the book inspired by the Chicago programs, he sums up the implications of this insight. He writes about an alternative metaphor for describing cognitive growth: that of the outsider standing outside a bounded area that defines community of discourse, the interpretive community consisting of us and our peers. This metaphor forces us to equate growth with socialization.

Thus the conditions for joining the academic community or the interpretive community of each discipline includes our telling the student what counts as behaving like a member of our community. We are forced to become our own ethnographers, so that we can articulate the "intellectual customs" of these communities. But how do we accomplish this task once we have brought these "ways of knowing" to our own consciousness?

Writing assignments were still front stage and center, but this time with an emphasis on embedding the characteristics of the professional discourse of the discipline in the assignment task after helping students to understand these characteristics through the analysis of professional writing characteristic of the field. Gregory Colomb's presentation, "Hidden Expectations: The Secrets of Interpretive Communities and the Novice Student," demonstrated how to accomplish this task when assigning papers in literature classes. Colomb was teaching at the University of Chicago at that time, in the Little Red School House program, an upper division writing program for teaching students how to write in the major.

The 1987 Conference program attracted a "blizzard" of writing specialists, including Kenneth Bruffee and John Trimbur who introduced "conversation" as an important pedagogy for teaching writing, relating it to a social explanation of the development of intellectual growth. Bruffee's conversation pedagogy can take many forms, such as the teacher-student writing conference, collaborative writing groups and peer tutoring. In "Thinking and Writing as Social Acts" also in *Thinking, Reasoning, and Writing*, Bruffee explains the rationale for using "conversation" to teach writing: "When we write, according to this alternative social constructionist way of talking, we re-externalize a linguistic process we had earlier internalized. That is, the 'writing process' begins as we continually internalize the language forms given to us by our community, along with the various processes of using them approved of by that community and many of the things said ('ideas') that are approved by that community" (215). Not surprisingly, in May, 1988 "Collaborative Learning" is one of the conference's main topics. Tori-Haring Smith who was the Director of the Writing Fellows program, a course based peer-tutoring program, at Brown University, became a "regular" on the Institute Faculty for several years afterwards.

The Institutes continued through 1993, revisiting earlier themes as well as moving in new directions. The last Institutes can be viewed as a segue to the Association of American Colleges and University conferences on General Education which continued through the 90's and are still going strong. The link is Carol Schneider, who has since been appointed President of the Association of American Colleges and Universities.

THE EFFECTS OF THE CONFERENCES ON WAC

It's hard to remember now that until 1997, the year that the first national WAC conference was held, that WAC was "homeless." Presentations about WAC were confined to a program strand in conferences such as NCTE or CCCC. But WAC did find a home, even if it was only a temporary one, in Chicago. Although the Institutes on Writing and Higher Order Reasoning did not have the strengthening of the WAC movement as their major objective, in fact that may have been their most important contribution to higher education. The Chicago Conferences represent the "coming of age" of the Writing Across the Curriculum Movement. WAC became respectable in Chicago

In "The Future of WAC," Barbara Walvoord calls for "additional ways to enlarge the debates about WAC beyond writing specialists (8)." The Chicago Conferences did just that—big time. WAC theory suddenly expanded to include diverse views on the relationship between writing and intellectual development. Writing in the disciplines was discussed within context of research in related fields. Joe Williams says that it became clear that models of moral/human development provided a pretty useful map of the development of writers from the most concrete form of behavior to the most abstract. He adds, "I think that was a particular contribution of the conferences to the field."

"Chicago" had more impact on those of us who were interested in teaching students the rhetoric of academic writing than it did on our colleagues in the expressivist camp of composition. Notice I do not make the distinction between the "write to learn" enthusiasts versus the "learn to write" supporters, which is a flawed distinction at best. "Chicago" reinforced that idea that the act of writing itself is a powerful mode of learning.

Linda Bergmann speaks for many of us when she says (in an email message to the author),

> Although I had read and had tried to believe that the practices of composition were soundly grounded in an intellectual base, my knowledge of it seemed scattered and diffused compared to my knowledge of literature and literary history. The development of my thinking about teaching and learning writing that ensued after the experience of this conference provided a sound base for my later design and development of WAC programs and Writing Centers providing a grounding that shields me from the kind of catch penny administrative expediency that can characterize administrative work at its worst.

But the conference benefits were not limited to theory. The conferences helped us to understand better the power and versatility of writing assignments to teach the conventions of writing in the disciplines. Writing assignments had always held great interest for me. In my own dissertation research I developed a freshman composition course based loosely on James Moffett's theories of the development of writing ability. However, at the Institutes, I was able to compare different paradigms for sequencing writing assignments and learn how to adapt these paradigms to the needs of the non-composition instructor. Also, all of us learned how to apply collaborative learning strategies beyond the composition classroom. In addition, the conferences provided us with a variety of course models for teaching writing in the disciplines, while the conferences themselves became models for future conferences.

"Chicago" helped many of us who were developing writing intensive course requirements or junior level writing courses. The Little Red School House program at Chicago became a model for courses at other institutions. We were able to compare this curricular approach to others. Linda Bergman underscores this point when she says, "Since I had worked with the Little Red School House, what was particularly use-

ful was to see it in context of other approaches to teaching and thinking about writing. Its placement in this context helped me to see how
it fit into and contrasted with more expressivist theories that seemed to
dominate composition studies at the time, and gave me the confidence
to pursue the more disciplinary-oriented approach to teaching writing
that I have always held."

Many institutions define their writing intensive courses by the
number of pages of writing or by mandating that students in these
courses submit drafts of all papers in the course. The Little Red School
House program teaches students how to write in their major disciplines. At La Salle the writing intensive course guidelines stipulate that
these courses will teach students the stylistic and organizational features of writing in their disciplines. To highlight the importance of
writing in all courses, at La Salle, we also developed a student publication, "Writing in the Disciplines," featuring the best writing in the
major, a practice followed in other schools as well.

"Chicago" brought likeminded WAC administrators to their first
conference together. We were hungry for those contacts, which have
sustained so many of us through our WAC "trials and tribulations."
After the 1985 conference, Barbara Olds wrote to me, "I am very interested in the hand-outs you sent about your summer workshop on
WAC. We're trying very hard to get something started here at CSM
(Colorado School of Mines) and your workshop sounds excellent. Do
you have any other information about it you would be willing to send
me? I'd love to be able to fly to La Salle and talk it over with you, but
times being as they are, the mails will have to do for now. Suggestions
about pertinent essays, books, etc., and other similar programs would
also be welcome. And many good thanks for your good work in Chicago. I'm looking forward to hearing from you again soon."

"Chicago" also supported composition instructors' collaboration
with their colleagues in other disciplines. William Sullivan and I
began to pool our "intellectual resources" on issues related to writing
after he had participated in the WAC workshop at La Salle. Chicago
offered us a forum at which to discuss these ideas. We coauthored
one article, "Demystifying the Academy: Can Exploratory Writing
Help?," and I wrote three other essays based on our presentations at
Chicago. Several years later, we received a grant from the National
Endowment for the Humanities for to conduct a series of seminars on
"Finding a Common Language: Integrating the Curriculum Through

the Humanities." These seminars were enriched by our experience at the Chicago Institutes, especially the one on "Critical Thinking and the Formation of Values." At this conference developing the capacity to think critically in a specific field was linked to "articulating and affirming its implicit values."

"Chicago" inspired us to return to our campuses and revamp our WAC workshops to include opportunities for faculty to become "ethnographers" of the discourse in their disciplines. At La Salle we added an "advanced writing across the curriculum workshop" conducted by William Sullivan (my Institute partner) and me for those faculty who had already participated in the "basic" workshop. The new workshop included readings by many of the Institute presenters, such as Joseph Williams, Elaine Maimon, Charles Bazerman and William Zeiger. We titled our workshop "Critical Thinking and the Major" (how original) and gave faculty the opportunity to compare different definitions of critical thinking and models of intellectual growth. We asked faculty to think about the intellectual goals of the major and urged them to develop writing assignments for making them explicit to their students. The instructors in the workshop examined the rhetoric of discourse in their discipline as part of the workshop.

Until "Chicago" the growth of WAC had depended largely on program development in individual schools and much of the early literature on WAC was primarily of the "how to" variety (Walvoord). WAC relied on composition theory and research aimed primarily at teaching writing in writing courses as opposed to teaching writing in non-composition courses. The demand for WAC workshops outpaced theory and research. As Walvoord points out, this phenomenon led to "settling for narrow goals and limited visions." She adds, "The emphasis on writing as the answer [to not only writing problems but learning problems] allowed the questions to be left vague: What sort of learning did WAC aim for? What were WAC's central goals beyond getting teachers to use more writing?" (61). Although the conferences did not give "equal time" to other possible answers to this question, such as the role of classical rhetoric in defining these aims, the conferences reinforced efforts to define these aims through research on the rhetoric and discourse structures as reflections of the questions and inquiry strategies characteristic of different disciplinary knowledge communities.

When I began this chapter, I said that my purpose was to assess the impact of the conferences on the WAC community and give readers some sense of the excitement we experienced in Chicago. I hope I have succeeded. But, what I did not anticipate, were the personal benefits I would reap from taking what amounted to "refresher course" on the Institute topics. One of the perils of academic life is to assume that "I've been there, learned that," and now I can tuck my notes away in the folder marked "Chicago" for some future time (which may never come) when I will need them again. It's a bit like finding the old notes from a course one once taught and thinking, "Wow—that was a great course. Why don't I teach American Literature that way this semester?"

Rereading the publications which grew from the conference presentations reminded me to be more aware of the problems associated with students "boundary crossings" from one interpretive community to another. In higher education, we have created a whole new set of knowledge communities in the last ten years through linked courses and other interdisciplinary programs. Chicago reminds me that we must repeat the process of defining the "customs" of these new communities and finding ways to make those customs explicit to our students.

Writing this chapter has also reinforced my conviction that to sustain the interdisciplinary dialogue about writing among our colleagues, there is no substitute for intellectually challenging discussions at which the participants are actively engaged in framing the issues and the debates surrounding them. As we plunge ahead into new contexts for WAC, such as interdisciplinary learning communities, the Chicago conferences provide models for tackling new issues related to teaching writing in the university.

NOTE

[1] Unless otherwise noted, the quotations that follow are from email exchanges and telephone conversations with the various participants in the Chicago Conferences.

WORKS CITED

Basseches, Michael. "Recent Research on Cognitive Development: An Integrative Survey." Presentation. The Seventh National Institute on Intellectual Development in the College Years, University of Chicago, November, 1985.

Bruffee, Kenneth. "Thinking and Writing as Social Acts." Maimon, Nodine, and O'Conner, 213–22.

Daly, John A., and Michael D. Miller. "The Empirical Development of an Instrument to Measure Writing Apprehension." *Research in Teaching English* 9.3 (1975): 242–49.

Maimon, Elaine P., Barbara F. Nodine, and Finbarr W. O'Connor. *Thinking, Reasoning, and Writing*. New York: Longman, 1989.

Larson, Reed. "Emotional Scenarios in the Writing Process: An Examination of Young Writers' Affective Experiences." *When a Writer Can't Write: Studies in Writer's Block and Other Composing-Process Problems*. Ed. Mike Rose. New York: Guilford, 1985. 19–42

Lovin, Robin. "Rethinking Values Formation: The Educational and Political Contexts." *Soundings* 68 (1985): 5–20.

Perry, William. *Forms of Ethical and Intellectual Development During the College Years*. San Francisco: Jossey-Bass, 1999.

Russell, David R. *Writing in the Academic Disciplines, 1870–1990: A Curricular History*. Carbondale: Southern Illinois UP, 1991.

Soven, Margot and William M. Sullivan. "Demystifying the Academy: Can Exploratory Writing Help?" *Freshman English News* 19.1 (1990): 13–16.

Walvoord, Barbara. "The Future of WAC." *College English* 58.1 (1996): 58–77.

Williams, Joseph. "Two Ways of Thinking About Growth: The Problem of Finding the Right Metaphor." *Thinking, Reasoning, and Writing*. Maimon, Nodine, and O'Conner, 245–55.

6 Writing across the Curriculum in the Ivy Consortium

Peshe Kuriloff and Linda Peterson

Linda: *If I were writing as a biographer, I would record that I first encountered "Writing Across the Curriculum" at the 1979 Conference on College Composition and Communication (CCCC) in Minneapolis. That convention took "Writing: A Cross-Disciplinary Enterprise" as its theme, due largely to Toby Fulwiler and others' urging of Frank D'Angelo, the conference chair, to make the new movement prominent in the composition community. As a newly appointed writing program director, I attended CCCC to gain broad knowledge about the teaching of writing, in preparation for implementing a college-wide writing program at Yale. With another colleague, Joseph Gordon, I had been designated to develop first-year writing courses in the English department, to design a tutorial program for all students, freshmen through seniors, and to implement a "Writing Intensive" program in departments other than English. At the 1979 CCCC, we would have noted (and may have attended) sessions on "Writing Across the Curriculum: A Symposium for Professional Exchange," "Organizing Faculty Workshops: Writing Across the Curriculum," "Cross-Disciplinary Writing Programs: Funding and Experimentation," or one of a series of five titled simply "Writing Across the Curriculum."[1] Panelists included Toby Fulwiler, Art Young, Elaine Maimon, Eugene Hammond, Ann Raimes, and others now recognized as the founding fathers and mothers of the WAC movement.*

Because I am writing as an autobiographer, however, my memories tell a different story. My first clear recollection of WAC dates instead to the first meeting of the Ivy Consortium, a two-day event held on November 15–16, 1982, Attending that first meeting were leaders in the new WAC movement: Harriet Sheridan, then Dean of Arts and Sciences at Brown University; Tori Haring-Smith, Director of the Writing Center at Brown University; Patricia Belanoff, then Assistant Director of the Writing Program at New York University; and Elaine Maimon, Associate Professor at Beaver College but that year also Adjunct Associate Professor of English at the University of Pennsylvania. Elaine Maimon especially was a moving force. With Writing in the Arts and Sciences *newly published and brimful of ideas for integrating writing within courses college-wide, she made certain that participants discussed more than approaches to freshman English.*

Peshe: *During the year Elaine Maimon spent at Penn, on leave from Beaver College, she inserted the concept of writing across the curriculum into a humanities across the curriculum proposal that appealed to the English department members, especially the chair, Robert Lucid. The humanities project never received funding, but the writing component found fertile ground. In 1983, when I took over Penn's fledgling Writing Across the University Program, popularly known as WATU, I relied not only on Elaine Maimon's research-based concept but also on Margot Soven's extensive knowledge and network. Through these contacts and others, I learned about WAC theory and practice and came to rely heavily on the established WAC network as I implemented a model, based loosely on Yale's, for Penn.*

CIRCULATING IDEAS, SHARING CONCERNS (LINDA)

The agenda for the 1982 Ivy Consortium meeting shows that the opening session included four topics: "the idea of a consortium," "curriculum-wide writing programs," "funding the writing program," and "staffing the writing program." Paula Johnson of NYU addressed the first topic. Elaine Maimon addressed the second, giving a spirited rationale for curriculum-wide writing programs, one she had articulated fully in the "Preface" to *Writing in the Arts and Sciences.* In that preface

Maimon argued that students entering college are "all beginners in the world of higher education. They must learn to cope with books, lectures, and papers assigned by scholars trained in a variety of fields." She went on to suggest that disciplinary traditions "appear to the student as mysterious rites of passage," but that it was our responsibility as teachers and scholars "to cast light on those mysterious academic rites that until recently have been open to too few" (Maimon, xi).

Elaine was not just visionary; she was also practical about the difficulties of instituting a WAC program and especially about the need for external funding to develop its curriculum. Although Yale's "writing intensive" program had originated independently of Penn's and Brown's, she quickly joined forces with Charles Long, former Assistant Professor of English, then Associate Dean of Yale College, who had drafted Yale's successful grant proposal to the Pew Memorial Trust. Given the success of the proposal, which brought Yale over $1 million during a five-year period, Dean (soon to be Provost) Long spoke from an authoritative position on grant writing and external funding. In the 1980s Maimon and Long would frequently speak on panels or in private conferences at other institutions about funding issues, and thus Yale's rhetoric of writing across the curriculum would merge with Maimon's rationale.

In its official statements, Long, speaking for Yale, argued that "instructors working with familiar materials feel knowledgeable about the conventions of written discourse in their fields," and thus in their regular courses faculty can, with the help of graduate teaching assistants, instruct students about writing in subject areas in which students have a demonstrated intellectual interest. "Systematic instruction in writing," Long urged, "might go on in sections of large lecture courses, if frequent short writing assignments that grew out of and led back into the lectures could replace the term paper and if students could have sufficient opportunity for rewriting their drafts" ("Consortium," 13–16).[2]

Yale and Penn were not, of course, the only universities with new programs or pedagogies to present ideas at the Ivy Consortium. Five other institutions sent representatives: Brown University, Dartmouth College, Harvard University, New York University, and Princeton University.[3] Not all of these institutions had initiated WAC programs, nor were all interested in creating them. Princeton's efforts focused on Literature 151, its "Exposition and Literature" course; Dartmouth's on English 5, "Literature and Composition." Both institutions were concerned with placement issues. Harvard, then under Richard Marius's direction, concentrated on "Expos," its first-year required writing course. "No entering student is exempt," declared Marius; "if God enrolls in Harvard, she must take a course in Expository Writing." In 1982, only Brown, Penn, and Yale included WAC efforts in the program descriptions that were circulated in advance of the meeting.

Those descriptions became important rhetorical documents, however, in the development of Ivy writing programs because they outlined the different models for WAC that other institutions would adopt and adapt. Brown, for example, had devised a Writing Fellows Program that selected twenty outstanding undergraduates, primarily sophomores and juniors, who were trained in a one-semester pedagogy course and then assigned to large, introductory lectures throughout the curriculum. The Writing Fellows served as first readers for student papers. Students enrolled in the lectures would first submit their work to a Fellow, who would evaluate the papers' strengths and weaknesses and then make constructive comments for revision, but who would not assign letter grades. This writing across the curriculum program was, according to Brown's description, "compatible with any discipline and allows faculty members throughout the university to increase the emphasis on writing in their courses without feeling obligated to teach writing itself" ("Consortium," 2–3).

In contrast, Yale designed a program that relied on graduate teaching fellows rather than peer tutors. Yale concentrated on redesigning already existing courses and on training TA's to address writing issues in special sections of such courses. The pedagogical rationale for this approach was explained as follows: "Instructors working with familiar materials will feel knowledgeable about the conventions of written discourse in their fields, as they deduce these conventions from their reading and engage them in their scholarly work" ("Consortium," 13). What was less explicit in the 1982 description was the need to fund graduate students (a large group during the 1980s) and the desire to train them in the pedagogy of composition.

Penn's program in 1982 emphasized new directions in the English department, particularly a graduate-level pedagogy course that trained teaching assistants in the English department to work effectively on students' writing in first-year courses. Like Brown and Yale, however, Penn had also initiated a "Writing Across the University" Program

(WATU) to expand the teaching of writing beyond the English department. The WATU program, housed in a new Center for Writing, conducted colloquia featuring workshops by specialists from both inside and outside the university; the targeted audience, according to Penn's description, included "fifty instructors, resident advisers from the dormitories, graduate fellows from the College House System, and graduate students assigned to assist in the writing across the university courses." Although this intended audience for colloquia was quite broad, the primary participants in the WATU program were graduate students from departments across the university.

Absorbing Information, Creating Models (Peshe)

It was Robert Lucid who first mentioned the Ivy Consortium to me. He had attended the 1983 consortium meeting at Dartmouth and recognized the importance of the new approach to writing instruction that various participants were trying to advance. I attended my first Ivy Consortium in the fall of 1984 at Williams College, where I discovered a community of writing program directors eager to have an impact on student achievement. Because issues related to writing instruction tended to have structural implications, we divided into two groups, one for small college directors, another for university directors. We presented and discussed the various approaches that participating schools were taking and tried to help each other think through individual situations. From this and following meetings, I learned a profound lesson: that each institution is unique and that different institutional solutions are required to address common pedagogical problems. I was stimulated by our common concerns, yet I found myself taking a little bit of several programs and reshaping them to suit the particular needs of my own institution. In this way, the Penn program, along with so many others, evolved.

The ideas that circulated within the Ivy Consortium during the 1980s helped a number of institutions pursue innovations. No program reinvented itself overnight, but several absorbed the new thinking about discipline-based instruction and ran with it. Penn's program, for example, drew heavily on the models created other Ivy programs— programs at Yale, Brown and Cornell—as it developed.

As is often true of WAC programs, Penn's began with extensive legwork in an attempt to find common ground between traditional English-department based writing instruction and writing in other departments. While Elaine Maimon, consultant to Penn, designed and tried to find funding for the humanities program, Robert Lucid, the chair of English, sent out a group of graduate students, fondly referred to as "moles." They were to investigate the discourse practices of other disciplines. A series of productive conversations ensued with faculty in different departments and schools, all of whom shared a commitment to the centrality of writing in academic inquiry. These conversations enabled WATU to broaden its base and attract senior faculty well positioned to help the program put down roots. By 1984–85, as a result of the groundwork, the Penn program had begun to gel. The help of other Ivy directors ensured that we were firmly grounded philosophically and practically as well.

For large research universities in the Ivy Consortium, WAC was a good fit. First, it respected everyone's expertise; it neither overvalued the knowledge and experience of English professors, nor undervalued the capacity of other faculty in the social, physical, or biological sciences to contribute to discussions about written discourse. Second, in a large research university, WAC needed only a small critical mass of faculty supporters, rather than a consensus of all faculty, to get up and running. That critical mass proved relatively easy to identify and engage at Penn, Yale, Brown, and other Ivy institutions. Third, WAC loosened the stranglehold the English department had traditionally held on monies connected with writing instruction by spreading financial support among departments. Sharing both the pedagogy and the resources proved a popular, and administratively wise, decision. So did sharing WAC scholarship. As many leading figures in the field of composition and rhetoric, from James Kinneavy to Richard Lanham to E. D. Hirsch, made appearances or gave lectures on Ivy campuses, we were able to initiate an extensive scholarly discussion about the role of writing within the curriculum. Our programs were well launched— pedagogically, intellectually, administratively.

The next decade, from approximately 1985 to 1995, developed into the "golden age" of WAC at Penn and other Ivy schools. With support from the national WAC network, annually provided at the 4Cs, and with yearly meetings of the Ivy Consortium, which became a fall ritual, multi-faceted models emerged for writing instruction across the university. Take Penn's "golden years," for example. Based on Yale's model, Penn created a group of writing-intensive lecture courses, featuring special sections in which students wrote drafts, participated in writing conferences with their graduate instructors, and revised their papers. Inspired by Tori-Haring Smith's writing fellows program at Brown, Penn also initiated a writing advisors program; in a special English seminar, undergraduates were trained to provide feedback to their peers at selected locations across campus. Further impressed by the Knight Writing Program at Cornell, Penn added "Chimicles" courses (named after the donor who funded the graduate fellowships), now called "Critical Writing Teaching Fellowships." These are first-year writing seminars in many different disciplines taught by graduate students trained and supervised through the writing program. And a centralized writing center staffed by graduate students provided advice and feedback to students from many different departments and professional schools, thus giving Penn's program yet another way of reaching out to student writers and ensuring that many encountered writing instruction in one of its several guises. (An on-line writing advice service, staffed by undergraduate writing advisors, was added in 1996.)

LEARNING FROM EXPERIENCE, DEVELOPING A THEORETICAL FRAMEWORK (LINDA AND PESHE)

As both of our narratives suggest, Ivy institutions learned from each other and from the examples of WAC programs across the country. Yet, from the start, Ivy WAC programs tended to adopt one of two models: 1) a model based on peer tutors, assigned to large lecture courses and charged with the responsibility of responding to fellow-students' drafts (the Brown model); or 2) a model based on graduate teaching assistants, also assigned to large lecture courses but responsible more fully for instruction in the content of, as well as writing in, their disciplines (the Yale-Penn model). Institutions with small or no graduate programs imitated the Brown model, whereas universities with large graduate programs tended toward the Yale-Penn model.[4] Except at Brown, where crucial leadership by Harriet Sheridan and later by Elaine Maimon, who served as Associate Dean from 1986 to 1988, helped to maintain the WAC program throughout the 1980s and 1990s, the Ivy institutions that developed the strongest programs were the large research universities. The idea of teaching undergraduates the principles of good writing, not only for communicating with the general public but also for exchange within a scholarly community, was an idea the general faculty found convincing. It was also an idea relatively easy to implement, given the high numbers of graduate students admitted to these universities during the 1980s—students whose funding derived primarily from teaching sections of lecture courses.

In retrospect, however, the most striking feature of the WAC programs within the Ivy Consortium is their emphasis on "writing in the disciplines." In her introduction to *Writing Across the Curriculum: A Guide to Developing Programs,* Susan H. McLeod distinguishes between two approaches to WAC: the first, "sometimes referred to as *cognitive,* involves using 'writing to learn,'" whereas the second, "sometimes termed *rhetorical,* involves learning to write in particular disciplines, or in what researchers have begun to think of as *discourse communities*" (McLeod and Soven, 4–5). Penn, Brown, and Yale emphasized the second approach. Although leaders like Sheridan and Maimon at Brown, later Peterson at Yale and Kuriloff at Penn, introduced and encouraged techniques associated with writing-to-learn, such as in-class writing, journal writing, and peer review, the primary rationale for upper-level writing courses remained discipline-based. As Penn's description in the 1982 "Consortium" document reveals, the Writing Across the University Program (WATU) began with the premise "that scholars in all disciplines already have the potential to help students with work in progress because all scholars are themselves writers" and because "research in any field remains incomplete until reported."

Why did this emphasis on discipline-based writing emerge at this moment in Ivy history? Part of the answer must be practical. The connection between writing and critical thinking, integral to the practice of WAC, came up frequently at meetings of the Ivy Consortium. Participants expressed concern about the growing number of non-native speakers among their student populations and the challenge of meeting their pedagogical needs. The concept of socializing students into discourse communities, part of the conceptual framework of WAC, became a useful construct for thinking about how to support these new student populations. Whether explicitly or implicitly, ideas embedded in the WAC movement influenced Ivy writing instruction as a result of conversations and presentations at the Consortium's meetings.

Yet the answer must also be historical and cultural. In his *Writing in the Academic Disciplines, 1870–1990,* David Russell reviews the socio-economic influences that led institutions to find it necessary to re-emphasize writing. According to Russell, as long as access to education was limited to mostly upper- and upper-middle-class students

who were well prepared for college, institutions did not find it necessary to invest in the teaching of writing. When a more diverse group
of students sought higher education, from the period of the GI bill
forward, the need for writing instruction became more apparent. An
important article by Patricia Bizzell ("What Happens When Basic
Writers Come to College?") makes this point even more concretely.
Bizzell illustrates in forceful terms two alternative ways of thinking
about writing instruction, one based on the assumption that students
gradually acquire skills over time, the other based on the idea that
students need to be socialized into unfamiliar discourse communities. The argument that students cannot master writing through skills
acquisition alone and that all students need to be socialized into discourse communities has provided a powerful rationale for WAC, in
the Ivy League as elsewhere.

In sum, the development of WAC in the Ivy institutions during the
1980s came about at least partially because of a renewed need to social-
ize students less familiar with academic conventions into the discourse
communities of the university. WAC provided a positive way, without
stigmatizing anyone or admitting student deficiencies, of addressing institutional needs. Ivy students received the guidance they required, and
the faculty the support they needed, to ensure that all students could
meet the high standards that Ivy League universities and affiliated colleges demanded. The Ivy Consortium furthered this goal of maintaining high standards by enabling writing program directors, along with
faculty responsible for writing instruction, to share strategies about
pedagogy and, equally as important, to integrate ideas about higher
order thinking and intellectual skills into their teaching.

CREATING EXPERTISE, CIRCULATING AUTHORITY

As preceding analysis suggests, Ivy WAC programs assumed the pedagogical expertise of their faculty. This was as much a political tactic as
a pedagogical reality. By stating that scholars in all disciplines always
already have the potential to help student writers because "all scholars
are themselves writers," Penn avoided the uncomfortable position of
suggesting that its faculty possessed scholarly, but lacked pedagogical,
expertise. Yale engaged in a similar rhetorical maneuver when it argued that faculty were "knowledgeable about the conventions of written discourse in their fields" and thus could help students, through

reading and writing exemplary articles, understand those disciplinary conventions.

In fact, many young Ivy directors drew on local expertise to further the goals of their programs. At Yale, for example, Professor of History Robin Winks created a junior-level seminar on "Writing History," and he was frequently asked to speak on panels about writing in his discipline, as was Kai Erikson, Professor of Sociology, who had developed a similar course for graduate students in the Social Sciences.

More often, however, expertise came from outside, with Ivy WAC directors inviting each other to speak to faculty and graduate students about writing initiatives at their universities or about writing in specific fields. Elaine Maimon regularly came to Yale for the fall meeting with teaching fellows in the "Writing Intensive" program; she gave a version of her preface to *Writing in the Arts and Sciences,* along with much practical advice about introducing writing in discipline-specific courses. Richard Marius from Harvard's expository writing program frequently visited other campuses, sometimes to speak about his program, sometimes to share his writing experiences as a journalist and historian. Tori Haring-Smith from Brown also visited other Ivy campuses and small private colleges in the New England region, sometimes to explain the peer fellows version of the WAC program, sometimes to discuss Brown's new seminar in composition theory and pedagogy.

More problematic, however, was outside expertise. Although Ivy WAC directors frequently invited nationally-known scholars to lecture or speak to small groups, the faculty of Ivy League institutions were then, and to an extent still remain, inbred; when they wish to initiate a new pedagogical venture, they look to each other for guidance rather than to small private colleges or large state universities. If, as Thomas Miller argues in *The Formation of College English: Rhetoric and Belles Lettres in the British Cultural Provinces,* innovations in composition have typically begun at the "margins," not at the older, established universities (86–88), then Ivy institutions face the threat of being left behind—a threat its directors have resisted.

One successful tactic was to invite another Ivy director. Another was to organize a large conference or symposium. Early in the history of Yale's writing program, Jasper Neil, then Director of the ADE, helped us put together a symposium on current issues and new directions in the teaching of writing. Invited speakers included Richard Lanham, author of *Style: An Anti-Textbook* (1974) and *Revising*

Prose (1979); E.D. Hirsch, Jr., author of *The Philosophy of Composition* (1977); and Stanley Fish, not author of a book on composition but a frequent commentator on collaborative learning and other pedagogical ventures.[5] Attended by virtually all members of the English department and faculty from other disciplines, this event informed the university community of the current state of student writing, writing instruction, and composition theory—as the latter was discussed and debated by the participants. No specific action resulted from that symposium, but it is fair to say that the serious attention given to writing by senior scholars in English studies did much to aid the development of Yale's comprehensive writing program.

Paradoxically, these attitudes toward expertise—that faculty already have the expertise to teach writing, that information about writing theory and practice can best be garnered from other similar institutions, that the best approach to teaching writing can be determined by internal discussion—account for the success of the Ivy Consortium. By relying on existing faculty knowledge—indeed, by insisting that faculty already possess knowledge—Ivy universities were able to challenge faculty across the disciplines to participate in a comprehensive writing program. By offering examples from peer institutions, program directors in the Ivy League were able to validate their claims about how writers develop and about new methods of instruction that might further such development. Whatever knowledge or expertise faculty lacked was readily available at a sister school, and once a place with the caché of Harvard or Yale, for example, had invested in a new approach to writing instruction, the other Ivies stood up and took notice.

Although during the 1980s the Ivy Consortium focused only occasionally on WAC, it deserves credit for spreading the word and helping to make the concept and practice credible. Only a few of the Ivy participants made it to the annual CCCC's meeting, but those who did brought back useful information and better practices that the rest of the group absorbed. Those who were able to join the national WAC network had the best of both worlds. We were able to merge the research base to which we were exposed at the national conferences with the local knowledge offered through the Ivy Consortium. As insulated as the Ivies can be from curricular and pedagogical trends, we were not insulated from the WAC movement as a whole. On the contrary, the WAC programs implemented at institutions such as Yale, Brown,

Penn, and Cornell have become national models, and the Ivy Consortium deserves at least partial credit both for exposing Ivy institutions to new ideas in the WAC world at large and for, in turn, sending new ideas back into that world.

NOTES

[1] See "Writing: A Cross-Disciplinary Enterprise," program of the CCCC, 30th Annual Meeting. My thanks to Toby Fulwiler for retaining and sharing his copy of this historic program with me.

[2] Prior to the first meeting, the hosts assembled a document, "Consortium of Ivy League Writing Programs, New Haven, Connecticut, 15–16 November 1982," which included descriptions of the writing programs of the participants and was distributed at the first consortium meeting.

[3] Although not an ivy institution, NYU sent Paula Johnson and Patricia Belanoff, Director and Assistant Director of the Writing Program, largely I suspect because Paula Johnson had served as Director of Undergraduate Studies at Yale when the initial research and first grant proposals for a university-wide program were written. As a private institution, NYU faced curricular and financial issues similar to those of participating universities, but to my knowledge, NYU participated in the Ivy Consortium only the first year. Cornell did not participate until 1983, when the meeting was held at Dartmouth.

[4] By 1983, the Ivy Consortium had expanded to include several private colleges in the New England region, largely because institutions like Brown and Dartmouth felt more affinity with private colleges like Williams, Wesleyan, and Smith and because the composition of the student population at the institutions was similar. Moreover, as the annual meeting traveled from place to place, local colleges and universities were added to the guest list. When Penn hosted the meeting in Philadelphia in 1988, for example, Swarthmore, Bryn Mawr and LaSalle joined the group. The meetings eventually generated so much interest that the numbers had to be cut back, but long-term participants agreed that much of the value in the meetings derived from the small size of the group and the intimate conversations that took place among fellow program directors about issues of mutual concern.

[5] Wayne Booth had also been invited but was unable to fly out of Chicago during a winter snowstorm.

WORKS CITED

Patricia Bizzell. "What Happens When Basic Writers Come to College?" *College Composition and Communication* 37 (October 1986), 294–301.

Rpt. Patricia Bizzell. *Academic Discourse and Critical Consciousness.* Philadelphia: U of Pennsylvania P, 1992.

"Consortium of Ivy League Writing Programs, New Haven, Connecticut, 15–16 November 1982." Photocopy.

McLeod, Susan H., and Margot Soven, eds. *Writing Across the Curriculum: A Guide to Developing Programs.* Newberry Park, CA: Sage, 1992.

Maimon, Elaine P., et al. *Writing in the Arts and Sciences.* Cambridge, MA: Winthrop, 1981.

Russell, David R. *Writing in the Academic Disciplines, 1870–1990: A Curricular History.* Carbondale: Southern Illinois UP, 1991.

Miller, Thomas. *The Formation of College English: Rhetoric and Belles Lettres in the British Cultural Provinces.* Pittsburgh: U of Pittsburgh P, 1997.

"Writing: A Cross-Disciplinary Enterprise." Program of the Conference on College Composition and Communication. 30th Annual Meeting. Minneapolis, Minnesota, 1979.

7 Montana, Mina Shaughnessy, and Microthemes: Reflections on WAC as a Community

John C. Bean

"You need to talk to Elaine Maimon at Beaver College. You'll be interested in what she is doing." The speaker was Harvey Wiener of LaGuardia Community College, future founder of the Council of Writing Program Administrators. The place was my backyard in Great Falls, Montana, over a couple of Coors beers, in summer 1978. I don't believe we used the term writing across the curriculum during that whole summer. And at any rate, I wasn't doing WAC at the College of Great Falls (a small Catholic liberal arts college in the middle of Montana). I was doing GAC (grammar across the curriculum) or HAC (Harbrace across the curriculum.). Whereas Elaine Maimon's story in this volume shows how a liberal arts college transformed a profession, my story shows how an emerging profession transformed me. Like the other stories gathered in this collection, mine is a story of serendipity and community.

I came to the College of Great Falls in 1972, a freshly minted PhD in Renaissance literature. With only three other full-time persons in the English department, most of my friends were from other disciplines. We talked a lot about student writing, and my colleagues explained sheepishly that they didn't know the technical terms needed to really "correct" students' papers. When the Lilly Endowment announced a 1977 competitive "Grants Program for Strengthening Communications Programs in Liberal Arts Colleges," I decided to try my hand at grant writing. We proposed a three-pronged program: First, I would conduct summer workshops for faculty on how to teach writing (oblivious then to my entrenchment in what would later come to be called the "current/traditional paradigm"). Second, the English and Speech Communication Department would hire an outside consultant/specialist in "remedial writing" to help us address the sentence correctness problems of a surprisingly diverse student body—commuting students from Great Falls, enlisted personnel from Maelstrom Air Force Base, a fairly large contingent of Native Americans, and first-generation college students from rural Montana. Our third prong was to create better articulation with feeder high schools, our agenda being primarily to persuade high school teachers to spend more time on grammar and sentence skills.

Writing this present article gave me the occasion to retrieve the old Lilly Endowment Grant from my files and try to reconstruct the way I thought about writing in the fall of 1976 when our proposal was being drafted. Here is my description of Prong One for the grant—my first articulation of a concept that, once planted, would evolve rapidly and profoundly:

> [Grant objective 1]: *Making excellence in writing and speaking a college-wide concern.* The English faculty is frequently demoralized by awareness that what we teach in composition is not reinforced by faculty in other departments. Motivation is low among many of our composition students because they know that inadequate writing "gets by" in classes outside the English department. We believe that if professors in other disciplines possessed greater skills in evaluating student writing and if they demanded clear thesis statements, adequate paragraph development, and other rhetorical skills in the student themes written for their classes, the quality of writing campus-wide would increase measurably.

I note here my focus on sentence correctness, my formalist understand of "rhetoric" as a matter of thesis statements and paragraph development, and my patronizing attitude toward non-English faculty, who, in my view at the time, didn't seem to care about good writing and lacked the skills needed to uphold proper standards. Not once throughout the eleven-page proposal do any of the following words appear: *ideas, learning, thinking, engagement, inquiry, audience, process, revision, multiple drafts, peer review, genre,* or *disciplinary argument.* I am amazed that my colleagues went along with the workshop regimen of grammar and sentence drill that I was proposing in the grant. Now, more than a quarter of a century later, I warmly remember my College of Great Falls colleagues, deeply thankful for the community we formed. What held us together was a shared passion for teaching, a commitment to writing in a way that we hadn't yet articulated, and the strength of friendships formed in a small college environment.

Having described my starting point, I can now begin to sketch the stages of my transformation. The first seeds were planted on the day an external evaluator hired by Lilly Endowment came to our campus to assess our proposal. His name was Ed White, who, as I learned later, had an emerging reputation in the assessment of writing through his work in placement testing in the California State University system. I picked Ed up at the airport, sick with nervousness, and spent the day in invigorating conversations about pedagogy. He regarded writing as an emerging research area, talked about writing curricula and about assignment design and sequencing, and didn't seem to share my preoccupation with grammar and correctness. This was my first in-depth encounter with a composition professional. Evidently satisfied with his on-site visit, during which time he met with many faculty from across the curriculum, Ed recommended funding of our proposal. As a required early stage of the grant, the Lilly Endowment sent my department chair and me—along with representatives from nine other institutions receiving communications skills grants—to Indianapolis for a workshop in writing assessment conducted by White. My most vivid memory in this early period was an argument with my chair over the scoring of "Bear Bear"—one of White's sample student essays. I had never before been asked to articulate my criteria for a grade, nor felt the exasperation of a colleague who disagreed with me. "How could you give "Bear Bear" a 5?" I remember asking my chair with incredulity. "It's mindless, it's sentimental, it's silly! I gave it a 2." "I like the voice and the details," my chair replied, and the argument heated up.

Once we got the grant in fall 1977, our next step was hiring the external consultant to come to Great Falls in summer 1978. My colleague Sr. Maryann Benoit, recently returned from an education conference, announced that she had heard "a most wonderful woman" give a talk—Mina Shaughnessy. Sr. Maryann called Shaughnessy personally, asking her to come to Montana for the summer. Professor Shaughnessy gracefully declined—she was even then dying of cancer—but she listened with interest to our program, offered encouraging advice, and gave us the names of several other possible consultants skilled in the teaching of basic writing. The first one we called, Harvey Wiener of CUNY, accepted our offer, and on a hot June day in 1978, I picked up Harvey at the Great Falls airport along with his wife Barbara and their two children. We drove them to the faculty home they would occupy for the summer, its living room replete with the trophy heads of deer, elk, mountain goats, and moose mounted on the walls. If Montana created cultural shock for the Wieners, so did they bring cultural shock to us with their stories of life in New York City and with Harvey's descriptions of writing classrooms in CUNY, the heart, as far as I was concerned, of the composition universe. That winter I had read *Errors and Expectations,* a watershed moment for me when the teaching of writing started to feel like a calling rather than a duty. By the time Harvey Wiener arrived in Great Falls, I could feel myself already catching the spirit that dominated Mina Shaughnessy's book: I wanted to bring her glorious wakeup mornings to Montana's high mountain plains.

My first summer workshop for faculty focused primarily on teaching my colleagues the accurate use of the marking symbols on the endpapers of the *Harbrace College Handbook.* I brought to the sessions freshly dittoed copies of the same drill and skill exercises I used with my students. But even then we sensed that finding sentence errors was not the center of our real interest. Our real interest was in how students learn, in how writing engages students with the ideas of a course, and in how differently each of our disciplines looked at writing. Let me list a few examples from my memory bank:

- We decided to reinforce writing skills across the curriculum by developing disciplinary versions of the rhetorical modes assignments in Wiener's *Creating Compositions,* the textbook the English department had selected for our first-year composition program. Each department would try to invent a description assignment, for example, as well as an explication assignment, process analysis assignment, comparison/contrast assignment, and so forth. But we soon discovered that the rhetorical modes didn't easily adapt to the kinds of questions disciplinary teachers wanted to ask. My sociologist friend Mike Lowe didn't mind giving his students a "description" assignment, but only in the context of sociological interpretation. In Lowe's view, one might describe a room for the purpose of analyzing its occupant's class status or social group identification. But to describe a room belletristically, for the aesthetic pleasure of evoking the sensations of touch, sight, sound, and smell, made little sense to him. The design of a simple one-paragraph writing assignment engaged us in epistemological inquiry about the nature of our disciplines.

- We discovered too that students had trouble moving from the narrative modes of description and narration to the mode of exemplification, where details were arranged hierarchically to support a topic sentence. We asked why our students had difficulty organizing a point/support paragraph. We pushed the question further: What constituted a point in our disciplines? What constituted evidence? How could one distinguish between point and data unless one knew how the discipline asked questions and made arguments? By some unarticulated teleology that we didn't understand, Grammar Across the Curriculum was evolving toward WAC.

- A particularly vivid memory for me is the exemplification assignment developed by sociologist Mike Lowe. "Explain what is meant by the sociological term 'role conflict' and illustrate role conflict with several examples from your own life." The resulting papers revealed students' struggle with the concept of "role conflict" itself: Problems with writing, critical thinking, and conceptual understanding were all linked to learning how to see within a discipline. Writing about role conflict was a way of extending and deepening students' engagement with a new concept. Shortly thereafter I discovered Janet Emig's 1977 article "Writing as a Mode of Learning," which helped me clarify the insights emerging from Mike Lowe's assignment.

- During a faculty meeting in the year following the first workshop, my chemist friend Dan Goodman came back from a chemical education conference excited by a presentation on Jean Piaget. Chemists were abuzz with Piaget's descriptions of concrete versus formal operational reasoning, which helped chemistry teachers explain students' difficulty with abstract chemical concepts. Over lunch, Dan, several others, and I began applying Piaget to writing. Were students who struggled with the exemplification assignment stuck in the stage of concrete operations? Did Piagetian theory explain students' ease with narrative forms and their difficulty with thesis-based forms? Shortly thereafter I read Andrea Lunsford's "Cognitive Development and the Basic Writer" and was overwhelmed by her argument. Using Piaget and other cognitive psychologists, she created new kinds of writing assignments aimed directly at tackling the questions we had pondered in the lunchroom at the College of Great Falls—how to help students induce points from data, how to help them understand the hierarchical nature of organization.

I was now hooked on composition as a research field. I joined NCTE, subscribed to *CE* and *CCC*, and began reading these journals from cover to cover, seeking out articles by Nancy Sommers, Peter Elbow, Linda Flower and John R. Hayes, and dozens of our other foremothers and forefathers who helped our discipline burst into flower during those heady days. Meanwhile my copies of *PMLA* languished on my shelf. In 1980 I attended my first 4C's.

A second stage of my WAC career began in the fall of 1979, when my family and I moved from Great Falls to Bozeman, where I joined a vibrant composition community at Montana State University inspired by visionary teacher Jack Folsom. In 1982, four of us interested in writing—Jack Folsom, John Ramage, Dean Drenk (from the Department of Finance in the business school), and I—received a grant from FIPSE to begin "The Montana State University Thinking Skills and Writing Project." We positioned ourselves as a "thinking skills" project wedded to a "second generation writing across the curriculum project." Using the College of Great Falls and Beaver College as models of first generation programs, we proposed to integrate recent research in writing and cognitive development into a WAC model adapted to a large state institution characterized by large lecture courses rather than the small classes of a liberal arts college. Moreover, we proposed to link writing across the curriculum to the critical thinking movement exemplified by growing teacher interest in cognitive psychology (Flower and Hayes, Lunsford, recent interest in brain research, particularly hemisphericity), developmental theories (Piaget, Perry, Maimon), the informal logic movement in philosophy, and expressivist theories about writing and language as modes of learning (Vygotsky, Britton, Freisinger, Fulwiler and Young).

If the College of Great Falls project awakened me to the excitement of composition as a research field, the Montana State University Thinking Skills and Writing Project shaped the particular direction that my own approach to WAC would take. Many of the consultants that we brought to Montana State—particularly Kenneth Bruffee for his work in collaborative learning, Dick Hayes for his work on the cognitive processes of writers, Karen Spear for her work in small group theory, Joanne Kurfiss for her research linking William Perry to writing theory, and Harvey Wiener (a return engagement to Montana) for his work in basic writing—stimulated the faculty conversations that I now look back on as the most intense and fruitful academic collaboration I have ever experienced. The presence of exceptionally talented adjunct faculty in the English department, a supportive administration, and engaged and dedicated teachers from a variety of disciplines led to a steady succession of conference papers and academic articles from more than a dozen MSU faculty.

During this period, my colleagues Denny Lee in physics, Dean Drenk in Finance, and I developed the "microtheme" strategy for incorporating writing into large lecture classes (Bean, Drenk, and Lee). The strategy combined a short writing assignment—for example, a controversial thesis to be supported, a puzzling problem to be solved, a disciplinary reading to be summarized, or a list of data to be analyzed—with Ed White's use of holistic grading scales. Teachers could grade the microthemes rapidly on a 1 to 6 scale and then provide feedback to students in class discussions of the strengths and weaknesses of different student examples. We observed how the microthemes increased students' active engagement with course material outside of class while serving as informal assessment tools to help teachers monitor students' difficulty with course concepts. They also gave instructors powerful alternatives to long term paper assignments.

We also tried to immerse ourselves in theories of composition. In 1984, my colleague John Ramage attended an NEH summer seminar with Ann Berthoff at the University of Massachusetts on a philosophical/epistemic view of language, while I became immersed in the work of George Hillocks on the presentational, natural process, and environmental modes of teaching and in Kenneth Bruffee's philosophical justifications for collaborative learning. Teachers in the MSU Thinking Skills and Writing Project had discovered that microtheme assignments worked equally well as tasks for small group problem-solving, so that use of small groups could become an alternative teaching mode in a large lecture courses as well as composition courses. This strategy created, in Hillocks' taxonomy, an environmental mode of teaching in which students collaborated to create arguments in response to teacher-designed problems. In 1984–85, Joanne Kurfiss (later the author of a significant monograph on critical thinking) moved to Bozeman for her sabbatical year to study our project's use of collaborative learning in different disciplines. The English department's work with Joanne Kurfiss, stimulated further by the innovative pedagogical projects of colleagues across the disciplines, helped us develop a praxis for small group work linking writing across the curriculum to disciplinary inquiry and argument.

Near the end of the three-year project, John Ramage and I began collaborating on our first textbook together, *Form and Surprise in Writing: Writing and Thinking Across the Curriculum* (Macmillan, 1986). In *Form and Surprise,* Ramage and I tried to integrate the strands of theory and research from the Montana State University Thinking Skills and Writing Project into a sequence of activities and assignments for first-year composition. The approach to WAC that emerged from our work focused on a handful of guiding principles:

- Writing assignments can be used to engage students in a disciplinary question or problem and help students learn to see and think within the discipline's perspective.
- Critical thinking tasks used as formal writing assignments can be used equally effectively as small group tasks for collaborative learning or as exploratory tasks for journals or thinking pieces. Also writing assignments can be short—employing the principle of conceptual leverage: a small amount of writing preceded by a great deal of thinking.
- Writing is rooted in a rhetorical context where it is intended to have an purposeful effect on an audience.
- Simultaneously, writing is an epistemic, meaning-making activity often best stimulated by expressivist assignments that encourage inquiry, learning, personal engagement, and idea-seeking. This epistemic function helps explain why transactional prose often requires multiple drafts in which early drafts reflect a struggle to find or make meaning.

- Collaborative learning is a valuable teaching tool at any stage of discourse—to help students discover ideas, wrestle with alternative points of view, construct arguments, understand audience, and assess their own drafts-in-progress.
- The "homework" portion of a course is as important as the in-class portion. The development and sequencing of writing assignments is a crucial part of course design. Formal and informal writing assignments (or collaborative learning tasks) become a chief way of teaching disciplinary discourse.
- Writing in a discipline means learning to think in the discipline; each discipline's characteristic genres and styles expressed the discipline's values, assumptions, and ways of making knowledge.

What finally emerged at Montana State University was an immersion approach to WAC rather than formalized "W" courses. A new general education program, partially stimulated by our thinking skills and writing project, stipulated that out-of-class writing assignments were to be incorporated into every general education course. The university created a large peer-tutoring Writing Center and gave the English department a new tenure track line for its director. Our new Writing Center, under the direction of Mark Waldo, then became the home of writing across the curriculum, a structural model for WAC that Mark later carried to the University of Nevada, Reno. It is difficult to tell how many faculty at Montana State University were influenced by the WAC initiatives in the first half of the 1980s, but a nucleus of faculty from civil engineering to agricultural economics, from finance to physics, formed a lively community of teachers practicing the active pedagogy that WAC stimulates and helps sustain.

For me, personally, the ten-year journey was marked by radical transformation. I evolved from a formalist teacher of grammar to a composition inquirer rooted in various communities of teacher/scholars fascinated by how students learn to question and argue within and across disciplines. At the heart of these WAC communities, I now believe—what made them so vibrant and sustaining—was a shared spirit first manifest to me by Mina Shaughnessy. I refer to her unconditional positive regard for students, her belief in their personhood, their dignity, and their potential. It is her spirit, I think, that makes writing across the curriculum so special.

Works Cited

Bean, John C., Dean Drenk, and F. Denny Lee. "Microtheme Strategies for Developing Cognitive Skills." *Teaching Writing in All Disciplines.* Ed. C. William Griffin. New Directions for Teaching and Learning, No. 12. San Francisco: Jossey-Bass, 1982. 27–38.

Bean, John C., and John D. Ramage. *Form and Surprise in Composition: Writing and Thinking Across the Curriculum.* New York: Macmillan, 1986.

Berthoff, Ann E. *The Making of Meaning: Metaphors, Models and Maxims for Writing Teachers.* Upper Montclair, N.J.: Boynton/Cook, 1981.

Britton, James. *The Development of Writing Abilities (11–18).* London: Macmillan, 1975.

Bruffee, Kenneth A. "Collaborative Learning and the 'Conversation of Mankind.'" *College English* 46.6 (1984): 635–52.

Emig, Janet. "Writing as a Mode of Learning." *College Composition and Communication* 28 (1977): 122–28.

Flower, Linda. "Writer-Based Prose: A Cognitive Basis for Problems in Writing." *College English* 41.1 (1979): 19–37.

Flower, Linda and Richard Hayes. "Problem-Solving Strategies and the Writing Process." *College English* 39.4 (1977): 449–61.

Freisinger, Randall. "Cross-Disciplinary Writing Programs: Theory and Practice." *College English* 42.2 (1980): 154–66.

Fulwiler Toby and Art Young, eds. *Language Connections: Writing and Reading Across the Curriculum.* Urbana, IL: National Council of Teachers of English, 1982.

Hillocks, George, Jr. "What Works in Teaching Composition: A Meta-analysis of Experimental Treatment Studies. *American Journal of Education* (1984): 133–70.

Kurfiss, Joanne Gainen. *Critical Thinking: Theory, Research, Practice, and Possibilities.* ASHE-ERIC Higher Education Report No. 2. Washington, D. C.: ASHE-ERIC, 1988.

Lunsford, Andrea A. "Cognitive Development and the Basic Writer." *College English* 41.1 (1979): 38–46.

Maimon, Elaine P. "Talking to Strangers." *College English* 30.4 (1979): 364–69.

Perry, William G., Jr. *Intellectual and Ethical Development in the College Years: A Scheme.* New York: Holt, 1970.

Piaget, Jean. *The Language and Thought of the Child.* 1926. New York: World, 1955.

Shaughnessey, Mina P. *Errors and Expectations: A Guide for the Teacher of Basic Writing.* New York: Oxford UP, 1977.

Sommers, Nancy. "Revision Strategies of Student Writers and Experienced Adult Writers." *College Composition and Communication* 30.4 (1980): 378–88.

Spear, Karen. *Shared Writing: Peer Response Groups in English Classes.* Portsmouth, N.H.: Boynton/Cook, 1988.

Vygotsky, Lev. *Thought and Language.* Trans. Eugenia Hanfman and Gertrude Vakar. Cambridge: MIT P, 1962.

White, Edward M. *Teaching and Assessing Writing.* San Francisco: Jossey-Bass, 1985.

Wiener, Harvey S. *Creating Compositions.* 2nd ed. New York: McGraw, 1977.

8 Still a Good Place to Be: More than 20 Years of the National Network of WAC Programs

Christopher Thaiss

Most of the essays in this history of the WAC "movement" limit themselves to the "getting started" part of the story. I'll devote the bulk of this piece on the National Network of WAC Programs to the early years, interspersing my narrative with the memories of others about those years; but I want to use that narrative of beginnings to draw attention to the present—and to speculate about the future. The most salient fact about the WAC Network is that, by design, it has remained pretty much as uncomplicated as it began. It has grown much in size but not significantly in scope. That would not be remarkable, except that the network remains, more than twenty years after its birth, the closest thing that WAC as a burgeoning community still has to a national organization. And the haunting implications of that will be the focus of the final part of this essay.

How the Network Began

In early 1979, I attended a meeting set up by Bob Weiss of West Chester State University at 4C's in Minneapolis as a beginning effort toward a network of WAC programs. I recall it as a well-attended meeting of enthusiastic people, though I don't recall anything that went on there, except that I put my name on a mailing list. I attended the meeting because we at GMU, in cooperation with the new Northern Virginia

Writing Project, had begun our first series of WAC workshops for faculty the preceding fall. I wanted to find out what others were up to and perhaps share my experiences. I knew Bob through the National Writing Project, he as director of the Pennsylvania Writing Project, I as associate director (under director Don Gallehr) of the NVWP. We had met at NCTE the fall before and knew a bit about one another's fledgling WAC efforts.

Bob and I continued to talk at conferences over the next year, and in early 1980 he called me to ask if I'd be interested in "taking over" a short mailing list, about 30 names, of interested WAC folks and pursuing the idea of a network. It was a good time for him to have called. GMU and the NVWP, along with three other Virginia schools, had just received a substantial state grant to build a network of Virginia WAC programs (see Thaiss, "University-Schools Partnership," this volume). We had also been funded to create what we called the Writing Research Center, which would give small grants to individual faculty applicants from diverse disciplines in Virginia universities to conduct and report on classroom research projects in the uses of writing in teaching. We had an office, two staff assistants, Louise Moore and Kathy Kennedy, and some release time from teaching, so why not take on the task of a national network, too?

I didn't envision the network as a major undertaking. It would be an adjunct to the networking we were already doing in Virginia, might involve a meeting or two each year at national conferences for interested parties, and would be in general a low-key affair, an opportunity for WAC developers to keep in touch, share questions and concerns, create first contacts that might become productive professional relationships. Since I was a 32-year-old assistant professor with no background in national, nor even state organizing, my only model for what such a network might do was the NWP, itself only six years old, but already, under the leadership of UC Berkeley education professor Jim Gray, achieving national prominence through a productive partnership with the National Endowment for the Humanities. I had attended with Don and others from the NVWP the NWP directors meetings at NCTE in fall 1978 and fall 1979; I had admired the energy and camaraderie, the shared sense of an important purpose, the cooperation between public school and university curriculum leaders and teachers.

At the NWP directors' meetings, I most enjoyed the many opportunities for open exchange among people from around the country in small breakout sessions, each focused on a theme, some institutional (finding funding, building a state network, building collaboration between schools and universities, etc.), some organizational (designing the summer institute for teachers, recruiting good teachers, designing follow-up courses), some pedagogical (grading writing, creating student publications, using freewriting and journals). There were sessions for directors and teachers, all informal, all open to everyone, none lasting more than an hour. I found this a productive way to exchange good information quickly and to give each person an opportunity to (1) have others address at least one of that person's specific concerns and (2) have a national audience, at least for a few minutes, to hear what that person was doing as a teacher or program builder. The leader of each breakout session was a facilitator, not a lecturer, though I could see that the leaders had been chosen for their experience in the target area and so their ability to answer questions posed by the group.

Using suggestions from Bob and Don, I set about proposing a panel at the 1981 CCCC convention, to be held in Boston. The structure would be similar to that of the breakout sessions at the NWP meetings, with

- small groups devoted to topics
- participants able to choose any group
- each group facilitated by an experienced person
- the agenda set by the participants.

In my short life as an academic, I'd already been at enough conference sessions to know that I didn't want the network meeting to be yet another rigidly structured series of talking heads, as useful and informative as those might be. This would be something different.

THE FACILITATORS: THE "BOARD OF CONSULTANTS"

My initial task was to build a group of facilitators. The best-known WAC scholars in the States at that time were Elaine Maimon of Beaver College and Janet Emig of Rutgers (Nancy Martin in England was the best-known WAC theorist anywhere). Elaine had been developing writing in the disciplines at Beaver since the early 1970s (see Maimon, this volume) and had sponsored an NEH seminar on the topic. Elaine and her colleagues Barbara Nodine (psychology) and Gail Hearn (biology) had come to GMU to lead a workshop in fall 1979. Janet's 1977 *CCC* essay "Writing as a Mode of Learning" had given us at GMU, among new programs at many places, a good theoretical base for our efforts with faculty. Janet, as director of the new New Jersey Writing Project, had visited GMU in 1978. But both were already otherwise committed for the 1981 4C's. Happily, my invitation was accepted by Toby Fulwiler, whose first essays on journals in the disciplines had appeared during the previous two years and who was part of the stellar team building WAC and the Writing Project at Michigan Tech (see Fulwiler, this volume); Barbara Walvoord, who was creating the Baltimore Area Consortium in Writing across the Curriculum (the euphonic BACWAC) and who had run perhaps the first U.S. WAC workshops in 1970 at Central College in Iowa (see Walvoord, this volume); Keith Tandy, director of the multi-college Writing Project consortium in Minnesota and director of his own new WAC program at Moorhead State; Leslie Whipp, director of the Nebraska Writing Project; and Richard Graves, director of the Sun Belt Writing Project.

The NWP connection was both available to me and, in retrospect, fortuitous. Even though WAC in later years would have its own trajectory of growth significantly apart from the NWP, at that point in the history of the discipline of composition and rhetoric the NWP served as a principal network of and incubator for new leaders (it continues to be both network and incubator today, though the many rhet/comp degree programs that have sprung up since have supplanted it as primary in these roles, certainly at the college and graduate levels.)

I can't recall who suggested the name "Board of Consultants" for our facilitators, but it captured the responsive role that that they were to play at meetings—assuming, of course, that there would be subsequent meetings. That wasn't at all sure. How would we know what to expect in Boston? What would be the level of interest in a WAC Network?

When the proposal was accepted, we sent a letter to those on the mailing list and invited them to let others know. We also sent a notice in a multi-purpose mailing to the other NWP sites around the country. We relied on the CCCC convention catalog to alert others. Looking back to those pre-computer days, I'm impressed by how much of our office time was consumed by planning and carrying out print mailings that would reach comparatively few people. But print and the phone were the whole ballgame for most offices then, so we could be assured of a pretty high rate of attention by those we wanted to reach. While we certainly talked about and bemoaned information overload in 1980, we couldn't even have imagined what faces us each morning now when we connect to the Internet.

The Directory

Besides creating the consultants board and ensuring a meeting place and time, my other main concern was developing the mailing list. If a network were going to be that, we had to have a vehicle so that people could keep in touch with one another and we with them. So we decided that a frequently updated directory would be the network's primary "publication," and that we would charge a nominal fee for it at subsequent meetings as the primary way to pay for copying and postage.

What would the directory contain? All we had pre-Boston was a list of names and college addresses. We knew nothing about any of these folks or the programs they might be trying to start. For the Boston meeting, I designed a one-page form (that we mimeographed, of course—do you remember mimeograph?) I would ask at the meeting for those who wished to join the network to fill out the form, as the basis for the directory. The "dues" I'd ask people to contribute would help us set up this first directory and mail it.

On the form I asked for name, school, address, and phone. In addition, we would code into the directory, to save space, answers to a series of questions about the program:

Year it began?
How funded (federal, state, private, institution, none)?
Name of source?
Kinds of documents that others could ask for, if interested? (program descriptions; reports to funding agencies; syllabi, assignments, articles by participants, etc.; evaluation instruments; "other")
Fee to requestors?
Newsletter that one could request? Fee?

We also left a space for "comments," which we'd not include in the directory but that I, as coordinator, would either try to respond to (if a response were asked) or refer to one of the consultants.

We settled on a dues of three dollars, just enough to cover our costs and just enough to let folks know we were serious, but also way less, even in 1980, than what they would pay for other national groups— and not so much that they would expect us to do more than we were offering. Our goal was to get a network going, our expectation that, if we were successful, further organization and expansion of WAC would be carried out by other groups that would emerge. I never envisioned the network as a national organization, a counterpart of the NWP or NCTE.

BOSTON, MARCH 1981

I can't remember the number we counted at the first meeting at 4C's, but I distinctly recall the mingled euphoria and panic of having too many enthusiastic people for the size of the room. We were able to conduct a set of energetic "small" groups of twenty or more each on such topics as "running a workshop for faculty," "funding," and "ways to use writing in teaching." And I recall staying in the meeting room for many minutes after our allotted time as participants queued up to hand in forms and pay dues. We came out of that meeting with more than 75 names on the mailing list and a firm basis for subsequent meetings.

THE NATIONAL NETWORK OF WAC, ELEMENTARY-UNIVERSITY

Given my ties to the NWP, it had been my intention in taking over the mailing list from Bob Weiss to build the network as K-University. That was part of the rationale for inviting NWP leaders to serve as consultants. The expectation was reasonable, given that the British movement in language across the curriculum, which had sparked the American movement in WAC, had focused on secondary schools, not universities. Hence, the next meeting was scheduled for NCTE the coming fall, and I had no reason to believe that the participation would not be as great.

Attendance was good, almost the same as the number that had overflowed the room in Boston, but I was surprised that even this group contained more college people than K-12. I realized that if the network were going to be as attractive to K-12 teachers and administrators as to their college counterparts, I'd need to build an alternative group of consultants: elementary, middle school, and high school faculty and curriculum leaders. The NWP site leaders already on the Board had many ties to the K-12 schools, but were not themselves K-12 teachers or administrators.

But was this "alternative WAC board" really needed? The NCTE fall convention already featured the NWP directors meeting, with its array of interactive breakout opportunities, which were beginning to include sessions on WAC; individual NWP sites, such as our own, were reaching out to other disciplines besides language arts through inservice courses and invitations to the summer institute. I decided that I didn't have the time or energy to coordinate a second board, but I did invite as additional members two excellent Northern Virginia teachers, Bernadette Glaze of the history faculty at Thomas Jefferson High School, and Albert Lengel of Louise Archer Elementary, both skilled in faculty development.

> *I ran my first WAC workshop in the summer of 1982, knowing a bit but not much about the larger WAC community (see Holder and McLeod, this volume). The Academic Vice President of my institution sent me to the Chicago Conference (as a reward for running a successful workshop) to meet Elaine Maimon, who advised me (among other things) to join the WAC Network. Elaine told me to contact Chris Thaiss, whom I called at George Mason. Chris gave me the information about the next meeting, at NCTE in Denver in 1983. I bought a plane ticket immediately.*

> *At that NCTE conference, one of the resolutions passed had to do with WAC: "Resolved, that NCTE affirm the position that students should write frequently in every course as a way of learning the subject matter and of sharpening their writing skills[. . .]" (www.ncte.org/resolutions/wac831983.html). WAC was clearly a hotter topic than I realized, operating alone in a department that did not take the teaching of writing as a serious intellectual enterprise. At the meeting of National Network, the room was packed with excited people, including myself—I couldn't wait to talk to the others about what they were doing. Chris managed to bring some order out of the chaos and in a few moments I found myself in a group with Barbara Walvoord, who drew us all into the conversation about what we were doing and where we wanted to go next with our programs. That 1983 National Network meeting was a defining moment for me; for the first*

time I found myself in a group of colleagues all of whom had the same goals, the same passion for bringing about educational change at the university level. I had found a disciplinary home. Not long afterward, Chris invited me to serve on the Board of Consultants; our annual meeting remains one of the most energizing events of CCCC for me.

—Susan McLeod

EVOLUTION OF THE MEETING STRUCTURE

Following the first CCCC and NCTE meetings in 1981, participation continued to grow, largely through attendance at the annual CCCC meetings. By the late 1980s the directory had grown to more than 600 names, with requests for membership coming regularly through the mail as well as through meeting attendance, which averaged 60–80 at C's and 20–40 at NCTE. For the first several years, attendance at the C's meetings overwhelmed the rooms we were given, and for our breakout sessions we used any available hall space.

After introductions, announcements, and new subscriptions, Chris divides up forty-seven participants according to special interests ("people with funding concerns up front with Sue and Margot"; "newcomers over here with Barbara and Pam; veterans in back with Toby and Lex"). With forty minutes left, fourteen faculty members arrange loose chairs into a ragged circle and introduce themselves (a community college, a small private college, a four-year public university, Big Ten, Ivy League, etc.). With thirty minutes left, everyone freewrites about a specific problem that brought them to this Special Interest session ("follow-up sessions are poorly attended"; "the new provost doesn't support WAC";" original enthusiasm has waned";" my chair thinks it should be 'grammar across the curriculum.'") With twenty-five minutes left, people pair up, exchange freewrites, and answer each other's questions: ("serve food, invite guest speakers"; " invite the provost to attend a one-day workshop"; "start a 'new' program called 'critical thinking across the curriculum'"; " offer the WAC program through the writing center"). With ten minutes left, partners talk rapidly to each other, elaborating upon suggestions, asking questions, exchanging e-mail addresses, and

> *laughing a lot (because moral support, more than specific an-*
> *swers, seems to keep people and programs going).*
>   *Language for learning is the foundation of writing across the*
> *curriculum.*
>
>   —Toby Fulwiler

By the mid 1980s, with WAC having become established at many schools, we evolved a discussion structure based on WAC experience, a structure that continues today: at the start of each meeting, I asked those in attendance to identify their programs as either "established" or "just getting started." When I first started using this distinction, I defined "established" as "beyond the first faculty workshop," a signifi-cant point of difference in those early days. (Now I let people define it as they will, and those who choose the "established" group tend to be those who've been running a program for at least five years and for up-wards of fifteen.) Then the consultants divide, some setting up groups of the "established" and the others leading groups of the "getting start-ed." It has become a standing source of amazement among long-time participants that every year, even in 2004, close to half of the attend-ees identify their programs as "just getting started"—although WAC has now been around long enough that some of those programs "just starting" are really second efforts at schools that formerly had had pro-grams that had withered for lack of leadership or money; or they are programs that are established in one way, say in conducting annual workshops, but are now venturing into new territory (e.g., a writing-intensive requirement, or response to a state assessment mandate).

> *What I remember as a leader of the WAC Network sessions at*
> *NCTE and CCCC meetings is how, over the years, the par-*
> *ticipants' needs have changed from "How do I get started?" and*
> *"What is WAC anyway?" to issues such as continued funding,*
> *second stage WAC, reviving a comatose program, ensuring con-*
> *tinuing leadership, and dealing with long-term campus politics.*
> *At the same time, there continues to be a substantial percentage*
> *of the group that still asks the start-up questions. Long after I*
> *thought that WAC was well known throughout higher ed., there*
> *would be people to whom it was a new idea that they had just*
> *encountered. It taught me how slowly innovations move into*
> *some corners of higher education.*
>
>   —Barbara Walvoord

The meetings have also changed over the years by the addition of more announcements and handouts of materials by participants at the start of the meetings—to announce conferences and publications—so our breakout time has diminished slightly. There has never been enough time to do justice to everyone's questions and concerns. Now that many programs and initiatives are more complex, the stories more involved, it's even more common than in earlier years for the sessions to spill over into the next time slot, and for participants' dinner plans to be even more delayed.

> *It is 6:45 on a Thursday night at a recent 4 C's Annual Meeting. I enter the WAC SIG session expecting to see only my friends who are on the Board of Consultants. Once again, I am proven wrong. The hardy conference participants start coming in, looking a bit weary after a long day of presentations. Some are newly appointed WAC directors wondering "where to begin." Others are seasoned WAC administrators wondering "where to go from here?" Some are old friends who just come to say "hello" and join us for the customary dinner that follows the SIG session. The mood is informal and relaxed as Chris gets up to give his pitch for the membership fee and to make announcements. But once we break into groups, the mood changes. Suddenly everyone is talking about funding problems, unruly faculty, administrators who want a WAC program up and running, immediately, if not sooner, etc. The mood becomes more intense. Can we answer all of these questions in the half hour that remains? We try our best, but 7:45 arrives all too soon. Email addresses are hastily exchanged; we promise to send materials after returning home—and then Susan McLeod starts counting heads for that all-important dinner. Another WAC SIG session has ended, and we are ready to party!*
>
> *—Margot Soven*

Of course, one way to extend the meeting time is to continue the conversation into dinner. It's become a tradition for the facilitators who have not made other plans to go out en masse after the meeting to a restaurant and to invite along participants who want to continue the conversation informally.

Move to the Annual Meeting Structure

The meetings at NCTE continued into the 90's, just as had our policy of updating the directory twice a year, after each meeting. But the attendance at the NCTE meetings never attained the numbers or the K-12 representation we'd hoped for, so we decided in 1994 to concentrate on the C's meeting only. At the same time, we went to annual updating of the directory, a move that has saved work for the very busy staff of the NVWP (primarily in the person of office manager Mark Farrington), the NVWP continues after all these years to serve as the clearinghouse for the network. This past year, the network directory caught up with the times and is now on line.

Growth of the Consultants Board

As the membership of college and university programs swelled, the consultants board grew. Toby Fulwiler, who moved from Michigan Tech to the University of Vermont in the 1980s, has been a member of the board since the beginning, as has Barbara Walvoord, now of Notre Dame. Since the mid-1980s, long-time members still current have included Susan McLeod, now of the University of California at Santa Barbara; Richard Larson of Lehman College, SUNY; Margot Soven of LaSalle University; Linda Shohet, Dawson College, Montreal; Lex Runciman of Linfield College; and Pamela Childers of the McCallie School, Chattanooga. More recent additions to the board have been Teresa Redd of Howard University and Vicki Tolar Burton of Oregon State. Keith Tandy and Dick Graves of the original board served well into the 1980s; Joyce Neff, first of Prince Georges (MD) Community College and now of Old Dominion University, and Bernadette Glaze, Fairfax County Public Schools, served from the 1980s into the 90's. It's not really possible to calculate how much these consultants have done for the many hundreds of teachers and program developers who have come to the meetings over more than 20 years in search of feedback and answers; but the consultants' willingness to spend those prime early evening hours in these sometimes difficult conversations after a hard day of convention-going surely has inspired more souls than me.

While I don't want to minimize what the board members have contributed, I also don't want to minimize the contributions of those who don't serve on the board per se yet who contribute by their regular participation in the meetings. For fear of leaving out deserving persons, I won't name names; but year upon year there are experienced WAC professionals, administrators and scholars, who attend the meetings and who contribute mightily to the groups. I hope they come to the meetings because they find a congenial group to discuss what they love. I know it does many a beset and frustrated new program director good to hear a well-known scholarly writer asking for advice from the group on yet another new problem in his or her program, and to have these well-known, veteran WAC administrators listening closely to others' concerns and offering suggestions.

EXTENDED WORKSHOPS AND PUBLICATIONS

Since the network has always been informal in its operations and membership, it can't be said to have truly *sponsored* any other activities besides the directory and the annual meetings. In that way, the network has never gone beyond our original intention that it be merely a way of bringing together people around a common interest. The board members and the significant group of regular participants have built individual scholarly and academic careers perhaps aided in some part by the network, but these careers are in no way beholden to it.

Nevertheless, network members have collaborated on some ventures that have come out of or been furthered by conversations at network meetings. For example, network consultants and members have organized and conducted three half- or full-day CCCC workshops on aspects of WAC program design and administration (perhaps four by the time this volume is published, since we are proposing one for 2004). Three volumes of essays, appearing in 1988 (McLeod), 1992 (McLeod and Soven), and 2001 (McLeod, Miraglia, Soven, and Thaiss) respectively, have chronicled and attempted to forecast important administrative and curricular issues as they relate to writing across the disciplines. Part of the impetus for all these ventures has been the energy of the annual meetings, the shifting focuses of issues and questions that are brought to the meetings, and the obvious burden we feel every year as the hour ends and we must close the conversation for that evening. I know that my own contributions to these volumes and my other WAC writings have been strongly influenced by the concerns that meeting participants voice. The three extended CCCC workshops have attempted in small part to address the diverse needs expressed at the SIG meetings. The volumes of essays have tried to address the requests for more extensive information on an array of issues

and have given those who have written these pieces the craved opportunity to reflect on what we hear at the meetings from colleagues and
to synthesize meanings from the exuberant conversation.

THINKING ABOUT WHAT THE NETWORK HAS BEEN, WHAT IT MIGHT HAVE BEEN, AND WHAT MIGHT BE

WAC has been around as a self-conscious faculty development initiative in the U.S. since circa 1970, as David Russell and others have
noted. In that time, no national organization on a par with, say, the
International Writing Centers Association has been built, not to mention an organization with the administrative complexity and standards
of the National Writing Project, of similar age. WAC is no less powerful an idea than that of the writing center or of "teachers teaching
teachers" or "teachers of writing must write," the basic principles of
the NWP. Indeed, it might even be said that the basic WAC notions
of "writing as a tool of learning" and "every teacher responsible for the
teaching of writing" underlie both the idea of a writing center and the
principles of the NWP. So why not an international WAC organization with all its trappings of administration, standards, and authorized
publications?

There are several possible explanations. Perhaps most likely, and
the one behind the original conception of the network, is that the idea
of WAC is sufficiently powerful and sufficiently tied into other powerful ideas, such as those mentioned above, that it has not needed a
hard-driving central lobbying effort in order to spread. The network,
as I'd pictured it, would succeed if it put ambitious imaginations in
contact, and they would carry the concept forward in their own ways.
Certainly this growth has occurred: we have an impressive literature
of WAC research, pedagogical tools, and program development guidance. Because of this literature and because of the consulting work of a
number of peripatetic scholars, WAC is a reasonably well-understood
idea in almost all educational settings, not only in the U.S. but in a
number of other countries. We have the WAC listserv, established at
the University of Illinois in the early 90's, and an impressive array of
local WAC websites, more and more of them linked to Colorado State's
WAC Clearinghouse, an excellent effort led by Mike Palmquist. (The
WAC Clearinghouse also now houses *Across the Disciplines,* edited by
Sharon Quiroz). Since 1993, we have had the biennial National WAC
Conferences, a South Carolina initiative that has now shared leader-

ship with other states. The IWCA, the NWP, the Council of Writing Program Administrators (WPA), and other organizations, many of whose members have attended network meetings or served on its board, understand WAC principles and teach them. So it might be argued that a more complex central organization for WAC would be redundant.

Nevertheless, a mere network lacks the ability of a more formal organization to do many things: create an agenda to focus efforts, issue position statements, establish and publicize standards, conduct statistical surveys of members, and, maybe most basic, ensure continuity through an orderly process of succeeding leadership. None of the other organizations I've named, their support of WAC principles notwithstanding, has as its express aim the building of a truly cross-disciplinary writing culture. Research on writing in disciplines, despite the years of successful activity by a number of excellent scholars, including several represented in this volume, is still in its beginning stages, with most academic writing cultures unmapped and untheorized except in the most abstract ways. Relatively simple demographic questions— e.g., the number of schools with a writing-intensive or writing-emphasis requirement in fields—keep coming up on listservs and no one can give an authoritative answer. Even basic questions of definition continue to be debated (a phenomenon not limited in academic circles to WAC, of course). Sometime in the 1980s I first heard at a conference someone speak as if writing across the curriculum (WAC) and writing in the disciplines (WID) were mutually exclusive concepts, a dichotomy with as far as I know no historical or theoretical basis. Yet I recently took part in a correspondence with several experienced writing program directors in which WAC was matter-of-factly described as "writing-to-learn exercises" and WID as the preparation of writers for the professional workplace, as if WAC did not encompass that concept. If WAC's inclusive interest in all aspects of writing in schools is not universally acknowledged by those familiar with the term, then the power of the concept is severely limited. A strong national, even international, organization could do something about all of these basic problems.

Further, it can be argued that, had a national WAC network specifically for K-12 teachers been pursued twenty years ago, by me or by anyone else, writing across the content areas K-12 would be a more recognizable phenomenon than it is today. Although the NWP, to cite one influential group, continues to support WAC as a basic concept, the influence of WAC as a driving pedagogical force in the K-12 schools is minimal at best in subject-matter professional groups, a lamentable fact especially now as state assessment programs, based as they inevitably are on high-stakes multiple-choice tests, become more aggressive.

This historical reflection is not perhaps the place to do a focused analysis on whether or not WAC needs an international organization, and why it doesn't have one; it's certainly not the place for a manifesto. However, I admit to wondering at times if the network, by its presence for more than twenty years, hasn't misleadingly given the appearance of being the national organization that WAC might need and so diminished the desire or incentive to others who might have built one. Or could it be that the community of WAC scholars and leaders at large is still waiting for the network to become that organization? I and others have written elsewhere (e.g., "Theory in WAC"; Walvoord) that one of the great strengths of WAC leaders on campuses has been their ability to locate support in—and have an impact on—other, often better-funded initiatives, such as technology, that become popular. But this adaptability and collaborative spirit can have their dangers, too, if they lead to a loss of identity for WAC.

So what is the next step for WAC and for the WAC network? Should we and, if so, how can we move to a more central, formal, assertive WAC structure? Surely there is more to be accomplished. Nevertheless, I will remember to enjoy my continuing surprise after more than twenty years that even without an International Association of WAC Programs the concept has become as pervasive as it has, and that these unpretentious little annual meetings of people who love what they're doing are still playing a role in that spreading of a good idea.

A final and perhaps most powerful lesson from the Network meetings has been how many dedicated, wonderful people there are in higher ed., working hard every day in the trenches, trying to innovate in the face of sometimes daunting obstacles, just figuring things out and moving forward as they can, with great love and commitment to their institutions and their students.

Works Cited

McLeod, Susan, ed. *Strengthening Programs for Writing across the Curriculum*. San Francisco: Jossey-Bass, 1988

McLeod, Susan, and Margot Soven, eds. *Writing across the Curriculum: A Guide to Developing Programs.* Newbury Park, CA: Sage, 1992.

McLeod, Susan, Eric Miraglia, Margot Soven, and Christopher Thaiss, eds. *WAC for the New Millennium: Strategies for Continuing Writing across the Curriculum Programs.* Urbana, IL: National Council of Teachers of English, 2001.

Thaiss, Christopher, "Theory in WAC: Where Have We Been? Where Are We Going?" McLeod, et al., 299–326.

Walvoord, Barbara, "The Future of WAC," *College English* 58 (1996): 58–79.

9 Gender and Discipline in Two Early WAC Communities: Lessons for Today

Barbara E. Walvoord

When Elaine Maimon and several faculty from Beaver College in Pennsylvania used part of their new NEH grant to travel all the way to rural Iowa to see what we were doing with WAC at Central College, we all sat there in our meeting room looking out over the Central College College campus and beyond to the rolling fields and the prairie sky, and we realized that we had a powerful national idea. We saw that we could help to make a new place for writing and learning in American classrooms.

As a WAC program builds its community and establishes its networks, a major challenge is to transcend boundaries of discipline and gender. Often beginning in English departments, perhaps among largely female writing faculty, the WAC program must become more than a female ghetto at the bottom of the status ladder in the English department. Two early WAC programs that I led in the 1970s and 1980s faced that challenge. The five strategies they used to build communities across boundaries of discipline and gender are still viable for WAC communities today and in the future.

1. Work with cultural values that transcend disciplinary and gender boundaries

2. Use avenues for networking by which women and English faculty can transcend boundaries of discipline and gender.

3. Address a perceived need that affects both men and women, administrators and faculty, across disciplines.

4. Gather resources that support a cross-disciplinary and trans-gendered initiative.

5. Attract leaders from both genders and multiple disciplines.

The need for these five aspects in any reform movement are widely demonstrated in the literature on change. This chapter, however, shows how WAC leaders used these components to transcend the boundaries of discipline and gender in two early WAC programs that are still lively today—the "skills" program of Central College in Pella, Iowa, in the 1970s and the Maryland Writing Project in the 1980s. The chapter then draws lessons for WAC programs in the future.

CENTRAL COLLEGE: GENDER AND DISCIPLINE IN A SMALL COLLEGE IN THE 1970S

The faculty workshops I led at Central College in Pella, Iowa, in 1970 have been cited by David Russell as the beginning of WAC in its current historic iteration. The program, still vital more than 30 years later, used the five strategies to transcend boundaries of discipline and gender. I had come to Central College in 1965 on a tenure track. A four-year, liberal-arts institution of about 1200 students, Central is affiliated with the Reformed Church in America, a conservative mainline Protestant denomination. As the daughter and granddaughter of Reformed Church ministers, I had a certain cultural acceptance and basis for leadership.

The culture of the English department was a strong advantage to the formation of WAC. In those years, at the beginning of the women's movement, many English departments had no women faculty, or women served only as adjuncts or as teachers of composition. Discrimination against women in higher education was blatant, as women in those years were beginning to document in complaints filed with federal agencies. Yet here in this small Midwest Christian college, the tenure-track faculty in English included two women—myself and the department chair—plus two or three men and no adjuncts. All English faculty, women and men alike, senior or junior, taught a share of the composition courses each year. That gender equity and the concern of the English faculty for writing shaped and supported Central's early WAC effort.

My leadership of WAC at Central College began with an impulse to transcend disciplinary boundaries to address a common problem. In spring of 1970, when my Chaucer seminar failed to make its enrollment quota, I was worried that the department chair would give me another section of comp with another 25 weekly themes to read. So, ironically, WAC began when a young, overburdened faculty member tried to escape having to deal with more student writing. Because there was a steady stream of complaints among faculty about the quality of student writing, I suggested to my department chair that I advertise among faculty to gather a group of volunteers who would meet every week during the semester to investigate student writing in courses across the disciplines. She said, "good idea." We English faculty were all tired of being blamed for students' writing problems. A key resource—my time—was in place. Also in place was support from key administrators—in this case the department chair and dean.

We had chosen a need that was widely-acknowledged among faculty across disciplines, and among both women and men. Student writing was viewed as a serious problem, and people wanted to address it. Fourteen of the college's 65 faculty members from a wide variety of disciplines volunteered to meet for an hour every Tuesday afternoon during that spring semester in 1970. The group was primarily male, and it included some of the most influential faculty on campus. We quickly widened our scope to include reading and listening—a scope that took us beyond the English department, and a scope that the Central College program retains today.

Because there were no writing "experts" among us, few resources, no grant support, and no centrally-constructed paradigm, each person had to take responsibility. The problems we identified were couched in our own terms at that time: student writing was awkward, inept, and not in control of edited standard written English. Students didn't seem to know how to construct coherent analyses and arguments. Each faculty member brought an assignment and several samples of student writing for group discussion. I took a facilitating role, rather than an "expert" role, thus avoiding the situation where a woman writing expert tells male faculty what to do. All these strategies helped us transcend boundaries of gender and discipline in that early workshop.

The program also built upon Central's culture of strong female leadership that extended beyond the English department. Of the 65 college faculty, six women held senior positions: five department chairs and the librarian—a highly unusual representation in a college or university during those years. Several of these women had instigated programs that were very important to the college's life and prosperity: for example, the chair of English built a strong program in English as a Second Language, including collaboration with Central College's site in Mexico. Thus, although the college's central administrators were men, there was a critical mass of senior women and there were models of female leadership. Women's power came from their willingness to work very hard, their initiation of valuable programs, their local departmental power, their participation in college-wide faculty governance, and their networking and persuasive skills among colleagues and administrators. The WAC program, under my leadership, used all these modes of power to build a community that transcended gender and disciplinary lines. I myself became another of those women who built important and enduring programs for the college.

There were also several important institutional avenues that the "skills" program at Central could use to nurture cross-disciplinary and cross-gender collaboration among faculty. Among these were a faculty lunch room where most faculty and academic administrators met each noon to sit at long tables with whomever was next in the buffet line. Faculty and administrators talked broadly with various colleagues rather than forming exclusive groups. The college had a long history of strong faculty governance and of collaboration between administration and faculty. All secretarial services were in one office in the center of campus, so we all had to walk the same campus paths to pick up our mimeographed syllabi or handouts. All faculty mailboxes were centrally located in the student union, in full view of the adjacent coffee shop, so a trip to get your mail could easily be sidetracked as you saw several of your colleagues around the large round tables, enjoying coffee and a Dutch almond pastry. It's not just that Central College was small; it had these particularly strong avenues of collegial interaction through which those interested in WAC could exercise power and leadership beyond their disciplinary and gender boundaries. Other institutions, be they large or small, will have different cultures and different avenues for collaboration, but the lesson is the same: WAC programs that are led by women and that originate in English departments need to identify and use all the avenues that the local culture offers for expanding the influence of the program across gender and disciplinary boundaries.

The skills program also could build on Central's strong cultural values for community service and egalitarianism, and its openness to the social movements of the time. I wrote a successful grant and then directed a county-wide project that addressed sexism in employment, schools, and counseling. The project also widened my knowledge of emerging feminist thought. The college in those years recruited larger numbers of African-American students, who organized themselves and began to question the established structures. I and several other faculty sponsored the first gay and lesbian student organization on campus. Six faculty families, including mine, adopted interracially and began to deal with how children learn language and form identities in a racist and sexist society. Several faculty were completing doctoral work and bringing back to campus the new ideas they gained. As I completed my own doctorate at the University of Iowa, ninety miles away, I took Black Studies and Women's Studies seminars in sociology, psychology, and history. At the university, I met feminist radicals who, despite my reputation in Pella as a radical "women's libber," thought I was hopelessly bourgeois, and stretched my thinking still farther. These involvements expanded our thinking and our ability and willingness to lead change. It is difficult now, in the twenty-first century, to imagine how stirring and how unusual such initiatives were for a small, rural religious college.

A successful WAC program in any era must allow the cohabitation and collaboration of a wide variety of political and sociological views of human nature and of education. It must provide a field of action and experimentation for the most creative minds on the faculty, both men and women. The "skills" program at Central served as a fertile ground for integrating new ways of thinking about race, gender, culture, and language, while also appealing to faculty and administrators who worked within a more traditional cultural paradigm—helping students meet the college's expectations for good writing as faculty defined it.

The Central College skills program moved from faculty workshops into campus-wide structural issues, using the five strategies to extend our workshop community beyond boundaries of discipline and gender. The 1970 workshop was so popular that the next year, twelve more faculty asked to form a second group. Now we had more than 1/3 of the faculty on board, including influential senior faculty, and we began to address larger issues.

One such broader initiative was two "labs," as we called them, to tutor students in writing and reading in all subjects. The labs forced us to talk with colleagues in other departments about what their students needed. Initially, I ran the writing lab out of my back pocket with a few student tutors and no released time. A few years later, the writing lab received a grant to hire a full-time (but not tenured) director, and it moved into a lovely room at the entrance to the new library, where there were lots of student and faculty traffic. The labs were soon reaching the majority of the student body. The grant and the labs gave WAC stature and visibility within the Central community.

As we moved from a workshop group of faculty into student services and new hires, we met a problem: the leadership group now consisted of a disproportionate number of nontenured women. Hired on a tenure track, I had reduced my teaching load to take care of children, thus falling off the tenure track. The writing lab director was full-time but untenured; the reading lab director was an adjunct. To combat this trend, we deliberately asked a high-status, non-English male faculty member to chair the newly-formed interdisciplinary "Skills Council," which formed policy for the skills program. This step helped address but did not entirely eliminate the gender and status boundaries that had arisen.

To ensure resources and to solidify our place within the college's culture, we needed a way to place the "skills" program firmly within the ongoing curricular and financial structures of the college. Thus we proposed, and the faculty passed, a policy that all graduating students had to be certified by their major departments as possessing the necessary writing, listening, and reading skills to function adequately in that discipline. Thus we carved a niche for ourselves within the established systems by which students moved toward graduation, a move that would become common throughout the nation (Walvoord "Future"). Though at some institutions curricular requirements were largely divorced from faculty development and/or it was enforced by tests administered by a ghettoized testing staff (White), at Central, faculty development remained strongly connected to the curricular structure, and the requirement was implemented by the departments, not by the writing program or the English department. Again, this structure helped us expand beyond departmental boundaries.

To get the certification proposal through the faculty, we leaders did considerable politicking. "Collegial" or "tribal" cultures such as Central's are relatively "flat" in their structure—there are few formal rungs in the power ladder; power is exercised informally; and espoused values focus on egalitarianism and consensus decision-making (Bergquist; Birnbaum; Smart and St. John). At Central, policy decisions were made in faculty meetings to which all faculty were invited and voted, and which were chaired by the (male) chief academic officer. This governance structure thus mirrored the male-dominated leadership of the central administration as a whole, but it also offered opportunities to all faculty for collegial interaction across disciplinary and gender boundaries. Women in collegial cultures tend to be excluded or undervalued in many ways, despite the rhetoric of inclusion, but because power is exercised informally, they can also exercise their skills of personal interaction and persuasion, and they can utilize their relationships with powerful males. Exercising such power, and with the support of the central administration and the faculty, we succeeded in garnering the necessary votes for the reading/writing/listening requirement. Later, the chief academic officer appointed me to serve on the committee that led a Core reform effort, in which the faculty made writing, reading, and listening skills a central part of Core curriculum structure and pedagogy.

In all these ways, then, Central College's skills program used the five strategies to form networks and communities that could transcend discipline and gender. The first community we formed was our own campus community, in widening circles from the first faculty workshops, to departments, and to the college as a whole. In addition, several major developments helped us connect to broader communities off campus.

Expanding into the world off campus, we offered credit-bearing WAC workshops to area high school teachers under the umbrella of Drake University's Continuing Education program. This gave us contact with Drake administrators and faculty, as well as with high school teachers and administrators in our region, and again made the program better known.

My mentors at the University of Iowa, though they focused on my doctoral work in literature, reinforced my expectation that I would be part of a scholarly community broader than Central College, and that I would contribute to that community in important ways. It was still difficult, but increasingly possible in those days, for women to obtain doctoral degrees and to be taken seriously by their professors, even if they had children and jobs in a distant town.

Other developments reflected avenues opening to women and extended our Central College community off campus. I began to be asked to speak about WAC, first to institutions in our region, and then nationally. I made presentations at CCCC and MLA conferences, enhancing my own knowledge and broadening Central's exposure. I developed my workshop materials into a book that was eventually published by *MLA (Helping Students Write Well)*. I also published about Central's program (Fassler). Elaine Maimon received a substantial grant for WAC at Beaver College in Pennsylvania, and used some of her money to visit Central with several of her faculty colleagues, thus putting us more firmly in touch with national colleagues.

Clark observes that faculty in higher education are connected to the outside world by multiple complex networks. The networks were opening to women in those years, though men were still disproportionately at the top. The WAC program utilized these avenues:

- Disciplinary conferences
- The practice of educators traveling to view model programs on site
- Publications
- Continuing-education graduate programs for K-12 teachers
- Grant funding structures
- Doctoral programs
- The practice on campuses of offering faculty workshops by outside speakers, creating a group of traveling consultant/evangelists for WAC.

In sum, the story of Central College's program, and of the networks that supported it and made it nationally visible, is a story of how, in a gendered and disciplinary world, amidst complex cultural dynamics, a significant and long-lived writing/speaking/listening initiative used the five strategies to transcend the boundaries of discipline and gender.

Gender and Discipline in a Regional Consortium

In 1980, I took a tenure-track faculty position to teach writing and
to begin a WAC program at Loyola College in Baltimore. I quickly became involved in founding and leading a regional program,
the Baltimore Area Consortium for Writing Across the Curriculum
(BACWAC), a consortium of representatives from Baltimore-area
colleges and universities. BACWAC soon launched the Maryland
Writing Project (MWP), under the umbrella of the National Writing
Project, which offered workshops and other services to area schools
from elementary through university. Using the National Writing
Project model, we identified outstanding teachers, K-university and
brought them into 5-week summer workshops where they wrote and
responded to one another's writing, read the literature, and prepared
workshop presentations about their own best teaching ideas. Then,
giving them the title "teacher-consultants," we sent them out to lead
workshops for other teachers. Soon the program was reaching hundreds of local teachers, K-university, and spawning other programs
such as student writing workshops and regional conferences for teachers. The BACWAC and MWP consortium included virtually every
public and private institution, K-university, in the greater Baltimore
area, and eventually in western, eastern, and southern Maryland as
well. BACWAC and MWP are still vital more than twenty years later,
with expanded programs but the same basic ideas at the core (www.
towson.edu/~bbass/mwp.html).

Baltimore was a much more complex environment for WAC than
Central College, and it presented enormous challenges for transcend-
ing boundaries of race, grade level, institution, geographic location,
and socio-economic class, as well as the boundaries of discipline and
gender that are the focus of this chapter. Nonetheless, the same five
strategies were important to transcend the boundaries, as this brief
history of the project will show.

The Maryland project addressed needs that were broadly acknowledged across lines of discipline and gender as well as race, grade level,
and geographic location. When we began, student writing was a
broadly visible concern, reinforced by the introduction of achievement
testing in Baltimore's K-12 schools during those years. Another strong
need was for collegial interaction among faculty. WAC proponents in
institutions a few miles from each other scarcely knew what the others were doing. At the same time, many faculty told me of their desire

to be more connected with colleagues at other institutions and in the K-12 schools. We all worked in educational systems where the prevailing culture sometimes seemed inimical to collegiality and wholeness for ourselves and our students. BACWAC and MWP connected to a strong counterculture that included men, though it was disproportionately female—a culture that Bergquist would call "developmental"—focused on education as development of the human spirit, and driven by hunger for human connection.

As at Central College, the spark to start the project was a series of events that made leadership available and created avenues by which the project could spread among institutions, disciplines, and genders. My growing national reputation led to invitations to conduct WAC workshops in Baltimore-area institutions of higher education. I was at that time married to the president of Towson University, so I met a number of faculty and administrators from Towson and other Maryland public institutions, in addition to the private college networks provided by my position at Loyola. I thus had unusually broad networks for a newcomer, based both on my own status and on affiliation with a powerful male.

When Gloria Neubert, a professor of education at Towson University, with wide networks in area K-12 schools and colleges, told her president that she had on her desk a grant application from the National Writing Project, the president suggested she and I get together. Gloria then brought in her friend Charles Allen, English Coordinator for the Baltimore City Schools. Now we had a leadership team that included both genders, public and private schools, English and education as disciplines, and grade levels from K-university.

Using our networks in local schools and colleges, we three leaders organized an initial meeting of about forty faculty from area schools, colleges, and universities. We worked hard to include both men and women of all educational levels and disciplines. The meeting was a love feast. As people stood to tell about their institutions' programs and their own dreams, the excitement and the warmth of collegiality were palpable. Participants delegated Gloria, Charlie, and I to take the lead in forming the Baltimore Area Consortium for Writing Across the Curriculum (BACWAC), which would encourage communication and collaboration among our institutions and would apply to be a site of the National Writing Project. For the first year or so, we held our meetings round-robin style at various campuses, stretching our map-reading and parking-place-hunting skills, but also extending our knowledge of one another's institutions, and crossing boundaries of institution, status, and race.

At Central, we had lacked an external program paradigm, so faculty in the initial workshops had empowered themselves to explore student writing. In contrast, the NWP had a well-formulated paradigm that empowered teachers across disciplines, made them experts and leaders in the program, helped them form support networks in schools, and garnered administrative support for their efforts. The paradigm gave us tested ways of attracting and empowering high school and college faculty from a variety of disciplines and of both genders, in a more complex environment than the Central College workshops.

The NWP also helped with resources. Their grant required that we raise matching funds right at the start, so with the help of Loyola College's development office, I made the rounds of local foundations, again extending our networks into centers of power and funding. I and the other co-directors also visited neighboring institutions' provosts to get their support and a small consortium fee to help fund the project. The widely-acknowledged need to address student writing gave us our entrée. As at Central, we operated within the dynamic where WAC leaders, primarily women, build in the trenches, creating centers of energy and collegiality that meet a common need, and where administrators, primarily male, support them. We made this system work to help us form a WAC community that, though primarily female, included men, and though primarily English teachers, also included faculty from other disciplines.

The resources for our effort were provided not only by grants and by the consortium institutions, but also by the system in which K-12 teachers enrolled in workshops and seminars for credit, with tuition paid by the school system. Teachers got promotions and salary raises based on the credits they earned. Here was money changing hands to pay for faculty development. The people who ran this in-service system were always desperate for good speakers, and the MWP provided them with outstanding teachers of both genders and multiple disciplines who had been well-trained in our summer workshops and who gave dynamic, practical, interactive workshop presentations.

For the college faculty, who did not need the master's level graduate credits, we held intensive workshops for outstanding faculty from our consortium institutions, then formed them into teams who would lead workshops at consortium colleges and universities, earning a small honorarium. We thus became a prime in-service provider both for K-12 and for colleges and universities, thereby ensuring our financial future. Our activities also facilitated rich cross-pollination among faculty around the region. We provided avenues for women, as well as men, and for math and history teachers, as well as English teachers, to become leaders in the WAC program.

An important resource was the institutions that hosted BACWAC and the MWP, and the aspects of their cultures that nurtured our community. Our first host was Loyola College, but my program head and my dean, both men, were unsure of MWP's long-term value to Loyola. The Loyola culture was a fine one for inception, because of its status and budgetary freedom as a private institution, but not as good a cultural fit in the long run. So after the first few years, we moved the headquarters of the project to Towson, which had a strong emphasis on education. MWP was highly valuable to Towson and richly consonant with its culture. MWP brought K-12 teachers to Towson's campus for workshops. Some of those teachers then enrolled in degree programs or took credit courses. Others just came to know the campus better and could advise their own high school students about Towson. Later, the MWP began to use its outstanding, well-trained K-12 teachers to lead summer writing workshops for selected outstanding high school and junior-high student writers. This program brought the local schools' best student writers to Towson's campus for a wonderful summer experience, ending with a luncheon at which the young writers showed off their own writing to their parents, teachers, and local school principals—an admissions officer's dream. Again, as with the system of faculty in-service workshops, the MWP was able to use for its own ends the existing avenues by which money changed hands—this time for admissions and public relations. WAC leaders were able to use their talent and energy, as well as their connections with powerful administrators, to establish the program.

In MWP leadership, as at Central, we worked hard to include both genders. After the first few years of leadership by the triumvirate of Gloria, Charlie, and me, Gloria alone became the director, followed by other directors, all women. So we worked hard to ensure that the project's executive council included men.

As at Central, the formation of our own community then led to networks in the wider world—networks that utilized the growing opportunities for women. At the NWP's national annual meetings of program directors, Maryland leaders spread the word about MWP's successes and gained new ideas. One of Maryland's directors was eventually recruited for a leadership position at the NWP headquarters in California. Some of our MWP teachers entered doctoral programs and moved throughout the region and nation, spreading the word. Schools and colleges outside our region requested workshop presentations. Our teacher-consultants gave presentations at national conventions and won grants to conduct classroom research.

We also began to publish about our work. Our program was described in Toby Fulwiler's *Programs that Work* (Walvoord et al., "Baltimore"). We began to do classroom research under the leadership of Gloria, and with external consultants such as Dixie Goswami of Clemson University—one of a number of outsiders who brought us new ideas and took away a knowledge of what we were doing. A number of us published classroom research, including *Thinking and Writing in College: A Study of Students in Four Disciplines* (Walvoord and McCarthy). We also received additional grants through the years.

Again, I refer to Clark's thesis about multiple complex networks. The networks were opening to women in those years, and we used them strategically to transcend boundaries of discipline and gender. The avenues of dissemination in MWP's case were:

- Faculty development workshops and "in-service" days
- A consortium, BACWAC, that brought together faculty and administrators from various schools
- Graduate programs that enlisted gifted teachers from the MWP and sent them out as faculty across the country
- The NWP, with its annual meetings, publications, and other forms of networking
- The practice in schools and colleges of inviting workshop leaders and conference speakers from around the nation
- Friendships and family connections
- Graduate programs
- College and university admissions efforts
- Teacher training systems that required collaboration between the institutions of higher education that trained teachers, and the local schools who engaged teaching interns and hired new teachers

- Existing systems of inter-institutional cooperation such as the state system of higher education, the public school system, the association of private schools and colleges, and the Catholic diocese

We used each of these avenues strategically to transcend boundaries of gender and discipline, as well as status, grade level, and geography.

Summary and Implications

The Maryland program was different from the Central College in many ways: in the 1980s, WAC was already familiar to many educators. The Maryland WAC effort had a guiding paradigm and rich national resources, right from its inception. The Maryland community was far more complex and fractured than Central. MWP had to reach across racial, socio-economic, status, institutional, and geographic boundaries as well as boundaries of discipline and gender. The segregation of women into K-12 classrooms and into the teaching of writing was more severe at most BACWAC institutions than at Central.

Despite these differences, however, the strategies by which the successful program in Maryland was launched and supported across the boundaries of gender and discipline had many similarities with the modes by which the Central College program had been launched a decade earlier in a different setting. Both programs used the five strategies to transcend boundaries of discipline and gender. We leaders, mostly women and mostly writing specialists, collaborated with men and with faculty from other disciplines, and we took pains to help those faculty become visible in leadership roles. We demonstrated our dedication and energy, using traditional avenues to get administrative support for our efforts to address needs that were widely perceived. We capitalized on ways in which money and other resources were already changing hands. We used our professional and personal connections to bring in powerful males. We transcended rigid boundaries of discipline and gender by finding forums in which women and men, scientists and humanists, could join on common ground to address mutual concerns, to connect more deeply with our students and to foster the collegiality for which all of us hungered. It was the ability both to work within the boundaries and also to transcend them that I believe were crucial to the formation, effectiveness, and long lives of the Central College and Maryland programs.

The world of higher education is changing rapidly now, but I believe the continuing prosperity of WAC still depends upon its ability to transcend boundaries. I have written about these issues in one way as I investigated WAC as a social movement (Walvoord "Future"). Here, I have approached the issues from a different angle, emphasizing the role of five strategies to transcend boundaries. Both approaches illustrate my belief that the continuing effectiveness of WAC depends upon strategies for innovation and change that are thoughtful, informed, deliberate, and theoretically sophisticated—strategies that use the culture yet transcend it, to do what all good reform movements do—help institutions better serve their constituents, call people back to their highest values, and foster genuine human community.

WORKS CITED

Bergquist, William H. *The Four Cultures of the Academy.* San Francisco: Jossey-Bass, 1992.

Birnbaum, Robert. *How Colleges Work: The Cybernetics of Academic Organization and Leadership.* San Francisco: Jossey-Bass, 1988.

Clark, Burton R. *The Academic Life: Small Worlds, Different Worlds.* Princeton, NJ: Carnegie Foundation for the Advancement of Teaching, 1987.

Fassler, Barbara E. [Walvoord]. "The Interdepartmental Composition Program at Central College." *Options for the Teaching of English: Freshman Composition.* Ed Jasper Neel. New York: Modern Language Association, 1978. 84-89.

Russell, David. *Writing in the Academic Disciplines, 1870–1990: A Curricular History.* Carbondale: Southern Illinois UP, 1991.

Smart, John C., and Elton P. St. John. "Organizational Culture and Effectiveness in Higher Education: A Test of the 'Culture Type' and 'Strong Culture' Hypotheses." *Educational Evaluation and Policy Analysis* 18.3 (1996): 219–41.

Walvoord, Barbara E., and H. Fil Dowling, Jr., with John R. Breihan, Virginia Johnson Gazzam, Carl E. Henderson, Gertrude B. Hopkins, Barbara Mallonee, and Sally McNelis. "The Baltimore Consortium." *Programs That Work: Methods and Models for Writing Across the Curriculum.* Ed. Toby Fulwiler and Art Young. Portsmouth, NH: Heinemann, Boynton/Cook, 1990. 273–86.

Walvoord, Barbara E. "The Future of Writing Across the Curriculum." *College English* 58 (1996): 58–79.

—. *Helping Students Write Well: A Guide for Teachers in All Disciplines.* 1982. Rev ed. New York: Modern Language Association, 1982.

Walvoord, Barbara E., and Lucille P. McCarthy, with contributions by Virginia Johnson Anderson, John R. Breihan, Susan Miller Robison, and A. Kimbrough Sherman. *Thinking and Writing in College: A Naturalistic Study of Students in Four Disciplines.* Urbana, IL: National Council of Teachers of English, 1991.

White, Edward M. "The Damage of Innovations Set Adrift." *AAHE Bulletin* 44 (Nov. 1990): 3–5.

10 Writing Across the Michigan Tech Curriculum

Toby Fulwiler, with Additions by Art Young

At Art Young's suggestion, I attended the (1977) National Endowment for the Humanities seminar at Rutgers called "Writing in the Humanities." When I read a volume called Writing and Learning across the Curriculum 11–16, *by Nancy Martin, et al., scales fall from my eyes. Writing across the curriculum.*

1976 (FALL)

Art Young, new chair of the Humanities Department at Michigan Technological University, appoints me, a new assistant professor of English, to direct the first-year writing program. My qualifications? I have a PhD in American literature from Wisconsin and have read Strunk and White's *The Elements of Style*—the only book about writing I remember reading. I have never taken a graduate course in writing or the teaching of writing, and I've never heard that teaching composition is serious professional work. Art knows otherwise. The first time he asks me about attending the four C's, I wonder what salad dressing has to do with teaching English.

1977 (SPRING)

I attend my first CCCC's in Kansas City wander session-to-session, learning as much as I'm able about directing a writing program. I'm especially interested in improving the "skill and drill" writing laboratory currently in place at Tech and want to learn more about a recent concept called "peer tutoring." I listen closely to Micky Harris of Purdue in a session called "Expanded Uses of Writing Labs." I also blunder into a session called "Teaching Composition: Strategies for Involving the Entire College Community" that includes panelists Jasper Neel, Frank D'Angelo, and Barbara Walvoord (then Barbara Fassler). Very interesting, but I'm not yet sure how it applies to my school.

During this time the job market for college English teachers is awful, allowing us to hire good people into our geographically remote department: Randall Freisinger, from Missouri, to develop a Bay Area Writing Project site; Peter Schiff, from Columbia, to help with assessment. Over the next several years we hire a dozen new faculty including Elizabeth Flynn and James Kalmbach to help with reading across the curriculum, William Kennedy to help with oral communication, Carol Berkencotter for research on composing, Diana George for the Writing Center, Cindy and Dickie Selfe for technological innovation, Michael Gorman and George Mc Cully for assessment, and Bruce Peterson, someone just bound to be helpful in some way. These new colleagues would prove to be key to the future development of our program.

1977 (SUMMER)

At the urging of Art, I attend the NEH seminar at Rutgers called "Writing to Learn in the Humanities," one of fifty participants who will study something about the role of writing in English, history, philosophy, and art. We work for three weeks with Lee Odell, Dixie Goswami, Robert Parker, Brian Newton, Marty Gliserman, and Steve Zemmelman whose mission is (I learn later) to introduce the British concept called "writing across the curriculum" to American colleges and universities.

At Rutgers I learn that people have, indeed, written books about the teaching of writing: Peter Elbow, *Writing Without Teachers;* Janet Emig, *The Composing Process of Twelfth Graders;* James Kinneavy, *A Theory of Discourse;* Ken Macrorie, *Writing to be Read;* James Moffett, *Teaching the Universe of Discourse;* Don Murray, *A Writer Teaches Writing;* Richard Ohmann, *English in America.* When I read a volume called *Writing and Learning across the Curriculum 11–16,* by Nancy Martin, et al., I discover writing across the curriculum, a term that emphasizes the role of informal language in thinking and learning: "The expressive is basic. Expressive speech is how we communicate with each other most of the time and expressive writing, being the form of writing nearest to speech, is crucial for trying out and coming to terms with new ideas. Because it is the kind of writing in which we most fully reveal ourselves to our reader—in a trusting relationship— it is instrumental in setting up a dialogue between writer and reader from which both can learn." (Martin, et al., 26).

> Art Young: *Dale Stein, the newly appointed Provost at Michigan Tech, visits me in his round of meetings with department heads. He challenges the department of Humanities to develop a program to improve the communication skills of all Tech students— this to be in addition to the already required full year of composition. If we develop it, he will fund it. We meet with engineering and science faculty and are awash in proposals: entrance exams (for placement), exit exams from first-year composition, junior exams (to allow for remediation before graduation), or technical writing requirements. Many of the proposals will result in teaching to a test; all will place responsibility for writing instruction solely with the English faculty. Isn't there a better way?*

We began to look at better ways. The British researchers, led by Nancy Martin and James Britton, believe that elementary and secondary students who use expressive language—freewriting, journals, small-group talk—will both learn and write better than those restricted to formal language instruction. Art and I believe that a similar approach might work with our Michigan Tech undergraduates: "We conceived writing across the curriculum as a teacher-centered program. Our program recognizes, computers and competencies notwithstanding, that teachers are still the center of the educational experience. . . . we hope to empower teachers to transform routine teaching and testing by developing pedagogies that thwart conformism and successfully encourage critical thinking" (Young, "Rebuilding" 13).

"In order to make the abstract concept of 'writing across the curriculum' more concrete, the Humanities Department of Michigan Tech planned, organized, and conducted a series of off-campus writing workshops to which teachers from all disciplines were invited. These workshops introduced participants to three premises which we believe crucial to developing a truly interdisciplinary writing program. We wanted teachers to understand (1) that the act of composing a piece of writing is a complex intellectual process; (2) that writing is a mode of learning as well as communicating; and (3) that people have trouble

writing for a variety of reasons; no quick fixes will 'solve' everybody's
writing problem." (Fulwiler, "Argument" 21).

1977 (OCTOBER)

We invite faculty from all departments to spend two days studying
the teaching of writing at the Keewenaw Mountain Lodge. With no
budget at this time, each department pays the expenses for one participant. Bob Jones and I lead a workshop for sixteen faculty modeled
after the approach I learned from Dixie Goswami and Lee Odell at
Rutgers: Lee asked questions, asked us to write and talk, kept time,
and didn't give answers. Every once in a while, Dixie provided answers. We run the workshop on a large screen porch, asking questions
for people to answer in their own informal language: What makes
writing hard for you? What makes it hard for students? We all write in
small notebooks we call 'journals' ("sharing will be voluntary"). The
journal writing serves both as a springboard for our group discussion
and, at the same time, a demonstration of how expressive discourse
generates ideas and insights. We argue as much as discuss (demonstrat-
ing the value of expressive talk), violate our planned schedule, take
breaks in the cool white pine woods and, when the academic work is
done, jog, eat, drink, and chat together well into the night.

In answer to the question, "What makes writing hard," participants list *Getting started. Being vulnerable. Finding time. Finding a
place. Spelling. Anticipating audience questions. Putting thoughts into
words. Organizing ideas. Editing. Not believing I have anything new to
say. Teaching four courses. Typing. Being alone. Being rejected.*

1978 (FEBRUARY)

Randy Freisinger and I are co-leading our second off-campus workshop, mid-winter, at the Ford Forestry Center. Most participants seem
to be having a good time. Bob Stevens, geography, isn't buying it. Bob,
who weighs two-twenty if a pound, looks skeptical. When we ask faculty to freewrite about "the best writing assignment they ever gave,"
Bob sits back in his tiny student desk, crosses his arms, and stares at
the ceiling. We both try to ignore his resistance, but cannot help a discouraged peek now and then: it never occurred to us that some faculty
wouldn't play. However, next year at a Christmas party, Bob takes me
aside and tells me he is sorry: "I was afraid somebody would see my

writing. You see, I got a D in freshman English, and when you told us to write, I was afraid somebody would see how I wrote."

> Art Young: *We tell the Provost we want to develop a WAC program to improve students' communication abilities—based on the premise that "writing is everybody's business," too important to be left to the Humanities Department. He agrees and asks us to write a proposal that he can shop around for external funding sources. Toby and I write thirty-pages describing the theory, practice, and goals of WAC. At the heart of the proposal lie intensive faculty workshops.*

1978 (JULY)

Michigan Tech joins Northern Michigan University in hosting the 28th site of the National Writing Project in Marquette called the Upper Peninsula Writing Project. Jim Gray—a union organizer masquerading as a college professor—visits and explains the concept of teachers teaching teachers and the importance of teachers being writers. Co-leader Mark Smith (NMU) and I learn to watch, listen, and get out of the way as twenty-five K-12 teachers share best practices about teaching writing and compose, share, revise, and edit their own writing.

1979

My first attempt to publish an article about the role of journals in across the curriculum is rejected by *CCC*'s editor Ed Corbett, who says the article recaps nicely everything that's already been said about teaching with journals. I am discouraged, believing he doesn't understand the importance of expressive writing to the new writing across the curriculum movement. I persist, finally placing "Journal Writing Across the Curriculum" in an NCTE anthology of Classroom Practices in Teaching English, 1979–80, called *How to Handle the Paper Load* (Stanford). I compose another piece from outtakes of this piece, call it "Journal Writing Across the Disciplines," and place it in *English Journal.*

This is the year that Frank D'Angelo adopts the theme of 'writing across the curriculum' for the CCCCs program in Minneapolis. He does so, in part because of all the lobbying at the previous convention by a lot of us at Michigan Tech and Beaver College now developing

WAC programs. In fact, Michigan Tech sends 25 full and part-time faculty to the Minneapolis, seven on the program delivering papers and all of us recruiting for new positions in writing. At the end of the day, in the hotel bar, a candidate is heard to say: "Whew! They've got a think tank up there."

For good or ill, our program becomes known for journal writing. As one sociology professor tells me, "If journals were Chevrolets, you'd be rich." Selling journals to interdisciplinary audiences becomes a personal mission: "Well used, journals can be exciting and humane educational tools. Journals keep students in the habit of writing regularly while they promote active learning and facilitate personal engagement. And they make teachers who assign them more aware of themselves and their teaching. Student journals might be the best interdisciplinary tool we possess, integrating personal with academic knowledge across the curriculum." (Fulwiler, "Journal" 21).

But implementing journal writing across the curriculum is not always smooth, especially at a technical university. Returning from one faculty workshop, Dick Heckle, chair of the metallurgy department, is all fired up about using journals in his engineering design classes. He assigns journals in three sections of sixty-students each and collects them all the same week. Trying to read one hundred and eighty journals, puts a severe strain on his enthusiasm. At the same time, he admits, reading the journals reveals that few students think in visual language—a necessity for successful engineers. He adds visual problem solving to his curriculum; in the future he staggers the due dates for collecting.

1980

Art Young: *The provost announces that the General Motors Foundation has awarded the Department of Humanities a grant of $250,000 over five years to develop a university-wide WAC program. We are ecstatic, but not everyone at Tech is pleased. The Dean of Engineering, for example, a "basic skills" guy, believes GM should support the College of Engineering, not the Humanities Department. And some literature colleagues in our own department wonder just what the humanities are coming to. However, I'm able to offer a one-course reduction from our four-course teaching load to any faculty member who wants to work on some aspect of WAC. Twelve accept the offer, and we* *now have a program, a team to develop it, and time to think and write about it.*

The GM grant provides modest stipends for MTU faculty to attend writing workshops ($50 day) which we now offer in two and four-day formats during both the summer and the academic year. Released time generated by the grant gives us time to write our first book: We co-write as we've learned to co-lead writing workshops, adopting a collaborative model of scholarship more akin to the sciences than the monk-in-the-cell model typical of humanities scholarship. NCTE publishes *Language Connections* (Fulwiler and Young, 1982). In the book's "Introduction" we articulate our objective this way: "We believe that a comprehensive program must start from certain pedagogical premises: (1) that communication education (primarily writing, but including reading, speaking, and listening) is the responsibility of the entire academic community, (2) that such education must be integrated across departmental boundaries, and (3) that is must be continuous during all four years of undergraduate education. Furthermore, a comprehensive language program must incorporate the several roles language plays in education: to communicate, to learn, to form values. While these roles are not mutually exclusive or exhaustive, we have found it useful to distinguish them in order to better understand and talk about them." (ix).

1981

"Showing, Not Telling, at a Writing Workshop," is published in *College English,* generating a wide-ranging publicity about the Michigan Tech workshops. That same year, I place similar articles in *CEA Critic* and *WPA: Journal of Writing Program Administration* in a deliberate attempt to disseminate WAC information to a wide range of English teachers—the target audience most likely to initiate and maintain WAC programs. We've found that, with a few exceptions such as DePauw and Bucknell, it's usually English professors who find WAC administration and scholarship directly related to promotion and tenure in their home departments. My colleagues and I are invited to other campuses conduct writing workshops and are paid consulting fees for doing so—a practice which puts English faculty on a par with our oft consulting engineering colleagues. We get a little more respect. We operate on a major principle: faculty must write. "Perhaps the most important sessions at faculty workshops require the teachers themselves to write something. Whether the workshop is one day or five weeks, teachers must generate a piece of writing based on personal experience and share that writing with other participants. They must also listen to critical commentary about their efforts." (Fulwiler, "Showing" 61).

Art Young: *But not everyone is happy. The Faculty Senate at MTU, led by its officers and faculty from the School of Business, conduct an "investigation" into the MTU writing programs. While none has ever attended a WAC workshop, they have heard rumors about expressive writing, journals, and the emergence of a touchy-feely curriculum. They propose to sanction the Humanities department for promoting writing in which basic flaws in grammar, spelling, and punctuation are tolerated, perhaps encouraged, insisting instead, that the Humanities Department return to a back-to-the-basics philosophy. In a heated Senate meeting, the proposal is narrowly defeated. Whew.*

1982

In a report to the Michigan Tech administration, we claim the following effects from five years of a WAC program: (1) by working together in an interdisciplinary setting, many instructors report a heightened sense of faculty community. (2) In learning new strategies for incorporating writing into courses, faculty learn techniques for creating a more active learning environment; many report the writing workshop as their first successful professional development activity. (3) The most innovative idea taken from WAC workshops is the concept of writing-to-learn. (4) The emphasis on revision provides now guidelines for assigning and responding to student papers. And (5) many faculty report an increased confidence in their own writing abilities—a completely unexpected by product of offering these essentially pedagogical workshops.

Art Young: *The powers-that-be are pleased with both the on-campus WAC program and the scholarship emanating from the Humanities Department. WAC has put Tech on the national map, and this time, not for an engineering program. No longer a service-only department, we are now designated a "pillar of excellence." The Provost awards five new tenure-line positions to the department, half of the total new positions available to the entire University this year. I'm able to move all tenure-line faculty to nine-credit teaching loads and to cap all writing-intensive courses at 35—real advances in light of previous teaching loads and enrollments in philosophy and literature courses that sometimes reached sixty students a section. In addition to strengthening the WAC program, our new stature enables us to strengthen our undergraduate degree programs in Scientific and Technical Communication as well as to begin planning a Masters in Technical Communication.*

1983

We conduct a WAC workshop exclusively for School of Business, whose faculty are the most vocal in their opposition to our ideas about expressive writing. Unfortunately, we had not yet learned the importance of an interdisciplinary mix at writing workshops. At the Business workshop, departmental pecking orders soon emerge, and many voices are silenced. We resolve never to work exclusively with a single department again. Despite our difficulties, the high-participation workshop strategies do their magic, and we gain quite a few allies in an otherwise hostile department.

As we hold more workshops, more questions are asked than answered: Do students really write better if their instructors attend writing workshops? Does journal writing improve content learning? What's your evidence? No matter how many workshops we conduct for an ever-increasing number of faculty, it's hard to see, let alone measure, real change across the vast Tech curriculum. Meanwhile, at the very time our WAC program asks professors to pay more thoughtful attention to their teaching, the university administration asks professors for ever more research and publication on the way to tenure and promotion. So, more questions emerge: Will new assistant professors who take teaching seriously, perish? Will only full professors have the time to put WAC ideas into practice? To answer some of these questions, we embark on a major collaborative research project and our second book.

> Art Young: *We embark on our second department book,* Writing Across the Disciplines: Research into Practice. *This time, we set out to assess a program now running for five years. With help from a second General Motors grant ($30,000), we buy summer time for a team of seven to write up the results of research conducted the previous two school years. We meet several times a*

*week, swap drafts, and re-frame for each other puzzling research
results. For example, when Cindy Selfe examines two otherwise
identical math sections, one using traditional quizzes, one using journals, when students take a common test, the math scores
are identical. Re-framed, we reason, "Well, the journal writing
was just as effective as the quiz taking." Bob Boynton and Peter
Stillman at Boynton/Cook go out of their way to help us publish
what they know will be modest selling volume on WAC research
at one institution; it is still in print nearly two decades later.*

1983 (August)

In search of a more moderate climate (you know, don't you, that
Houghton, Michigan, gets more than two hundred inches of snow
every winter) and more comprehensive culture in which to raise my
daughters Megan and Anna, our family leaves the Upper Peninsula for
the balmy climate in Burlington, Vermont.

Today

For more than two decades, I have conducted a writing across the curriculum workshops at my new home at the University of Vermont. In
recent years, the program has moved the center of its activities from
the English department to the Center for Teaching and Learning.
Our writing workshops commonly combine with other themes such
as critical and creative thinking, problem solving, and drawing. In
1987, Art Young moved to Clemson to establish that university's nationally renown program in "communication across the curriculum"
(CAC). Speaking for both Art and myself, those early years developing
the Michigan Tech WAC program were the most exciting professional
years of our lives. We were new in the profession, WAC was new on
the national horizon.

Though I've recently retired from full-time English teaching, I
continue to be active in a variety of Vermont's WAC programs—a lot
easier to do without full-time teaching obligations. Over the nearly
thirty years that I've worked with what might be called WAC ideas,
I've become more philosophical, if not downright discouraged, about
the chances of significant change in either individuals or institutions.
I know that student writing and learning abilities develop slowly over
time—sometimes very slowly. And I know that college curricula de-

velop slowly over time as well, and always through complicated long-term compromises.

At the same time, the popularity of interdisciplinary writing programs remains strong and, when asked, both Art and I continue to help colleges and universities develop them. Why? Because exploring good ideas with interested colleagues is the most exciting work we've learned to do. Expressive writing and speaking continue to make passive classrooms active. Process writing assignments remain the surest way to improve student writing. And teachers exploring ideas together continue to create faculty community in otherwise pretty isolated academic settings.

Works Cited

Elbow, Peter. *Writing without Teachers.* New York: Oxford UP, 1973.

Emig, Janet A. *The Composing Processes of Twelfth Graders.* Urbana: National Council of Teachers of English, 1971.

Fulwiler, Toby. "The Argument for Writing Across the Curriculum." *Writing across the Disciplines: Research into Practice.* Ed. Art Young and Toby Fulwiler. Upper Montclair, NJ: Boynton/Cook, 1986.

—. "Journal Writing Across the Disciplines." *English Journal.* 69.9 (1980): 14–20.

—. "Showing, Not Telling, at a Writing Workshop." *College English* 43.1 (1981): 55–63.

Fulwiler, Toby and Art Young, eds. *Language Connections.* Urbana: National Council of Teachers of English, 1982.

Kinneavy, James L. *A Theory of Discourse: The Aims of Discourse.* Englewood Cliffs, NJ: Prentice, 1971.

Macrorie, Ken. *Writing to Be Read.* Rev. 2d ed. Rochelle Park: Hayden, 1976.

Martin, Nancy, et al. *Writing and Learning Across the Curriculum 11–16.* 1976. Rpt. Portsmouth, NH: Boynton/Cook, 1993.

Moffett, James. *Teaching the Universe of Discourse.* Boston: Houghton, 1968.

Murray, Donald Morison. *A Writer Teaches Writing: A Practical Method of Teaching Composition.* Boston: Houghton, 1968.

Ohmann, Richard M., and Wallace Douglas. *English in America: A Radical View of the Profession.* New York: Oxford UP, 1976.

Stanford, Gene, and National Council of Teachers of English. Committee on Classroom Practices. *How to Handle the Paper Load.* Classroom Practices in Teaching English, 1979–1980. Urbana: National Council of Teachers of English, 1979.

Young, Art. "Rebuilding Community in the English Department." *Writing across the Disciplines: Research into Practice.* Ed. Art Young and Toby Fulwiler. Upper Montclair, NJ: Boynton/Cook, 1986.

11 My Story of Wildacres, 1983–1998

Sam Watson

Personal Knowledge. *Those are terms, which our culture keeps as separate as oil and water. If scientist-philosopher Michael Polanyi could articulate the chemistry which bonds them, if he could make good on that bold title of his, then he had something to say to me, a beginning teacher of writing. I wrote a dissertation to find out (1973), and ever since I've been plumbing those depths—or at least fishing in those waters. Writing wants to be more than reporting; our language involves our learning. Persons able to take those lessons to heart find their learning transformed—and their living.*

At least 280 different faculty members from all colleges and virtually all departments at UNC Charlotte. Some 225 additional colleagues from sixty other institutions in twenty states, as far away as Michigan, New York, and Missouri. Colleagues from across institutions and all disciplines, comprising groups from thirty to nearly a hundred. Those are the persons who came together for one—or, for many participants, for most—of the annual three-day working retreat, which the UNC Charlotte Writing Project sponsored at Wildacres, 1983 to 1998. Those are the numbers. But beneath numbers, any numbers, which really count, are stories. This article is largely my story of the writing retreats at Wildacres, over a sixteen-year span—the conditions under which they began, the nature of the Wildacres place and the retreats we held there, the reception they met back on the university campus. That is the story I am telling.

A full story calls forth other voices. So this article includes a representative sample of reflections from participants at the Wildacres retreats. (Quotations from Wildacres participants come from their written reflections and are printed here with their writers' permission). Finally Dr. Ron Lunsford, who attended the first retreat in 1983 as Writing Project Director from Clemson University and in 1991 was commissioned to study the status of the then-current "writing-intensive" movement at UNC Charlotte as he was joining our university as Chair of English, has agreed to write the epilogue on the Wildacres retreats and their influences. His perspective is an authoritative counterpoint to my own.

THE WRITING PROJECT

The story of the writing retreats for UNC Charlotte faculty at Wildacres is a series of accidents or, to use a more polite word, serendipities, and one stubborn person. The stubborn person would be me; the accidents, I say with neither regret nor self-congratulation, were ones which I helped cause, although they were the sort which no single person could ever bring about alone. And like Coleridge's ancient mariner, I feel that the story insofar as I knew it and have lived it, is now finished. All but its telling. It is a sobering story in some respects, and here I am telling it as frankly as circumstances allow me to. (For example I usually refer to university administrators without giving names. I have learned the hard way that they prize their anonymity.) Looking back now, I can see that the tradition of our Wildacres retreats arose from a confluence of factors that came together at a fortuitous time in our university's history, beginning more than twenty years ago. Though the retreats continued under leadership other than mine, it is difficult for me to imagine that anything like them could take root now. Thus it is important to understand the conditions under which the retreats arose. The most important single condition was the presence on our campus of an active site of the National Writing Project.

"All those people do, is drink coffee and laugh," muttered one of my professorial colleagues one summer morning as he stomped past the Writing Project classroom of our invitational institute. We *did* ingest lots of coffee and donuts (and some fresh fruit). We *were* having great fun. Maybe nothing more could be seen from outside, but a great deal more was being born within that room.

In 1979 Leon Gatlin and I had begun a Writing Project at UNC Charlotte. From within the Project, we had both experienced and seen its powers for personal renewal; we had come to believe in its potentials for effective educational improvement. Begun in 1973 by Jim Gray and other teachers in California and by now active in all fifty states, (http://www.writingproject.org/; Silberman; National Writing Project) the basic Writing Project model is simple in its assumptions. And common-sensical in its program designs. And revolutionary in its implications.

Among the Writing Project's bedrock principles are these:
- Those who teach writing need to do some writing themselves.
- Teachers know things.
- Across the dividing lines of grade levels, institutions, and academic disciplines, teachers deserve to come together to act on what they know and to articulate their understandings for themselves (often for the first time ever), making their knowledge accessible to other teachers.
- The best teacher of teachers is not an expert, not a theory. It is another teacher.

In sum, the Writing Project model is determinedly grass-roots, co-operative and collaborative, "bottom-up."

It is all too easy for policy-makers and legislators of education to overlook the obvious—"Teachers at the Center," as the title of Jim Gray's memoir of early Writing Project history puts it. The Writing Project is a grassroots movement of, by, and for teachers, welcoming them within a mutually-sustaining and energizing professional community of a kind which many have never before experienced. Within our own Project institutes and workshops, it *was* great fun, to be shaping our own words onto paper and sharing them—drafts, notes, warts and all—with colleagues who listened and helped. It *was* great fun temporarily to become "students" in one another's classrooms, experiencing classroom strategies for writing and taking stock of our own, in light of what we were learning. As Leon had put it, "The Project is about writing, sure. But even more, it's about *learning,* for teachers and students." It's all so very simple, really. So obvious. But, in part because this model is grounded in an epistemology very different from (if complementary to) the "delivery system" assumptions which tend still to shape universities and schools, it is also thoroughly alien to much educational practice (Watson "Teachers," "Writing," "Who," "Coming").

One day in the early spring of 1983 my telephone rang. Phillip Blumenthal, Charlotte-based philanthropist and Director of the private Wildacres retreat center, was on the other end. Wildacres had had a cancellation for May 5–9; could I fill that gap in the Wildacres schedule? I said "Yes," without any clear idea what to do next, or how. What I did was to call a brainstorming meeting, of a few faculty friends (virtually all of them from beyond the English department) who had taken an active interest in writing and a few K-12 Teacher-Consultants of our Writing Project.

That such a meeting could even be called suggests the considerable groundwork with respect to writing that was well under way at our university. From the beginning, our Wildacres story was a Writing Project story, in several respects. For one thing, the invitational Writing Project summer institutes provided many participating teachers their first graduate-level contact with the university, and a number of them had gone on to advanced degree programs here. They proved themselves excellent students; their confidence and abilities were beginning to influence the attitudes of some of their professors; their presence was contributing to a more positive atmosphere regarding writing, in the English department and beyond. And, as I have said, we had seen the energies and renewal, both professional and personal, enjoyed by participating K-12 teachers. Surely there could be some way to make such energies, such professional growth, accessible to our professorial colleagues as well. The Writing Project model bills itself as K-university, but it has rarely been that in practice. Furthermore, if there were ways to bring university faculty and K-12 teachers *together*, they would learn significantly from one another, the university teachers catching some of their K-12 colleagues' enthusiasm and fresh ideas, while their presence might also provide some "critical correctives" to enthusiasms which can flame out from their own excess.

By the time Wildacres began for us, we had been fruitlessly seeking tangible university-level support for the Writing Project. I in particular had made myself a pest among our administrators (when I showed one the numbers of K-12 teachers who had gone on to begin graduate degree programs, the response was, "If they didn't take these classes, I wouldn't have the expense of teaching them.") To requests for any university funding for the Writing Project, administrators' standard counter-argument was that while the Project might be fine for K-12 teachers and their students, it was doing nothing for the university itself. That argument was a challenge, an argument that begged to be removed.

Another condition was the happy accident of Dixie Goswami. Dixie had joined us for the 1982–3 year, on a half-time basis, thanks to a grant from the Blumenthal Foundation. The idea was for her to lay groundwork for what we would call a "Center for Literacy Education," which would have served as a clearinghouse for literacy concerns across our campus and throughout the educational community of our region and would have provided the Writing Project with a solid institutional base within the university structure. (At that point, the Project really reported to no one; it was seen pretty much as "what Sam and Leon do." An enviable status perhaps, but also one which, for the long haul, is bound to be unhealthy.) I had hoped that Dixie would become the full time director of that center, but when Phillip Blumenthal offered us Wildacres, she had just announced that she had taken a job for the next year elsewhere. While she was here, though, Dixie had held a Blumenthal Seminar on Communications on our campus, drawing on luminaries from IBM and Rennsellear Polytechnic Institute, and attracting some forty faculty from across the UNC Charlotte campus for a day-long, intensive discussion of their interests and needs in communications. She had established an effective teacher-research group at an elementary school that Shirley Brice Heath was later to call "a model school" and had worked with other teachers throughout our Writing Project. And throughout the year she had held conversations and workshops with individual university faculty and their classes in ways that perhaps only Dixie can.

Finally, and from an institutional perspective most importantly, change was afoot in our program of General Education. The intent was to move away from the smorgasbord, essentially political array of courses confronting students, to one that would help them develop abilities and understandings needed by educated people. Most notably, the new program would include "writing intensive" courses, where writing of a variety of forms and purposes would be integral *to* the courses and where class sections would be kept small enough to allow for individual attention. A set of flexible, intelligent guidelines was drawn up for these courses, and the new Council on General Education, which Leon Gatlin chaired, was empowered to approve those course proposals. But the large question loomed: Where would faculty come from, to propose and teach these courses across our curriculum? The university found itself facing an urgent need for faculty development in writing.

Those were the conditions we found ourselves within, when Phillip Blumenthal called: A Writing Project whose vitality had proven itself but that remained essentially "homeless" within the university structure; the part-time and effective presence of Dixie Goswami, and the need to help our university faculty prepare themselves for sorts of instruction that had rarely if ever been part of their experience. In our brainstorming meeting toward the first Wildacres retreat, we decided that we would invite Directors from across the National Writing Project network to share the Wildacres facilities with us, conducting essentially their own separate retreat (it was the first such retreat ever held within the National Writing Project). At the same time we would invite all UNC Charlotte faculty to join us for our own retreat, which Dixie and I would lead. Thanks to remaining grant money, each faculty member would be asked to pay just $30.00 for three days in a comfortable resort setting in the Blue Ridge mountains. And as part of their registration, we asked each to send us a brief statement of the particular interests and needs they would bring.

Those brief statements from colleagues gave them some investment in the retreat. As I read through them, time and again I found myself moved. Here were persons who saw the importance of writing, their own and that of their students. They wanted to help students improve, but they expressed little sense of how. They knew that writing was something that they too were expected to do, but many felt equally at a loss there. These colleagues seemed intimidated by writing, even cowed. As one of them put it, "My typewriter is my enemy." I could not resist taking some of their statements into an Expository Writing class I was currently teaching and reading them, orally and anonymously, to those students. Their spontaneous reactions were at once exciting, instructive, and sobering: "These professors have the same anxieties about writing that we do." "I didn't know there were professors like that at UNC Charlotte." "These are professors I would *want* to take courses with." "Who *are* these professors??" Of course, I gave them no names.

WILDACRES: THE PLACE

Dedicated to "the betterment of human relations"; that is the mission and motto of Wildacres, where a granite tablet in the stone fireplace of the north lodge reminds us, "Behold how good it is to dwell in harmony with nature and one another." Wildacres began quite differently, as a land speculation. In the 1920's North Carolina native Thomas Dixon, most widely remembered as author of the racist novel *The Klansman,* which became the movie *Birth of a Nation,* bought up land with the idea of establishing a cultural resort and selling spacious lots for expensive houses. The Great Depression ended that dream and in 1936 I. D. Blumenthal, now buried at Wildacres, put in the only bid at a court sale. His bid was so low that a clerk of the Texas-based court was sent out to inspect the property with him.

I.D. loved to tell the story of that day. It went like this: "I led him through the boarded-up buildings with a flashlight. Even outside, you couldn't see your hand before your face. Upstairs and down, from one lodge to the other took about twenty minutes. It was eerie, and the poor man soon had enough. He asked me if I was going to try to buy this God-forsaken place. I told him that when God gave Moses the Ten Commandments, the mountain was covered with a cloud. If it was good enough for Moses, it was good enough for me." Several days later, the offer of $6,500 was accepted. Wildacres belonged to I.D. Blumenthal. He regarded it as a miracle. At first he didn't know what he wanted to do with it, but he was truly religious, and he believed God had bestowed this gift upon him for a purpose. He never felt that his wealth should be used for himself ("Wildacres").

Beginning in 1946 Wildacres has hosted innumerable non-profit civic, cultural, educational, inter-faith, and crafts-based groups in retreats of varying lengths. Participants, up to a hundred or more, are housed in comfortable, motel-style rooms of its two lodges and provided home-cooked meals served family style, all at incredibly modest rates. (More than half the operating budget comes from Wildacres owner and sponsor, the Blumenthal Foundation.) Rocking chairs line the porches and the flagstone patio connecting the two lodges, looking up to Mt. Mitchell in the distance. There are numerous trails for mountain hiking, meeting rooms, a recently-built library and professional-quality concert hall. Rooms have no locks, and beyond cautions about the dangers of fire, pleas for water conservation, and prohibition of in-doors smoking, there are no rules. (We were once asked to mute the first "happy hour" of our retreat. It seems we were sharing Wildacres that night with a Temperance Union group.) There are no televisions, no Internet connections, just one pay phone, and the nearest towns are some fifteen miles distant. The only requirements are that each group must conduct some sort of educational program for its members and, of course, must be granted a slot in the crowded Wildacres schedule.

Our First Wildacres Retreat

The last hurrah for a failed effort; that's what I thought our Wildacres retreat would be. Efforts of a year and more had indeed come to naught. Dixie Goswami had taken a job elsewhere; the continuing projects we had hoped for would not happen, and we were spending the last of our grant money on the retreat itself. Dixie and I would lead the retreat; she would be saying goodbye to friends she had made throughout the year; I would be welcoming Writing Project directors from across the country, who would essentially be running their own separate retreat. But mainly I would be saying a sincere thank you to colleagues while we gave ourselves a three-day taste of what might have been.

Throughout that Tuesday afternoon participants straggled in, some thirty in each of the two groups. In our central meeting room I had laden a large table with textbooks on writing and monographs on writing across the curriculum, not hoping that anyone would read them but knowing that university colleagues are impressed by printed pages. Those books were there merely to suggest that there would be *substance* to what we would be doing.

Whatever that would be. Dixie was running late (of course). Our first agenda item was a predinner BYOB happy hour on the flagstone patio; while colleagues wandered awkwardly about, drinks in hand, not knowing quite why they were there, I quietly worried the same thoughts. Dixie arrived by the dinner bell; we huddled briefly; the loose plans we had laid for the retreat, while we had been still safely back on campus, began again to assume some sense of direction.

That evening, after a brief welcoming session, Writing Project directors went off to organize their own retreat. (As one UNC Charlotte colleague put it later, "Those Writing Project people came on like the New York Yankees in their pin-stripe uniforms. I felt like I was on a sand-lot team, the last player chosen.") Dixie and I gathered our sand-lot folks and went to work. It was a busy evening, but as non-threatening as we knew how to make it. We introduced writing as process, using a 3x5 card activity adapted from Don Murray. We briefly demonstrated the workings of a writing group, and asked people to form into small writing groups, which would continue to meet, at times, and places of their choice, throughout the retreat. Finally Dixie introduced double-entry journaling and handed out an Ann Berthoff article, asking that we write our way through it by the next morning. And we retired for the night, me to a well-earned stiff bourbon and, with others, a hymn-sing around the piano.

Wednesday and Thursday we held a couple of scheduled sessions each day, of a couple hours each, inviting people to consider the various ways we actually write and to consider ways that writing might be woven into courses they were teaching, such that it might strengthen the courses rather than being merely a burden to students and themselves. But most of the hours were left deliberately open, for writing groups to meet as they wished and for participants to do what they wanted. Dixie and I were available to talk with people, and the books were available for browsing (a few of them actually *were* picked up). Thursday evening was a read-around. We gathered around the stone hearth in the main Wildacres lobby. Anyone was free to read anything they had written, and a number did. Perhaps everyone in that room shared the feelings I found myself having; I was humbled by the courage my colleagues were showing, some of them timidly sharing some halting initial efforts, others reading their own eloquent words with an unexpected passion, all of us I think surprised and awed by the varied voices we were hearing.

Friday morning there was one final session with my UNC Charlotte colleagues. I asked that we write briefly, listing as many as three things we wanted to do differently, next fall back on campus, in light of our experiences at Wildacres. Then we reported out our wishes. One colleague from the business college hesitantly announced that he would be leaving us to return to graduate school in the fall. "But I know what I'm going to do," he said. "I'm going to establish a writing/learning group with other students." He was greeted with cheers and applause from across the room. Another colleague, who would be on sabbatical next semester, announced that after the three days he was already farther along than he had expected to be in a month of work alone. Others talked about ways they wanted to try incorporating writing into their courses, while others most wanted to be members of continuing writing groups, to encourage their own work. When we got to our philosopher colleague Steve Fishman, he said, "Sam, I'm going to flunk this test. I don't have three things, I have only one. I'm going to change my life." And Steve did just that. He has gone on to write and publish any number of powerfully written stories from his own childhood, and with Lucille McCarthy he has twice won the James Britton award for outstanding research ("Boundary"; *John Dewey*).

Throughout that closing session, I had heard a chorus of calls for support from our university administration for what we had been doing. We had come together and, amidst our anxieties and uncertainties, we had actually *written,* rather than merely talking "about" writing or bemoaning its status. The presence of Writing Project directors had been important to us in informal ways; over drinks and dinner tables, they had offered glimpses of educational successes that just might be possible. We had talked with one another in ways that the distractions and pretensions of campus life rarely allow; we had come to value each other anew as persons, friends, colleagues. Not the final celebration of a failure at all, our initial Wildacres retreat had clearly become a new beginning. I drove down the mountain that day with renewed gratitude for my colleagues in the Writing Project movement and, especially, a new sense of responsibility to my colleagues at UNC Charlotte.

OUR SUBSEQUENT WILDACRES RETREATS

Perhaps in any endeavor, there can be only one "first" experience. Teachers find that, who participate in a Writing Project more than once, and we found it in our subsequent Wildacres retreats. Only once can there be the initial uncertainties, anxieties, excitements and innocence. It's not that subsequent experiences are "not as good," but they are distinctly different.

Wildacres became an annual affair for our university, retreats held during the few days between spring exams and graduation. Funding was secured by begging a reluctant university administration and by a series of local Curriculum and Instructional Development grants; funding would never have been forthcoming, except for the pressure the university had placed upon itself, to develop writing-intensive courses adequate to its new set of general degree requirements. We began inviting other universities and colleges to send colleagues to join us at Wildacres. Their payments helped finance our retreats, for one thing. For another, I expected that university administrators back on campus, like my colleagues participating at Wildacres, would be quietly and usefully impressed that these retreats were good enough that people "from off" would attend.

The next several retreats, I ran myself. But doing the work of planning, administering, registering on-site and conducting sessions was too much for any one person. Even more important, any number of "old" participants kept coming back for subsequent retreats; I tried separating out "old" from "new" participants, conducting separate sessions for each: returning participants would have a distinctly different agenda, while "new" ones needed the re-orientation with regard to writing, and deserved something of the "high," that others of us had experienced at the first Wildacres. But the separations of groups did not work well; most participants wanted to be in both groups, afraid of "missing something."

So that everyone would at least get to hear some voice other than mine, I began bringing in a guest consultant for each of our retreats. The list includes Nancy Martin, Amanda Branscombe, Patricia L. Stock, Barbara Walvoord, Peter Elbow, Toby Fulwiler, biologist Craig Nelson of Indiana University, engineer Karl Smith of the University of Minnesota, and Darlene Forrest of Bard College, doing a masterful job of filling in for the just-deceased Paul Connelly.

I regret that I ceased inviting leading K-12 teachers from our own Writing Project to join us. Their presence had been important to the vitality of the retreats and the depth of discussion, but from university colleagues I was hearing reluctance to participate with their public school colleagues, and I needed to do everything possible, to expand the ranks of "new" participants from our own faculty.

The themes of retreats varied some from year to year, given the expertise of our guest consultants and perceived needs and interests at our university. For instance the Wildacres with Craig Nelson focused on using group work and writing in large classes; the ones with Karl Smith (he came twice) focused on instituting and effectively managing group processes, and Darlene Forrest led us to consider ways we could help our students become more effective readers of difficult texts.

In a way the most notable retreat was one in which I had no visible hand. The political climate on campus had turned particularly hostile that year, and when my anthropologist colleague Gary Ferraro called to ask about plans for Wildacres, I told him that there would be no retreat that May. Gary was determined that the tradition not die; he organized and conducted the retreat that May, with me merely helping from the background.

My own favorite retreat was one where we had no guest consultant and where our focus was not on "writing" but on "learning." I asked several colleagues to present illustrative classes from their respective disciplines. The rest of us served as students, learning as we could (I even achieved a toehold in the mysteries of calculus!) Then we reflected on the learning strategies we had been employing, the "mental muscles" we had been called upon to exercise. And only then did we consider ways that writing might serve to strengthen those "mental muscles."

The Thursday evening read-arounds continued as a staple of our retreats. In each, we continued to do some writing of our own and we formed small writing/discussion groups, which met, though perhaps never with the intensity of the first retreat. One colleague, an art historian who had told me how dreary he was finding the traditional academic writing he felt obliged to do, began writing of a different sort at one of the retreats. Before the next spring's retreat he called me: Could he read his writing at Wildacres? It turned out to be a 1900-page book from the perspective of Eric the Red (he read parts of it to the rest of us).

In each retreat we had a number of formal sessions, designed to leave participants with provocative questions and promising possibilities. Those sessions were necessary, but the most important hours were the many *in*formal ones, when participants were free to do whatever they wished. Various ones of us found ourselves thinking new thoughts while walking on a mountain trail, and time after time we were amazed to learn of the commonality and educational commitments we shared with colleagues, from whom disciplinary boundaries keep us largely separated while on campus. Those informal times were, I think, the real seedbed of importance at Wildacres, times within which we found personal and professional renewal and which led to lasting instructional changes back at the university. Partly for that reason I did everything I could, to encourage colleagues to come to Wildacres on time and to stay through the end. But we university folks are busy people and, perhaps even more than members of our harried culture at large, we measure self-worth by the demands we perceive on our time. (I recall one participant who came late, left early, and back at the university complained that he had not gotten a sense of "closure.")

Meanwhile, Back at the University

Wildacres became the most visible annual activity of a genuinely grassroots faculty development effort, always under Writing Project auspices, which both sustained the retreats and was sustained by them. In the year following the initial retreat we did establish faculty writing groups, three of them comprising some twenty-five colleagues, which met weekly through the year and in which members developed their own writing, both personal and professional; some members found themselves publishing professionally for the first time ever. As occasions permitted, on campus we hosted brief workshops and public lectures, by such leaders as James Moffett and Janet Emig. Perhaps most notably, Paul Ricoeur and Louise W. Phelps met for the first time in an evening of public lectures they gave here, while Louise was completing the issue of *Pre/Text* on Ricoeur's work that she was editing. As an intellectual community, I wanted us to be at least aware of the conceptual depths that writing across the curriculum has but seldom acknowledges.

Dr. Loy Witherspoon of Religious Studies provided initiative and funding for an annual writing contest in memory of a former student, Loch Walker. Students submitted essays reflecting on their own writing histories and experiences; where possible these were judged by former guest consultants of our Wildacres retreats, who also wrote commentaries on the essays and on our writing efforts at the university as they saw them. Winning essays and judges' commentaries were published in a newsletter to all faculty, *Writing Talks,* with the idea that we could learn valuable lessons by listening to our students and by seeing our work in the larger contexts our consultants provided.

Three different times, the university funded semester-length seminars for small groups of faculty, meeting weekly to discuss writing and its implementation in their classes. In 1990 Janet Smith and I edited and distributed to all faculty *What's Happening with Writing at UNC Charlotte? Writing Intensive Developments in Context,* a 125-page booklet whose heart consisted of interview and questionnaire responses from 55 faculty across the campus. Its Preface catches the spirit of

our on-campus efforts and suggests their indebtedness to the Wildacres retreats:

> A simple way to [define "writing intensive"
> courses]would be by administrative (or faculty) fiat,
> pointing to some one single model to which "writing
> intensive" courses implicitly should adhere or even
> by laying down some single set of rigorous guide-
> lines and standards to which any "writing intensive"
> course must conform.

There is another way and, thankfully, it is the way
the university has chosen: What is "writing intensive"
coming to mean as faculty come to incorporate writing into their coursework, in varieties of ways, across
varieties of disciplines? To ask the question in this
manner, is to allow the "writing intensive" concept
over time to achieve sharper focus and definition that
is clearer, richer, more variegated. It is to encourage
writing intensive work to become more surely woven
into the warp and woof of instructional methods and
the institution's life. It is to open toward kinds of active inquiry and continuing conversation, familiar to
us in our roles as scholars, which also can sustain our
efforts as teachers.

This booklet is a contribution to this continuing
conversation. At its center are descriptions, by faculty from a wide range of disciplines, of how and why
and with what effects they are incorporating writing
in their courses. These descriptions, useful in themselves, also will enable faculty to identify colleagues
with whom they could usefully talk. Such conversations contribute to an atmosphere of supportive discussion and mutual inquiry, on a topic that is important to the university and to our students' education.

The booklet presents sample strategies and identi-
fies potential resource persons on the faculty. It also
provides a sample of student experience, in the award-
winning essays of this first year of the Loch Walker

writing contest. And reflections by the nationally
known judges of that contest provide something of
an outsider's perspective on what we are doing. The
variety of voices and stances, which this booklet rep-
resents, helps us to infer questions, which invite our
further conversation.

"Continuing the conversation." That was the watchphraseand mo-
tive for our visible efforts on campus. Crucial to the continuing conversation was largely unseen work, at times virtually subterranean. A
small *ad hoc* groups of faculty continued to meet, regularly, to seek out
possibilities and chart directions. Our Wednesday afternoon sessions
were held in the student union, and anyone was welcome to come. Dr.
Ron Gestwicki of Religious Studies, whose patience and quiet persis-
tence made him the group's leader, kept reminding us that the task
was to figure what "next steps" should be, what would help "keep
the conversation going." But the group's attention turned more and
more to issues of institutional acknowledgement and administrative
support; from our perspective, university administrators were greet-
ing our efforts with bewilderment, denial, or hostility. (As I recall,
only one administrator ever sat in on these sessions, once. As he was
leaving he merely commented, "You people are working too hard.")
Grassroots faculty commitment was festering into frustration; my own
frustrations are suggested in the titles of professional talks I gave during those years, "As the Expressive in Writing Meets the Institutional
in Education" (CCCC, New Orleans, 1986) and "When the Voluntary Becomes Required: Failures of Convergence at UNC Charlotte"
(NCTE, Los Angeles, 1987).

In 1989 Dr. James Woodward became Chancellor of UNC Charlotte. Our group of committed faculty, which by then had become a
quasi-official "Writing-Intensive Advisory Committee," requested to
meet with him. Over the space of several months Chancellor Woodward met with us twice, lending a thoughtful ear to discussions that
laid out the accomplishments of our initiatives and made clear the
frustrations we were feeling. He decided that far more was indeed
being done than could be expected of any committee, and he directed
his administrators to establish a line position for someone to lead these
efforts.

There were a number of false starts, and two national searches
were held. In 1993 I was named as Director of University Writing

Programs. Though now officially sanctioned, in some ways the work became more difficult. In particular, faculty who had taken leadership roles, now tended to assume that their leadership was no longer needed. The holy grail of "research" was becoming an increasing preoccupation across our rapidly growing and changing campus; faculty writing groups and informal sessions to discuss classroom strategies dwindled to nothing. I had given everything I had, but mine was an increasingly lonely job; after five years of it, I resigned. The 1998 Wildacres was the last retreat I led or attended.

In 1993 I was honored with the university's NationsBank Award for Excellence in Teaching, at least in part as a result of the work I had done with faculty development across our campus. In accepting that honor, here is part of what I said:

> As part of this year's Teaching Week, yesterday some of us heard Dr. Fred Shair of the Jet Propulsion Laboratory, talk about scholarship and teaching. He ended by emphasizing the centrality, in all that we do, of *community*. That is a word we don't always know how to take seriously in academic circles; it is a quality toward which we often do not know how to work. I certainly don't have the answers, but I have learned this. In a university, perhaps in any complex institution, there is an understandable tendency to *listen up*, students to faculty, faculty to administrators, and to *talk down*. There is nothing wrong with that, but it needs to be balanced; we need also to *speak up* and *listen down*. We need not be locked into an either/or lie; it is a both/and world.

WHAT I MAKE OF IT ALL

Wildacres began by accident. But it became an annual anticipation for our faculty, something to which they could look forward at the end of a hard academic year. Its effects touched faculty who never participated directly and students who probably never heard of Wildacres. For example two students, who had experienced writing-to-learn activities as part of a Religious Studies course, approached their Business professor in a subsequent semester: would she be willing to add these writing practices to her own course? Wildacres became known as *the* premier faculty development initiative at our university, and within our general education program, the writing-intensive domain still is considered the only one which amounted to more than a reshuffling of what already was.

Within our teaching and across our institutions of learning, how do we do more than reshuffle what already is? That is a vital question, a foundational one. If my teaching is not also my learning, my teaching slowly dies and I with it. If our students are merely presented preexisting categories, they are learning from a distance. And their learning is probably temporary; they are untouched by it. If our institutions of learning merely repackage and re-present what is presumably already known, I do not see how they can seriously be considered institutions of learning.

The question of learning which matters, of educational and institutional change, which lasts, is a vitally important one. My story of Wildacres shows that I did not manage to enact answers adequate to it. Part of the answer, I remain convinced, goes back to the matters of "speaking up and listening down" which I mentioned above. To invoke a metaphor of electricity, it is as though our institutions typically are powered by "direct current" only; communication tends to go in only one direction, from faculty to students, from administration to faculty. Alternating current is more efficient, and it travels further. Any human world is a both/and world; our institutions and our classes need to live within such a world.

Our Wildacres retreats fomented a faculty development movement, which was genuinely grassroots. For the crucial first five years and despite my best efforts and those of other faculty, our administration shared no ownership of this movement. Don Gallehr once said to me, "If you get too far out front, you start looking like the enemy." There is no question that others and I were very much "out front." Our administrators did not know what to do with this movement, and there is good reason to believe that they felt threatened by it. In some respects they have my sympathy. Here was something so brimming with enthusiasm that it must be mainly froth; it couldn't be very good, surely, all this attention to writing that falls beyond (and I would say, lies beneath, informing) the strictures of traditional academic types. Before something bewildering, one response is to try to make sense of it. Another is to force it into familiar categories, under the mistaken assumption that one understands what one has categorized. Over time I think that is what happened with Wildacres and all that it represented; members of the movement were carried away with "writing to learn," whereas the proper business of the university is "writing to communicate." As though those have nothing to do with one another.

Much of my intellectual orientation is grounded in my understanding of scientist-philosopher Michael Polanyi (Emig et al.; Watson, "Polanyi and the Contexts"; "Polanyi's Epistemology"; "Polanyi"), and it is informed by the successes I have observed within the National Writing Project movement. I believe that lasting educational changes, like the development of renewed and deeper understandings generally, are rooted in grounds which are essentially informal, whether those be the "tacit" and "personal" processes of an individual learner or the "communal" ones of a group sharing similar standards and exploratory aims. Within my own classes and across our university I have done what I could to cultivate those grounds, never I trust as an end in itself or calling attention to itself, but as foundational to the achievements of personal assurance and of knowledge which we all desire and deserve. Perhaps because "foundations" do their work quietly, beneath the surface, we tend not to cultivate our own; mine is a view, which the academy tends not to acknowledge or perhaps even to share.

For several years I had a pair of cowboy boots hanging through a hole in the ceiling, in the corner of my university office. A reminder not to take myself seriously, those boots also led to some interesting conversations. Visiting students and teaching colleagues would notice them hanging there at some point, utter a shocked exclamation, then ask me to explain. *That's me, at the end of a bad day.* Or, *It's the last student who asked to be excused from an assignment.* Or, *It's a professor strung up for not publishing enough.* Occasionally an administrator would wander into my office. Administrators were different. At some point I could see them taking an instantaneous glance at those hanging boots. Then without comment, they would deliberately focus their eyes someplace else. The cowboy boots hanging from my ceiling did not fit into the world of their categories; the boots simply were not there.

Was the Wildacres experience really "there"? It was, though I understand how reasonable people could discount or dismiss it. But it is past for me, all but my telling of the story here. As I write these words, our university is again reconstructing its program of general education. I understand that "writing-intensive" courses will become ones of "writing in the disciplines," as though many of our students will ever go on to become members of the academic "disciplines" in which they are majoring. The change does not seem like progress to me.

My days of actively worrying such matters are thankfully past. In the privacy of my own classes I am working with students on matters of reflection ("WAC, WHACK"), which I increasingly see as the fertile ground for writing and learning and, for me, perhaps the most lasting lesson from the Wildacres retreats. And to encourage reflection I am asking students to explore with me the possibilities of a "mindings collage," a place where we write in many varied modes as we cultivate our own interests and, really, our own minds. And I am asking how best to live, what best to say, in the dark times, which our nation is entering. But all of that is, as they say, a different story.

To See Ourselves as Others See Us

I promised other voices. Written by participants, the following reflections express the spirit and suggest the contexts of our Wildacres retreats.

❧

As I sit in a weather-beaten rocking chair on the balcony of the rustic lodge, I gaze out over the tree-covered mountains and see a spectrum of shading, from the light green of the leaves in the sun to the darker green of the next level of hills and, finally, to increasingly darker shades of grayish purple.

Around me, people sit, just as I am sitting, and gaze at the same hills. I am surrounded by writers. One who sits in the corner rocking chair in front of me frequently raises her head— contemplating? seeking inspiration? Daydreaming? Another has placed her rocking chair in the shade. Her feet on another chair, Coke in hand, she writes on what looks like graph paper. Below me, other people write—feet propped up on the bench in front of them, most writing on yellow lined pads, just as I do. Another sits cross-legged on the flagstones; he's writing on white paper. Occasionally we gaze at the hills and silently rock. We are a community of writers. I don't know what they are writing about as individually they take something from the scene and make it part of themselves, as they put pen to yellow lined paper and make connections.

These connections, it seems to me, have different levels, different shades of intensity. We make individual connections. We refocus our connections. We are isolated. Yet we are a community of writers. I don't know—I can't remember—it isn't important which of us teaches English, history, math—we are a community of writers. I see some now-familiar faces, yet I can't recall the names. As I sit here, hearing the birds and the wind, I don't need to remember names—or even faces. We are a community of writers. In my small response group I may share this writing; I may not. I may hear someone else's writing; I may not. But even if I don't share their words, we still come together as a community of writers.

Someone in front of me moves her chair. She does it quietly so as not to disturb her fellow writers. She does not want to impose upon "my" space—nor do I want her to. There will be time for that later . . . or never . . . but no matter. We, as a community of writers, share the essential belief that writing can and does make a difference, for by writing and by introspection, we learn about ourselves as individuals. And we can't be a community of writers sharing a common bond unless we first come to an understanding of our SELVES. And we can't be a community of teachers of writers until we understand that.

The value of Wildacres, it seems to me, is to have a place where it's all right to sit in a rocking chair, to gaze at the mountains, to cover a yellow or white pad with scrawls—to share an unspoken, common bond with other writers and teachers of writers. As we respect each other's need for private contemplation, we find our sense of community.

❧

I want to get my thoughts down fast, before they fade. To me, [the booklet] What Is Happening with Writing at UNC Charlotte is a remarkable coming together of dedicated teachers who see writing as a major tool in disciplines as varied as ROTC, nursing, art, philosophy, political science, anthropology, etc. What this book tells me is that many students at UNC Charlotte will have not only the direct benefit of becoming more practiced and thereby, I think, more confident writers, but they also will have the experience of working with teachers who take seriously their task of helping students to learn how to learn. I assume that UNC Charlotte, like universities everywhere, has its share of dead wood, but in my three visits to Wildacres I haven't seen any of it. The people I have talked with there, listened to as presenters, or discovered through vignettes in the "green book"; all without exception impress me as teachers concerned to become better teachers.

I am impressed by the conclusions that intensive writing courses generally result in better writing, in a more lively classroom atmosphere, and in more enjoyable teaching. On page after page march many, many ideas about how writing is used, and all of these many ideas revolving in one's brain set off charges that produce writing activities uniquely tailored by your colleagues from "Off" for classrooms far away. Last year I came away from Wildacres with Sam's letter writing scheme, which I adapted for my senior level Milton seminar; this year, I have relearned some uses of freewriting and collaborative writing which will show upin my advanced English literature courses.

On the smaller campus where I teach, I believe it will be easier for teachers to be recognized for classroom innovation and research. But I imagine the percentage of people who open themselves initially to what is (for most) a new pedagogy will not be much higher than at UNC Charlotte. We'll see. We're just beginning our Writing Across the Curriculum program. I am impressed by what UNC Charlotte has already accomplished.

⚹

Here are some other comments from the booklet that I have copied out for my continued reflection as workshop leader in terms of what participants found most helpful.

"Teaching a writing intensive class encourages you to take chances." "I am convinced that our goal as educators must be to create universities where students learn to think and to educate themselves. Writing is an essential component of this process. . . ."

Larry Barden's use of double entry and especially his good feeling about it: *"I think it's probably the best thing that I do all semester, because the students really do a good job on this. It's amazing."*

The struggles of one professor that have led her to seeing the value of writing for the development of her students as worth the enormous time she must put into preparing and evaluating assignments.

The journal assignments of Shelley Crisp, which I will adapt for a Women Writers course I teach.

The awareness of students as developing writers: *"If they don't write well in this course, their grade may drop half a point, but that's all. Later, the results of poor writing may be far more damaging." (Ferraro)* I really like his assignment for students to analyze what people throw away, and I'm determined to try to adapt it for a freshman composition class.

"I also believe firmly that students don't learn anything if they don't see a connection between what's being presented to them and their own lives." The notebooks of Camus and Einstein and Darwin offer at least some evidence that frequent informal writing forms the seedbed for more formal, audience-oriented pieces. These informal writings are the scaffolding for later pieces, a kind of nest or safe place in which good learners record impressions, ask themselves questions, invite their unconscious to come forward with surprising discoveries.

"There seemed to be a possibility that 'this just might work.'" Good teaching is frequently the result of openness to the idea that "this just might work." I wonder with Dan what special problems foreign students might encounter in writing-intensive courses.

The connection between a writing assignment and a broader classroom goal: *"When we finish I use the letters as a starting point for class discussion of the article. This approach seems to break the ice, and reduces the uncomfortable silence that often accompanies, 'Let's discuss so-and-so article.'"*

"There are lots of reasons why students have been taught to avoid 'I,' having to do with the whole notion of objectivity, critical thinking, all those words that we hear. Schools, especially the universities, seem to be very suspicious of anything that is subjective, personal, or elusive. We still have great difficulty with this. . . . "

Students "seem to appreciate being empowered" through group work and consensus development. *"These definitions and answers to questions are 'theirs' as they had developed them, when in actuality the answers are very similar to the points I wished to raise with them."*

Ken Lambla's emphasis on the need for verbal skills for his architecture students is amazing to me, and showed me a new arena where writing is necessary. I am reminded of a similar discovery during my first Wildacres—about math. *"In justifying why [a computer problem] was correct, [students] discovered that it wasn't—their writing wasn't just describing something as a formality, but it became the essence of the project. It created a revision process and the internal feedback to compare what they did with known realities."* I love this kind of discovery.

"When people find something to say that they want to say, that gives power. If somebody has to say something, they find poetry. Not every time; you don't get a thousand percent batting average on this, but somehow the sense of urgency is felt in the language."

"So I'm thinking that maybe the authentic engagement from both the writing and the discussion is curiously having a positive impact, not only on the students' understanding of values, but also on their ability to memorize the details from the textbook."

"Those who use writing as a means to an end sometimes find the process of writing frustrating. A good word processor liberates the writer from much of the pain."

The Loch Walker essays are very special results of the emphasis on writing at UNC Charlotte. . . . After Michael Parker
read his Loch Walker essay at Wildacres, I told him I'd had
a similar experience of being accused of not having written
a piece of writing. (I didn't know the work plagiarism when
I was in the eleventh grade.) I think the hurt was less for
me because I was both older than Michael was when he was
accused, and also less impressed by my accuser. But I have
never forgotten the moment

Finally, here are some summary comments from two well-known
participants that give a sense of what two participants took away with
them.

*I want first to thank the sponsors of the Wildacres Seminar for
inviting me to participate in their 9th writing-intensive seminar. I feel extraordinarily grateful for the opportunity to spend
three days in extended conversations with fellow professionals
from different disciplines. Such opportunities in England today are rare, so the first thing I want to say, in addition to my
thanks, is that the nine annual occasions of the Wildacres gatherings are historical events; they happened, and, like all happen-
ings, they have had their effect (great or small) on everyone who
was there.*

*I came away with much optimism, both specific and general,
and delighted with the rich mines of practice. However, I sup-
pose it is a fact that most academics are vastly indifferent to the
nature of their colleagues' fields of study. For minorities, such as
those of us at Wildacres, the content of other people's disciplines
were of absorbing interest, and it seemed that many of the procedures used were eminently generalizable. Why should this be? I
had a stereotypic idea that sessions about other subjects would be
too obscure for me. The Faculty presentations at Wildacres made
me amend this notion and speculate about what the commonalities might be which made the content and procedures of alien
disciplines so accessible.*

*It was clear that the use of language in classrooms was one such
commonality; all the presentations gave important place to var-*

ied uses, and the focus mostly was on language, but in some sessions it shifted to examine the nature of the learning that seemed to be happening in the writings emerging from classes. This I think is the other main commonality—matters of learning, and of the teaching that is its context. One can see here the evolution of the notion that 'writing is to learn with' into more complex concepts embracing broader aspects of learning and teaching. I like to think that it is probably such a shift of focus into matters of learning, which will draw in more faculty members and create a more communicative culture throughout universities.

I came to Wildacres with two themes (threads), which were significant for me, which I had only begun to understand, and which I hoped might be seminal in our conversations. One was interpretation (or individual meaning-making); the other was the role of institutions in effecting cognitive bonds. The full force of the first changing focus hit me in the sessions connected with Steve Fishman's philosophy students where it was clear that he was as much concerned that they should articulate their responses to the ideas of the philosophers they were studying as to be articulate about those ideas. So much academic work is concerned with the transmission of accepted ideas that to encounter something different in action (not just in discussion or report) had a thunderstorm effect on me. I had a similar shock of perception at the 'read-around' when I heard Marty Tourneur's piece;—and again, going away in the van, when at my request, he produced an account of last year's retreat, and I listened to his report of the impact of the presentation on his own thinking.

In addition to looking at good practice, we should always look at the conditions in which that practice grows. I had with me an essay from Sam Watson which began, "I live institutionalized . . . Like most of you I live in a University . . . I live also in a Writing Project. . . . Those institutions, the University and the Writing Project are where I live." Powerful words. I couldn't ignore them, so I returned the bid, as it were, by raising the issue of the social bond between institutions and cognitive thinking as significant in our discussions. I think we tend to lay too much responsibility on individuals for their success or failure in initiating change. Without being too deterministic, I am sure that conditions, contests, historical circumstances, all powerfully affect ideas, actions and psychological climate; yet many of us don't make these kinds of analyses.

⚡

I have been writing this letter in my study in London looking out over my June garden and imagining myself to be listening and talking in the great lounge at Wildacres with the wind and the rain as a background to our talk. I send you all greetings, and thanks for all that you gave me. (Nancy Martin, University of London)

My twelve visits to Wildacres have always been for programs sponsored by UNC Charlotte's Writing Project, and the first time was spring, 1983. In the years before that, I had always been embarrassed when friends chided me for missing the good conferences at Little Switzerland. I really had no excuses. Often I had heard I.D. talk about Temple Israel's summer meetings at Wildacres, and Herman was always kind about sending me invitations to one academic conference after another. And then there were the Lusky and Ackerman and Pranksy families, year after year, praising the enrichment of their Yiddish weekends at Wildacres. But I resisted. I guess I am something of a stick-in-the-mud and anxious about travel and change. So it was a sort of mistake that I went in the spring of 1983, a sort of backing into it. And if I have to blame someone, it's got to be Sam Watson of our English department.

In March of that year I had seen lots of signs around campus about a first-time UNC Charlotte writing retreat. A few announcements even invaded my department mailbox. Still I continued to ignore them until I got a handwritten note from Sam. He asked if there was any chance I could come, even going so far as to promise I'd have a good time.

Of course, I dismissed his promise as innocent rhetoric. But what got me was the handwritten note. I figured Sam Watson had to be pretty desperate if he was writing me, since he knew well enough that travel, adventure, and fun weren't my things. I con-

cluded no one from our campus was going and Sam was grasping at straws. When I left for Wildacres that May weekend I traveled thinking I would help save a drowning man. It turned out I was correct, only it wasn't Sam I saved, it was myself.

Lots of things hit me when I arrived the first evening. There was I.D.'s grave, the man who once told me—as the North Carolina Hebrew Academy struggled—that if we saved one student, it would be as if we saved the world. And the dusk that evening was clear and purple cold. I started to run along the top of the mountain, clumsily jumping at tree branches, somehow filled with the vision of Wildacres, filled with the spirit of those who created and nurtured it. The simple, modest message—our deep care and love and genuine concern for one another, for all that we share, and the kind, patient, sympathetic listening for what we do not share—as in the buildings, trails, and dining hall meals. Wildacres was recognizable. I could see the Blumenthals in it and Sam Watson and a ton of pilgrims but also something of me.

Sam Watson likes to tell the story of the final session of that first UNC Charlotte writing retreat in '83. We were sitting in a circle in the large glassed room on the ground floor of the main dormitory. Afternoon sun streamed in as Sam asked us to reflect on our Wildacres experience and list three things we'd do on our return to campus. I was next to last, and I did write down three changes I would make in my teaching. They reflected the sort of writing we had been doing at Wildacres, work which had helped me see writing in new ways, as a tool of discovery and exploration, not just reporting. I listened to the other twenty or so faculty members read their lists, but when it came my turn, my own list suddenly became trivial and I put it down. 'When I get home," I said. "I think I'll do just one thing. I'll change my life." Lorraine Penninger, our school librarian who was last, then said, "I'll skip my list too. I'll just go home and watch Fishman change his life." Everyone roared. When I looked up I caught Sam from the corner of my eye, he had pulled his pipe from his mouth and he was doubled-over in laughter, banging his knee with his right fist.

*I came home and did change. And for those changes, for what I
always see mirrored at Wildacres—the quiet, generous, self-ef-
facing effort to bring us together and closer to our best selves—I
say thankyou I.D., thank you Herman and Anita, thank you
Phil, and thank you dark clouds from God who befuddled the
Texas bankruptcy court man clinging to I.D.'s arm on the day
long ago when we received our mountain. (Steve Fishman,
UNC Charlotte)*

EPILOGUE (RON LUNSFORD, UNC CHARLOTTE)

In referring to the reflections that follow his story, Sam Watson
calls them "a representative sample of voices from participants at the
Wildacres retreats." If these voices are representative of the 500-plus
people who attended these retreats, one would have to assume that
something very special happened at Wildacres. They are; and it did.

I was there from the beginning—that first retreat in the spring of
1983. Like many who came I suspect, I had little idea just what might
happen. But I knew that Sam would be there. And that was enough. I
knew his infectious enthusiasm would draw the kinds of exciting people that I would enjoy spending a few days in the mountains with.

I didn't know how breathtakingly beautiful Wildacres would be—
never having been there. I couldn't imagine the view from the lower
patio where we would congregate each evening with the "Bs" that we
brought (BYOB) and laugh and talk until the difficulties from the past
semester began to seem less insurmountable. I thoroughly enjoyed that
retreat, and I attended every subsequent Wildacres retreat I could—
well over half of the fifteen retreats.

What drew me to these retreats? It wasn't the programs, per se. I
must confess that I often came to retreats without noticing who the
guest speaker(s) were. Sometimes I was thrilled to find who they were
after I got there—people like Peter Elbow, Nancy Martin, and Patti
Stock. But the Wildacres experience was not defined by the speaker.
It was the people who attended: teachers of writing, of course; but
also, accountants; mathematicians—one year I roomed with a Russian
mathematician from UNC Charlotte; scientists; philosophers; historians, and more. Where else in the academy do we have time to sit
and talk, at length, with people who are about the same business as
us—teaching—but who have such varied teaching fields?

The atmosphere at Wildacres was electric. As I reflect on what made this so, I believe the electricity was in part due to the spirit of cooperation and shared learning that Sam and his UNC Charlotte colleagues brought to that first retreat. Sam and Dixie Goswami, and many others, had already been at work building a community, based on the principles of the National Writing Project, at UNC Charlotte. Among those principles were these: 1) writing is a powerful tool for learning in all disciplines; 2) those who would be teachers of writing must themselves be writers; and 3) all of us, workshop leaders and participants alike, have much to learn from one another.

At that first, and all subsequent, Wildacres retreats, I found a critical mass of people—from various disciplines—who subscribed to these principles. Together, we listened to exciting ideas presented by various speakers. But more importantly, we were given time to reflect individually and in small groups on the ways in which writing could be made to matter in our lives and in the lives of our students. At times, I worked on my own writing; at other times, I examined ways to use writing in various courses I teach. At all times—I felt empowered by my time at Wildacres.

Empowered—it's worth thinking a minute about that word. No other word can capture as well the Wildacres experience for me. The retreats always came at the end of semesters—at a time when the various frustrations of teaching and program direction seemed greatest. As I drove to the retreats, I could feel myself relaxing because I knew I would be given some time to analyze and write about issues that were on my mind. As my friend Bill Bridges loves to point out to his students, one of the benefits of writing is that it helps us to "name," and thus gain some sense of control over, those things in our lives that trouble us.

I always knew that writing at Wildacres would empower me in that way. But that was not all. Since I believe writing is also empowering to my students (helping them learn material, organize and gain insight into their lives, and communicate with others to achieve those things important to them), a large part of the excitement of Wildacres for me was reflecting on how I could help students discover the power in their writing.

As I look at what I have said about Wildacres to this point, it seems to do little to provide the "authoritative counterpoint" that Sam promised when he alluded to my epilogue in the beginning of his story. I was one of the most enthusiastic participants and supporters of Wildacres. When I came back to North Carolina in 1991 as Chair of English at UNC Charlotte (having served as Head of English at Southwest Missouri State University for five years), I had the opportunity to learn more about Wildacres and about the work that Sam had done in supporting writing across the curriculum here at UNC Charlotte. Upon my appointment as Chair, the Dean of Arts and Sciences commissioned me to write a report on the Writing Across the Curriculum program at UNC Charlotte. In writing that report, I read all the reports Sam had submitted after the Wildacres retreats to date, I interviewed over twenty UNC Charlotte faculty who had been key figures in writing across the curriculum efforts here and/or frequent attenders of Wildacres retreats. I also interviewed key administrators. My report concluded that the combination of grassroots efforts by Sam and others and institutional support for writing had helped foster an unusually rich climate for writing instruction at UNC Charlotte. I reported that the faculty at UNC Charlotte were unusual in the large number who were committed to using writing in their teaching and in the broad understanding they had of what roles writing might play in teaching.

The Writing Across the Curriculum program I found at UNC Charlotte was unusual. As I talked with those implementing this program, I found they had a real understanding of the writing process and of the ways in which writing can be used as a tool of learning. It was clear that those trips to the mountains were partly responsible—but not entirely. Many of these people had continued to study the role that writing could play in their teaching after coming back from Wildacres retreats. Sam had been able to convince the UNC Charlotte administration to fund semester-long sessions in which a cadre of teachers from various disciplines met to talk about writing across the curriculum. This funding was no small commitment by UNC Charlotte, since it allowed course reductions for those attending the seminars.

It seems I have arrived at one way in which I can provide a *counterpoint* to Sam's perspective. I would give more credit to UNC Charlotte than Sam seems to—both for supporting the Wildacres retreats for fifteen years and for other on-campus in-service work. This is not to suggest that any of this would have happened without the dedication and perseverance of people like Sam Watson, Leon Gatlin, Ron Gestwicki, Steve Fishman. It clearly would not have.

I will conclude by suggesting one final *counterpoint* to what Sam has written. I'll begin by agreeing with his assessment of what is happening in our new general education program at UNC Charlotte. As a member of the taskforce that fashioned this program, I think I'm in a good position to judge the claim that Sam makes about the writing in that program; as Sam puts it: "the change does not seem like progress to me." While I believe there is much that is good about our new general education program, I agree with Sam's observation. From what I can see, our new Writing Across the Curriculum Program has pretty much dedicated itself to helping students learn how to write—as opposed to helping them use writing as a way of learning. Having said that, I disagree with the tone of Sam's last few paragraphs. He seems disappointed that someone hasn't been able to pick up where he left off in the Wildacres retreats and in the writing across the curriculum work at UNC Charlotte. I agree with Sam that they haven't, but rather than bemoaning that fact, I would like to draw attention to what did happen here under Sam's leadership.

I would like to give my own answer to Sam's question; "Was the Wildacres experience really 'there'?" I agree with Sam that it was. Something very special happened at UNC Charlotte while Sam was in charge of the Wildacres Retreats and while he led the writing across the curriculum efforts here at UNC Charlotte. But what happened happened to individuals who were a part of this writing program— not to the writing program; not to the institution. By design and by definition, institutions are impervious to the enthusiasm, energy, and charisma of the individuals who labor within those institutions. But for the time that it existed Wildacres made a tremendous difference to those of us who were able to experience it, and, I would argue, to the students whom we taught when we came down from the mountain.

Works Cited

Emig, Janet, et al. "Polanyian Perspectives on the Teaching of Literature and Composition." *Tradition and Discovery* 17 (1990–1991): 4-17.

Fishman, Stephen and Lucille Parkinson McCarthy. "Boundary Conversations: Conflicting Ways of Knowing in Philosophy and Interdisciplinary Research." *Research in the Teaching of English* 25 (1991): 419–68.

—. (1998). *John Dewey and the Challenge of Classroom Practice.* New York: Teachers College P, 1998.

Gray, James. *Teachers at the Center: A Memoir of the Early Years of the National Writing Project.* Berkeley: National Writing Project, 2000.

National Writing Project and Carl Nagin. *Because Writing Matters: Improving Writing in Our Schools.* San Francisco: Jossey-Bass, 2003.

Silberman, Arlene. *Growing Up Writing: Teaching Children to Write, Think, and Learn.* New York: Times Books, 1989.

Smith, Janet, and Sam Watson, eds. "What's Happening with Writing at UNC Charlotte?" Charlotte: UNC Charlotte, 1990.

Watson, Sam. "Coming of Age in California" *The Quarterly of the National Writing Project and the Center for the Study of Writing and Literacy* 14 (1992): 24-27.

—. *Michael Polanyi and the Recovery of Rhetoric.* Iowa City: Diss. University of Iowa, 1973.

—. "Polanyi." *Encyclopedia of Rhetoric and Composition.* Ed. Theresa Enos. New York: Garland, 1996, 538–39.

—. "Polanyi and the Contexts of Composing." *Reinventing the Rhetorical Tradition.* Ed. Aviva Freedman and Ian Pringle. Urbana, IL: National Council of Teachers of English, 1980. 19–26.

—. Polanyi's Epistemology of Good Reasons. *Explorations in Rhetoric: Studies in Honor of Douglas Ehninger.* Ed. Ray McKerrow. Glenview, IL: Scott Foresman, 1981. 49–68.

—. "Teachers into Action: Heart of Writing Projects' Success." *English Education* 13 (1981): 93–96.

—. "WAC, WHACK: You're An Expert—NOT!" *Inventing a Discipline: Rhetorical Scholarship in Honor of Richard E. Young.* Ed. Maureen Goggin. Urbana, IL: National Council of Teachers of English, 1999. 319–33.

—. "Who Owns the Writing Project?" *Quarterly of the National Writing Project and the Center for the Study of Writing* 9 (1987): 1-4, 26-7.

—. "Writing Projects and Rhetorical Epistemology." *NWP Network Newsletter* 5.1 (1983): 1-3.

Wildacres Retreat. "History" (n.d.). 1 April 2003 <http://www.wildacres.org/history.htm>.

About the Authors

Charles Bazerman is Chair of the Education Department and Professor of Education at the University of California, Santa Barbara. In the fall of 1999 he was Knight Distinguished Visiting Scholar of Rhetoric and Composition at Cornell, and in Fall 1997 he was Watson Distinguished Visiting Professor of Rhetoric and Composition at the University of Louisville. His research interests include the psycho-social dynamics of writing, the rhetoric of science and technology, writing across the curriculum, rhetorical theory, and the history of literacy. His most recent book, *The Languages of Edison's Light,* won the American Association of Publishers award for the best book in the history of science and technology. A previous book, *Shaping Written Knowledge: The Genre and Activity of the Experimental Article in Science,* also won several awards, including the McGovern Medal of the American Medical Writers' Association and the National Council Teachers of English Award for Excellence in Technical and Scientific Writing. He has written and edited several other scholarly books including *Constructing Experience, Textual Dynamics of the Professions, Landmark Essays in Writing Across the Curriculum.* and *Reference Guide to Writing Across the Curriculum* (co-editor). Recent articles and chapters include several on the formation of the information age and the transformations occurring in socio-discursive systems as they become mediated by electronic communication.

John C. Bean is a professor of English at Seattle University, where he holds the title of "Consulting Professor for Writing and Assessment." He has been active in the writing across the curriculum movement since 1976. He is the author of *Engaging Ideas: The Professor's Guide to Writing, Critical Thinking, and Active Learning in the Classroom* (Jossey-Bass, 1996), which has been translated into Dutch and Chinese. He is also the co-author of several textbooks on writing, critical reading, and argumentation, including *The Allyn and Bacon Guide to Writing,*

4th ed., *Writing Arguments*, 6th ed., and *Reading Rhetorically*, 2nd ed. He has published numerous articles on writing and writing across the curriculum as well as on Renaissance literature, including Shakespeare and Spenser. His current research interest focuses on teaching and assessing rhetorical numeracy (arguing with numbers)across the curriculum.

Toby Fulwiler, Emeritus Professor of English, directed the writing program at the University of Vermont from 1983 until 2002. Before that he taught at Michigan Tech and the University of Wisconsin where, in 1973, he also received his PhD in American Literature. At Vermont he taught introductory and advanced classes in writing (in computer classrooms) and American literature. He currently teaches part time in Vermont's graduate program for field naturalists in the Botany department. He is the author of *College Writing, The Working Writer,* and *Teaching With Writing.* He is editor of *The Journal Book,* and co-editor of, among others, *The Letter Book, When Writing Teachers Teach Literature, Community of Voices, Angles of Vision, Programs that Work,* and Reading, *Writing, and the Study of Literature.* He conducts writing workshops for teachers in all grade levels and across the disciplines, riding to workshop sites, weather permitting, on his BMW motorcycle.

Anne Herrington is Chair of the English department and former Director of the Writing Program at the University of Massachusetts Amherst. She has been involved in program development and research work associated with writing across the curriculum since the mid-1970s. With Charles Moran, she is co-editor of two collections—*Genre across the Curriculum* and *Writing, Teaching, and Learning in the Disciplines*—and with Marcia Curtis, co-author of *Persons in Process: Four Stories of Writing and Personal Development in College,* winner of the NCTE 2002 David H. Russell Award for Distinguished Research in the Teaching of English. She has written numerous other articles based on research studies of writing and learning in classrooms across the curriculum. Her most recent work includes consideration of new technologies as they impact to assessment and genres of writing.

Carol Holder is Professor of English Emerita at California State Polytechnic University, Pomona, where, over a thirty-three year period, she taught writing, linguistics, and literature, directed Freshman English and Writing in the Disciplines, and worked with faculty as founding Director of Faculty Development. With grant support the first few years, Dr. Holder started the WAC program in 1979 and continued as program director for twenty years. By 1982 she was working with faculty at other CSUs interested in launching WAC programs for their own campus. She co-authored with Andrew Moss *Improving Student Writing: A Guidebook for Faculty in All Disciplines*, currently in its 10th printing. In 2000, she led the start-up of the on-line journal *Exchanges* and was executive editor for the first two years of the journal, while she was faculty director of the CSU Institute for Teaching and Learning. Since 2002 she has been assisting with the start-up of the newest CSU campus, Channel Islands (in Camarillo), focusing primarily on creating programs and services to support the faculty. She has assisted more than 50 colleges and universities, including 19 of the 23 CSUs, and continues to write, work part time, and consult on campuses to support writing programs, writing across the curriculum, faculty development, and the scholarship of teaching.

Peshe C. Kuriloff is currently Director of Communications, Policy and Planning for the College of Education at Temple University. She formerly directed the Mellon Writing Project at the University of Pennsylvania, where she was also an Adjunct Associate Professor of English, and conducted research focused on creating and evaluating new, electronic pedagogy. For 15 years, Kuriloff directed Writing Across the University, Penn's writing across the curriculum program. She regards electronic writing instruction as the logical extension of writing across the curriculum, distributing writing instruction to students when and where they most need it. Kuriloff has written a number of articles on teaching writing in different discourse communities and on teaching writing with new technology as well as a writing across the curriculum textbook.

Elaine P. Maimon is the Chancellor of the University of Alaska Anchorage, where she is also a Professor of English. In the early 1970s, Dr. Maimon initiated and then directed the Beaver College (now Arcadia University) writing across the curriculum program, one of the first writing across the curriculum programs in the nation. She was a founding Executive Board member of the National Council of Writing Program Administrators (WPA). She has directed national institutes (sponsored by the National Endowment for the Humanities) to improve the teaching of writing. Arcadia University annually presents the Elaine P. Maimon Award in Writing to recognize her achievements. In the1980s, Dr. Maimon's co-authored textbook, *Writing in the Arts and Sciences*, set the standard for classroom books using the writing across the curriculum approach. Today, the three handbooks she has published—*A Writers Resource* (with Janice Peritz and Kathleen Yancey), *The New McGraw-Hill Handbook* (with the same authors), and *Writing Intensive* (with Janice Peritz) testify to the fact that writing across the curriculum has become mainstream.

Susan McLeod is Professor of Writing and Director of the Writing Program at the University of California, Santa Barbara. Her publications include *Strengthening Programs for Writing across the Curriculum; Writing Across the Curriculum: A Guide to Developing Programs* (with Margot Soven); a multi-cultural textbook for composition, *Writing about the World*, now in its third edition; *Notes on the Heart: Affective Issues in the Writing Classroom;* and *WAC for the New Millennium: Strategies for Continuing Writing Across the Curriculum Programs* (with Eric Miraglia, Margot Soven, and Christopher Thaiss), as well as numerous articles on writing across the curriculum and writing program administration. Before taking the position at UC Santa Barbara, she served as Chair of the English Department and as Associate Dean of the College of Liberal Arts at Washington State University.

Linda Peterson is Niel Gray, Jr. Professor of Rhetoric at Yale University, where co-directed the expository writing program from 1979-2004. Her books include *Victorian Autobiography: The Tradition of Self-Interpretation, Victorian Women Artists and Authors* (with Susan Casteras), and *Traditions of Women's Autobiography: The Poetics and Politics of Life Writing.* She is general editor of the *Norton Reader,* a collection of classic and contemporary essays, and frequently teaches "Daily Themes," an upper-level writing course that has been a part of the English department's curriculum since 1907. Her current projects include a study of 19th-century women of letters and how they began their writing careers.

David R. Russell is Professor of English at Iowa State University, where he teaches in the PhD program in Rhetoric and Professional Communication. His book *Writing in the Academic Disciplines: A Curricular History* examines the history of American writing instruction outside of composition courses. He has published many articles on writing across the curriculum and co-edited *Landmark Essays on Writing Across the Curriculum,* a special issue of *Mind, Culture, and Activity* on writing research, and *Writing Selves/Writing Societies,* an online book on writing and activity theory. He has given many workshops and lectures on WAC, nationally and internationally, and he was the first Knight Visiting Scholar in Writing at Cornell University. He has also served as consultant to the NCTE/IRE standards project, and has co-edited a collection of essays, *Writing and Learning in Cross-National Perspective,* describing the role writing plays in the transition from secondary to higher education in six national education systems.

Margot Soven is Professor of English at La Salle University and is currently the Director of the Core Curriculum and the Writing Fellows Program. Her essays have appeared in journals such as *College Composition and Communication,* the *Journal of the Council of Writing Program Administrators,* the *Journal of Teaching Writing,* and *Freshman English News.* She is the author of *Write to Learn: A Guide to Writing Across the Curriculum, Teaching Writing in Middle and Secondary Schools,* and *What the Writing Tutor Needs to Know.* She has co edited two texts, *Writing Across the Curriculum: A Guide to Developing Programs* and *Writings from the Workplace.* She is also one of the editors of *WAC for the New Millennium.* She is currently working on a textbook for training peer tutors. Soven has conducted numerous workshops at the high school and college level on writing across the curriculum.

Christopher Thaiss is Professor of English at George Mason University, where he has chaired the Department and served for many years as director of the Writing across the Curriculum and English Composition programs. A regular consultant to writing-in-the-disciplines programs around the country, he has served as coordinator of the National Network of WAC Programs since 1981. He also works with teachers in the elementary, middle, and high schools through the Northern Virginia Writing Project. Books he has written, edited, or co-edited include *Dynamic Disciplines: Research on the Academic Writing Life* (with Terry Myers Zawacki), *The Harcourt Brace Guide to Writing Across the Curriculum, Language Across the Curriculum in the Elementary Grades, Speaking and Writing K-12,* and *WAC for the New Millennium.* He has also written or co-authored several textbooks, the most recent of which are *Writing about Theatre* (with Rick Davis),

Writing for Law Enforcement (with John Hess), and *Writing for Psychology* (with James Sanford).

Barbara E. Walvoord, is Fellow of the Institute for Educational Initiatives and Concurrent Professor of English at the University of Notre Dame, Indiana. Her publications include *Assessment Clear and Simple, Effective Grading: A Tool for Learning and Assessment* (with Virginia Johnson Anderson), *Academic Departments: How They Work, How They Change* (with others), *In the Long Run: a Study of Faculty in Three Writing Across the Curriculum Programs* (with others), and *Thinking and Writing in College: A Naturalistic Study of Students in Three Disciplines* (with others). She has served as founding director of writing across the curriculum programs at thre institutions, and of the kaneb Center for Teaching and Learning at the University of Notre Dame. She has consulted and led workshops at more than 300 institutions of higher education. Named Maryland English Teacher of the Year for Higher Education in 1987, she also received the University of Notre Dame President's Award in 2000.

Sam Watson states, "Beginning with my first teaching job in 1967 my most persistent professional goal has been to learn to teach freshman composition really well." Sam completed his PhD at the University of Iowa in 1973, with a dissertation on "Michael Polanyi and the Recovery of Rhetoric." He invested his teaching career at the University of North Carolina at Charlotte, establishing a National Writing Project site in 1979 and serving for seven years as Director of Composition in the English department. His Writing Project experience helped Sam see that the writing we are capable of, depends largely on the culture(s) we are members of, and that a deeper word for "writing" is "learning." To help the university culture become safe for both, he began the annual faculty retreats at Wildacres in 1983, and in 1993 he was given the university's most prestigious award for excellence in teaching. For five years (1993 to 1998) Sam held the position of Director of University Writing Programs. Then he returned happily to his own classroom, where he continued trying to learn how to teach freshman composition really well. Sam is now an emeritus professor, retired to the fishing village of McClellanville on the South Carolina coast, where he finds fulfillment in artistic possibilities of found objects from woods to words, in civic engagements of the village, and in welcoming friends to visit.

Art Young is Campbell Chair in Technical Communication and Professor of English at Clemson University. After helping to implement a WAC program at Michigan Tech in the 1970s and 1980s, in 1987, he moved to Clemson where he founded and continues to coordinate that university's Communication Across the Curriculum program. In 2002, the Conference on College Composition and Communication presented him with Exemplar Award for distinguished teaching, research, and service in the fields of composition studies and writing across the curriculum.

Index

Printed in the United States
65081LVS00004B/47